PERMANENT
CALIFORNIANS

PERMANENT CALIFORNIANS

*An Illustrated Guide to
the Cemeteries of California*

Judi Culbertson
and
Tom Randall

CHELSEA GREEN PUBLISHING COMPANY
CHELSEA VERMONT

Library of Congress Cataloging-in-Publication Data
Culbertson, Judi.
  Permanent Californians: an illustrated guide to the cemeteries of
California / by Judi Culbertson & Tom Randall.
    p.   cm.
  Bibliography: p.
  Includes index.
  ISBN 0-930031-21-0 (alk. paper)
    1. California—Biography.   2. Cemeteries—California—Guide-
books. 3. California—Description and travel—1981- —Guide-books.
I. Randall, Tom, 1945-   . II. Title.
CT225.C85 1989
920'.0794—dc19
[B]   .
                                                        89-30997
                                                            CIP

"It all started with a broken sibling,
In the words of the famous Rudyard Kipling."

Hence, with love to our brothers and their wives:

Dave and Liz Randall
John and Heide Chaffee
David and Margot Chaffee

Acknowledgments

Our deeply felt thanks to:

Roger Sinclair and Robert Siler, whose encyclopedic knowledge of Hollywood, and willingness to spend days showing us where the bodies were buried, greatly enriched this book.

Michael Chellel in Los Angeles, Mark Gordon in San Francisco, and Charlie Gerrans in Colma, who generously spent hours with us, pointing out significant spots and sharing local folklore.

Paul G. Bahn for his maps, Andrew Culbertson for his expertise, Dave Randall for his books and knowledge, Jim Morris for his help with photographic supplies, Marie Laudante for her help with Spanish translations, and the Port Jefferson Library staff for their help in acquiring the specialized information we needed.

Our aunts and uncles, Cliff and Mary Chaffee, and Bill and Edna Chaffee, who provided sustenance and interest, Elaine Mundy for her hospitality in San Francisco, and Gordon and Jean Thomsen who helped keep the home fires burning.

The production team who worked hard and with inspiration to create this book: Castle Freeman for his editing, Sally and Chris Harris for their design work, Julia Rowe for her cover work, Walter Jeffries for his map-making skills, and, as always, Ian and Margo Baldwin for their dedication and the high standards they bring to publishing.

Contents

Preface

A BOOK ON CALIFORNIA cemeteries must walk a fine line, the fault line that exists between San Francisco to the north — cool, cosmopolitan, sophisticated, and traditional — and Los Angeles to the south: warm, freewheeling, glitzy, innovative, and laid back. While exceptions abound, there is no doubt that both cities openly display their personalities in life and death.

A book on California's notable dead has to include both the settlers of Hollywood and the settlers of San Francisco. One need not compare the contributions of William Randolph Hearst and John Steinbeck to those of Marilyn Monroe and Jack Benny. While each illustrates the difference of region, they share a common humanity which we have tried to respect. With personalities ranging from naturalists (John Muir) to botanists (Luther Burbank), comedians (Lenny Bruce) to movie stars (Jean Harlow), politicians (George Moscone) to eccentrics (Emperor Norton), captains of industry (Claus Spreckels) to admirals (Chester Nimitz), rogues (William Sharon) to lawmen (Wyatt Earp), and opera singers (Ernestine Schumann–Heink) to writers (Theodore Dreiser), the dead of California cover a vast, diverse, and intriguing range of history and anecdote.

Nor is early history ignored. Indian graves, pioneer monuments, the dead in Mission Dolores, and the crypt of Father Junípero Serra all provide a look back to the harsh early years of Spanish settlement and frontier life.

While California suffers from the sterility of modern cemetery art just as the rest of the country does, there is nevertheless a full range of design and concept for the explorer. The memorial parks of Los Angeles offer bronze plaques laid flush with the ground, designed to emphasize the grace of the land and to provide easy care. What is missing in statuary is made up for by surprising epitaphs: "Too bad, we had fun." "This cat lived, and he was loved." and the playful, "I'd rather be in Las Vegas." On the same grounds visitors will find mausoleums, huge reverential halls filled with sarcophagi, urns, drawers, and magnificent stained-glass windows.

In Carmel the mission graveyard of plain crosses is near a flowering garden inhabited by hummingbirds. Salinas offers a cemetery filled with charming examples of Victorian stones, many marking Scandinavian families. It includes boys on horses, broken flowers, clasped hands, and sentimental verse. Cypress Lawn in Colma and Mountain View in Oakland provide more of the same, but on a larger scale befitting their urban settings.

Unique to this book in our series are the house tours where one can wander the grounds and homes of John Muir, Luther Burbank, and Jack London. They provide, perhaps, the most intimate view of all.

As always, one should respect the cemeteries, their rules, and their inhabitants. Lives are memorialized here, and whether the accomplishments were grand, scurrilous, or pathetic, they deserve the same respect and longevity. In many ways this is history at its best.

LOS ANGELES
AREA

San
Fernando

San Fernando Valley

⑤
⑪
118
405
Freeway
210
Foothill
Golden
210
Freeway
⑤
State
Burbank
170
⑩
②
210
101
Ventura
⑩
134
Freeway
Glendale
Glendale
210
Hollywood
⑨
134
Beverly Hills
Hollywood
101
Freeway
⑤
⑧
110
②
San
⑥
Monica
②
Blvd
⑦
Santa
Monica
Santa
LOS ANGELES
②
10
⑤
60
Diego
Santa
Santa
Monica
Freeway
①
10
10
⑤
Freeway
⑤
④
③
405
110
710
①
Inglewood

Santa
Monica
Bay

405

DOROTHY STRATTEN
FEBRUARY 28, 1960 — AUGUST 14, 1980
IF PEOPLE BRING SO MUCH COURAGE TO THIS WORLD
THE WORLD HAS TO KILL THEM TO BREAK THEM, SO
OF COURSE IT KILLS THEM. IT KILLS THE VERY GOOD
AND THE VERY GENTLE AND THE VERY BRAVE IMPARTIALLY.
IF YOU ARE NONE OF THESE YOU CAN BE SURE THAT IT
WILL KILL YOU TOO BUT THERE WILL BE NO SPECIAL HURRY
WE LOVE YOU, D R

Westwood Memorial Park

Hot night in August
So long to the Goddess
"America's fatherless child"
Immortal forever
That Queen of the camera
The master of winkin' a smile
And leaving her shadow behind.

"Marilyn Monroe — Neon and Waltzes"
— NANCI GRIFFITH

WESTWOOD MEMORIAL PARK is an accommodating cemetery. In the course of the year it receives several hundred
letters from all over the world, written to Marilyn Monroe.
Some are 14 or 15 pages long. If a letter has a return
address, Westwood personnel tape the letter to Marilyn's
crypt, take a photograph, and send it to the writer. They
want people to know that their letters have reached the
intended recipient. Westwood does not, however, respond
to requests for dirt from stars' graves. Enough is enough.

Like Trinity Churchyard in New York City, Westwood is
in the heart of the city and dwarfed by tall buildings. It is, as
is Trinity, a lunchtime oasis for nearby workers and students, though it is even more exquisitely planted than its
eastern twin. It is still an open cemetery; for $13,000 you
can buy a plot near the star of your choice.

Entering, you will first notice the substantial mausoleum
of the **Hammer** family to your left. The structure, only nine
years old, is plain but solid and appears built to last forever.
The black ironwork doors have an Egyptian motif.

Armand Hammer's offices are only two blocks away, in

the Occidental Building, so he visits his future home frequently. Recently a stereo system was installed which plays classical music when the door of the mausoleum is opened. Hammer, who has lived out the careers of five men — doctor, pharmaceutical tycoon, art collector, presidential adviser, and CEO of Occidental Petroleum — was born on New York's Lower East Side. His father, **Julius** (1874–1948), was also a doctor, as well as a pharmacist and an ardent socialist. Mama **Rose** (1873–1963) was working in a garment factory when they were married.

Armand's brother, **Victor Hammer** (*d.* 1985) is the last family member to be buried here. Victor, an art expert who died of a stroke, was eulogized by Louis Nizer: "If everyone who was a beneficiary of his goodness would place a petal on his bier, he would lie in a forest of blossoms. The only time Victor made anyone sad was the day he died."

Go past the Hammers to the first outdoor mausoleum wall. Part of the way up on the outside row of markers is the vault of **Heather O'Rourke** (1975–1988), the beguiling child in the series of *Poltergeist* films. Her plaque reads, "Star of Poltergeist One, Two, and Three." Heather also appeared in TV's "Happy Days" in the 1982–1983 season. Her unexpected death was caused by a congenital intestinal deformity; she died on the operating table of cardiac arrest and septic shock.

Until recently, the vault just above Heather's belonged to **Peter Sydney Lawford** (1923–1984) and had the inscription, "Beloved husband, father, friend." After persistent rumors that he was about to be evicted for nonpayment of rent, Lawford's ashes were removed by his widow and scattered at sea on May 19, 1988.

A	Armand Hammer Family	K	Dorothy Stratten
B	Heather O'Rourke	L	Minnie Riperton
C	Harry Warren	M	Will and Ariel Durant
D	Buddy Rich	N	Richard Conte
E	Marilyn Monroe	O	Darryl F. Zanuck
F	Oscar Levant	P	Natalie Wood
G	Helen Traubel	Q	Donna Reed
H	Gregor Piatigorsky	R	Sebastian Cabot
J	Dominique Dunne		

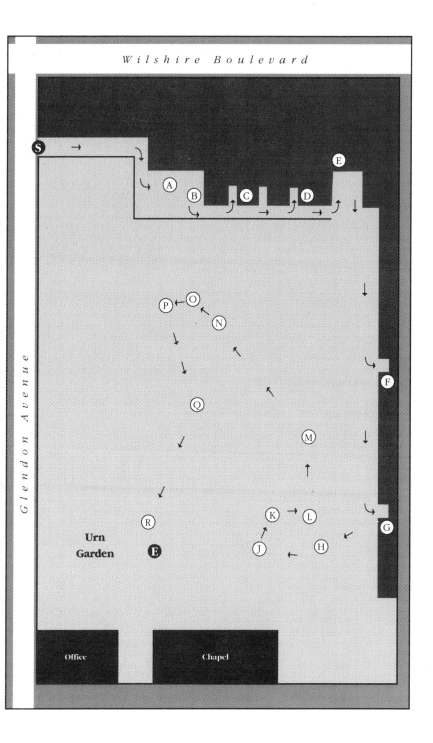

Hammer family mausoleum

If you enter the alcove behind the nearby mausoleum's wall, the Sanctuary of Tenderness, halfway in on the bottom to your right you will find the crypt of **Harry S. Warren** (1894–1981) with the epitaph, "Beloved husband, father, composer." The plaque bearing the epitaph is also decorated with a musical staff showing the opening notes of "You'll Never Know (Just How Much I Love You)." One of our greatest songwriters, Warren was born Salvatore Guaragna to a large and poor family in Brooklyn. He was essentially a self-taught musician, first on the accordion, then drums, and finally piano. He broke into the music business as an accompanist but soon started composing. Over the years Warren worked with many of the best lyricists around, but he is chiefly remembered for his association with Al Dubin and Mack Gordon. Among his many hits are "I Only Have Eyes for You," "42nd Street," "The Gold Digger's Song (We're in the Money)," "Chattanooga Choo-Choo," "Serenade in Blue," "I Know Why and So Do You," "Lulu's Back in Town," "Jeepers Creepers," "You're Getting To Be a Habit with Me," "Lullaby of Broadway," "You'll Never Know," and "On the Atchison, Topeka, and the Santa Fe." The last three won Warren Academy Awards.

In the third alcove, the Sanctuary of Tranquility, on the bottom right, second marker from the end, is **Buddy Rich** (1917–1987), designated here as "One of a Kind." Another

Brooklyn baby, Rich started as a vaudeville prodigy by dancing in his parents' act before the age of 2. By the age of 4 he was soloing as Baby Traps, the Drum Wonder. A wonder he was; a virtuoso drummer who maintained his incredible technique and control without practice and was thus without a drummer's callused hands. It was amazing that his fists did not become callused, however, as Rich was known for his hot temper and willingness to fight. His opponents ranged from his onetime roommate Frank Sinatra to any other musician or customer who had offended him.

Starting out with Joe Marsala's band in 1937, Rich subsequently played with such big names as Bunny Berrigan, Artie Shaw, and Harry James. When he left the James band in 1966, he was listed as the world's highest-paid orchestral musician, earning $1,500 per week. Rich started his own band, which performed until 1974. While musically successful, Rich had to declare bankruptcy in 1968 after becoming embroiled with the IRS. In his later years he gained control of his temper, attributing his newfound calm to his study of the discipline of karate. He died of complications from a brain tumor.

Also in the Sanctuary of Tranquility is **Nunnally Johnson** (1897–1977), a screenwriter and director who also produced *The Three Faces of Eve* (1957) and *The World of Henry Orient* (1964).

Continue walking, proceeding around the last wall. Facing you will be the simple vault of a woman who has as many admirers in death as she had in her life. Every August 4, on the anniversary of her death, the Marilyn Forever Fan Club holds a memorial service in Westwood. Two dozen or more Marilyn look-alikes attend, giving the eerie feeling of a resurrection gone mad. Although Joe DiMaggio no longer sends roses every day, there are always flowers near her vault.

MARILYN MONROE *b. June 1, 1926, Los Angeles; d. August 4, 1962, Los Angeles.* Norma Jeane Mortenson was a sensitive child who carried her childhood hurts into adulthood. Although she spent less than two years (1935–1937) in an orphanage and was in touch with her mother throughout her life, her image of herself was of an orphan. Her life was lived out of a cardboard suitcase in a series of makeshift family arrangements. Though there were opportunities for Norma Jeane to be adopted, her mentally ill mother refused to consider it. Having relinquished her two older children to her first husband, she refused to give up her last.

Gladys Mortenson was not the only one to fail Norma Jeane. There were memories of a boarder in one of the homes where she lived who tried to molest her; the little girl was further humiliated when her story was not believed and she was scolded for telling it. When she was 16, her guardian, Grace McKee, solved the problem of where Norma Jeane would next live by arranging a marriage between her and Jim Dougherty. The teenager still felt obliged to work for her keep. She kept their apartment scrubbed, dressed prettily in white, and tried to cook. But when Dougherty joined the Merchant Marine and sailed for Shanghai, it felt like another abandonment.

Norma Jeane moved in with the elder Doughertys and took a wartime defense job at the Radio Plane Company. There she was photographed by an Army photographer as "doing her bit"—spraying dope on plane fuselages. The photos brought Norma Jeane to the attention of a large modeling agency run by an improbably named woman, Miss Snively. Soon the dark-haired Norma Jeane was a blonde named Marilyn; her new last name came from her grandmother, Della Monroe. Too voluptuous to model clothing, Marilyn was signed on as a starlet by Twentieth Century–Fox and then Columbia Pictures.

A small part in a Marx Brothers movie, *Love Happy* (1950) attracted some attention and helped Marilyn's agent and lover, Johnny Hyde, arrange roles for her in *The Asphalt Jungle* (1950) and *All About Eve* (1950). Her next roles created the Marilyn Monroe persona: *Gentlemen Prefer Blondes* (1953), *How To Marry a Millionaire* (1953), and *The Seven-Year Itch* (1955). She was ambivalent about the dumb-blonde typecasting, but her success in these pictures gave her the confidence to enter Lee Strasberg's Actors' Studio and to negotiate films with greater scope. These included *Bus Stop* (1956) and *The Prince and the Showgirl* (1957), the last with Laurence Olivier.

Monroe by then had become a myth. Her chirpy child's voice, cotton-candy hair, and sensuous body were a blank screen on which Americans could play out their own fantasies. A few had the chance to do it in reality. Joe DiMaggio tried to turn Marilyn into a homemaker in Peter Pan collars; Arthur Miller took notes on her. The men with whom she had briefer affairs—Yves Montand, Marlon Brando, and Frank Sinatra—did not take her seriously enough to remake their lives for her. To be fair, Marilyn could not articulate what she wanted, other than constant emotional attention. At the end of their marriage, Arthur Miller was as worn out as if he had been parenting a difficult adolescent.

Marilyn's growing sense of her importance in the world was allowing her to make long-suppressed demands. She drew satisfaction in being hours late to appear on a film set, knowing that nothing could happen without her. In one instance, however, the parent turned stern. *The Misfits* (1961) had been successfully filmed despite her tardiness and temperament. But in *Something's Got To Give*, completion was impossible; even when Marilyn wasn't late or absent or ill, her on-screen performance was too poor to be used. The tranquilizers and other medications she was dependent on did not help enough.

Twentieth Century–Fox fired her and eventually shut down the set. To compound her stress, her relationship with Robert F. Kennedy appeared to be ending. In June he disconnected the private phone line which she had used to call him. Although Kennedy came to Los Angeles several times to explain why their friendship was over, Marilyn still had fantasies of marrying him and living in the White House.

The last Saturday of her life Kennedy may have flown down from San Francisco to talk to her about it again. It is known that one of the people Marilyn spoke to after taking the overdose of pills that killed her was Kennedy's brother-in-law Peter Lawford. He and Bobby Kennedy, alarmed by her condition and what she was saying, may have gone over to the house to try to rescue her. An autopsy showed that her body had been moved after death, and the police were not called for four hours. Years later Lawford was said to have confessed to his then wife, Deborah Gould, that evidence embarrassing to the Kennedys, such as a suicide note, had been removed.

Marilyn once characterized herself as "the kind of girl they find dead in a hall bedroom with an empty bottle of sleeping pills in her hand." As if rehearsing, she attempted suicide several times by barbiturates. But many people have doubts about what happened that August night. Books have been written suggesting Marilyn was murdered—by organized crime, by the FBI, by the Kennedys, by parties unknown. Unfortunately, those who are in the best position to know—Peter Lawford, Bobby Kennedy, J. Edgar Hoover, and Marilyn herself—have taken their secrets to the grave.

Farther down on the same wall as Marilyn is **Jay C. Flippen** (1899–1971), a character actor whose face is more familiar than his name. "Colonel" Flippen appeared in more than 50 movies, and broadcast the New York Yankee's games in the 1930s. He is perhaps most familiar to audiences as the chief petty officer on the "Ensign O'Toole" TV series. While filming *Cat Ballou* in 1963, Flippen developed a sore on his right leg. He tried treating it himself, but the infection spread, and the gangrenous leg had to be amputated. In the tradition of Sarah Bernhardt, Lionel Barrymore, and Suzan Ball, he continued acting from a wheelchair.

Turn right and continue on the perimeter path until you reach the Sanctuary of Love. In the bottom vault on the right, against the back wall, is:

OSCAR LEVANT *b. December 27, 1906, Pittsburgh; d. August 14, 1972, Beverly Hills.* To hear Oscar Levant tell it, he had run away twice by the time he was 10 months old, and what he aspired to as a child was to become an orphan. This latter revelation, made on Jack Paar's TV show, shocked the audience into an uneasy silence. Such "humorous" remarks were typical of Levant. There seemed to be no end to his acerbic wit, which was pointed at any target that leapt to his nimble, free-associating mind. Anyone was fair game: friends, soon to be ex-friends, enemies—but above all himself. Mired in an obsessive-compulsive, depression-ridden psyche that worsened with age, Levant displayed amazingly few inhibitions in his verbal output. His marriage, neuroses, hospitalizations, and drug addictions were the subjects of the humorous, if morbid, outpourings in his books and on his many television appearances.

Levant grew up in a Jewish family in Pittsburgh. His father was a watchmaker who ran a small jewelry shop. Through his youth Levant developed a guilt-based devotion to his mother and a fierce ambivalence toward both parents. Displaying his musical precocity early on, Levant was in constant demand all over the city as an accompanist for other budding musicians. Shortly after his father's death, Levant left high school at 15 to study piano in New York. Starting with stag shows, roadhouses, and elegant dining rooms, Levant played at a wide range of jobs in order to pay his way. In doing so he quickly enlarged both his worldly experience and his musical repertoire. Moving on to a society orchestra, he played for Clifton Webb's dance act.

Word of Levant's talent quickly spread, and he was engaged by Brunswick records to record "Rhapsody in Blue" in a competing version to George Gershwin's own. Gershwin invited Levant over and asked him to bring the record along. After listening, Gershwin magnanimously declared that his version was decidedly better than Levant's. This did not stop the development of a firm, long-lasting friendship. Unfortunately for Levant, the relationship led too far into the realm of hero worship. So awed was he by Gershwin's abilities that his own already suspect self-confidence suffered even more when he compared his own works with his friend's.

Not that Levant lacked talent. He had been composing since the 1920s and had musicals under his belt (one of which included the beautiful song "Blame It on My Youth"), a sonatina which had impressed Aaron Copland,

and several other pieces. By the late 1930s he was studying with Arnold Schoenberg, who was impressed enough with Levant's compositions to arrange for him to be heard by Otto Klemperer, the great German conductor. On the occasion of a party when all three were in attendance, Klemperer invited Levant to play one of his pieces. Sitting down at the piano, the ever self-destructive Levant rippled off "When Irish Eyes Are Smiling," while lustily supplying the lyrics.

Levant did go on to have some of his pieces published and even played by major symphony orchestras. As a pianist he was in great demand throughout the 1930s and 1940s. Known as the foremost interpreter and champion of Gershwin's music, Levant also played the standard repertoire, including Tchaikovsky and Rachmaninoff, and had over one hundred recordings to his credit. Nevertheless he was best known to the American public for his radio and television appearances, where his wit entertained, lacerated, and shocked. Starting as a one-night substitute on "Information Please," Levant proved to be so popular that he was invited back as a regular and remained for six years. Later he had his own TV talk show and was fired more than once for his off-color or impromptu political remarks. He was also a favorite and frequent guest on other shows, most notably Jack Paar's.

By 1952 Levant was suffering from nervous exhaustion. Around that time he became addicted to various medications. By the next year his condition had worsened, and he began a series of both voluntary and enforced stays in mental hospitals which lasted for many years. His life was marked by extreme depression and lethargy and a drive to seek sublime unconsciousness through the use of drugs. To this end he experimented with many kinds of drugs and enlisted the aid of an unethical doctor, who would make house calls in the wee hours of the morning to dispense medication. When Levant's wife, June Gale, found out about this and threatened to kill the doctor, the two began meeting in the doctor's car, where Levant would receive his pills and injections. In his better moments Levant was still able to conduct himself in public and on TV, but he was victim to hypochodriasis and of many compulsive rituals which inhibited his functioning. His life was, as he described it, "a morbid rondo," with his psychosis returning "obsessively and repeatedly."

Those who remember Levant in his later days recall a hyperkinetic chain smoker whose hands shook violently. While his wit was unimpaired, he had "divested himself of all [his] abilities." By the mid-1960s Levant had retired and become more and more of a recluse, still seeking oblivion. His wife, June, devotedly stayed with him, though his illness and his antics brought the marriage to the breaking point more than once. Levant stated that "There is a thin line between genius and insanity, and I have erased that line." Levant's own self-analysis best sums up his life. "In some situations I was difficult, in odd moments impossible, in rare moments loathsome, but at my best, unapproachably great." It was a heart attack which brought this strange, talented man the final oblivion he sought.

Outdoor mausoleum alcove

Finally, in the Sanctuary of Remembrance against the back wall, you will find the great soprano **Helen Traubel** (1903–1972), whose unlikely married name was Bass. Traubel started voice lessons early and seriously by leaving high school at the age of 13 for full-time training. She made her debut with the St. Louis Symphony and by the age of 23 was offered a contract by the Metropolitan Opera. Feeling she was not ready for opera, Traubel declined and continued her studies while supporting herself as a soloist for a local church and synagogue in St. Louis. Eleven years later, after being discovered by Walter Damrosch, she made her debut at the Met in *The Man without a Country*. Still dissatisfied with her voice, she continued lessons, but by 1939 she became established with her moving portrayal of Sieglinde in *Die Walküre*. In 1941 she replaced Kirsten Flagstad as the company's leading soprano in the German repertory, and for years she remained a Metropolitan favorite.

Traubel left the Met after her well-publicized run-in with its general manager, Sir Rudolf Bing. Objecting to her nightclub performances and radio and television appearances on the basis that they lacked dignity, he loftily requested that she contractually cease and desist. Traubel's answer was to return her contract unsigned and to perform with Jimmy Durante, George Gobel, Jerry Lewis, and Red Skelton. "Appearing with them is entertainment in its highest form," she asserted, while maintaining that "Dignity is something a person maintains, whatever her surroundings." It was the Met's loss.

The rest of the tour is on the grassy area in front of the chapel. Walk to the first full row of markers. About ten markers in, you will see the plain plaque of **Gregor Piatigorsky** (1903–1976), a literal and figurative giant among cellists. At six feet, three inches, Piatigorsky dwarfed his instrument, which itself was large enough to require its own seat on an airplane. He was a performer from the Romantic school who played with virtuosic ease, drawing large, luscious tones, emphasizing the line, and favoring big ritards.

Born in Yekaterinoslav, Russia, Piatigorsky survived an adventurous childhood including enduring a pogrom and his seduction at 13 by a young employee of a local "nightclub." His skills, aided by his unique early-morning silent practicing, quickly advanced, and he performed with Chaliapin and became the first cellist for the Bolshoi Orchestra. In 1921 he escaped to Poland by swimming the border rapids with his cello held over his head. It was rumored that his orchestral entrances, with his cello triumphantly held aloft as he made his way forward through the orchestra, grew out of this experience.

Piatigorsky's skills soon drew the notice of Wilhelm Fürtwangler, the famed German conductor. In time his solo career took off, and he made his US debut in 1929. For the next 20 years he toured throughout the world, becoming a familiar and beloved performer. Gregarious by nature, he accumulated a vast collection of stories and humorous anecdotes about his fellow musicians. In his later years he settled down in Los Angeles, teaching at the University of Southern California and giving occasional performances with Jascha Heifetz and other well-known musicians.

Although plagued by bouts of stage fright throughout his career, Piatigorsky urged his students to "Be a show off. . . . You must be able to say with great feeling, 'I hate you,' or 'I love you.' Once you are able to say that, you will find you can play the cello." They were words he certainly lived by.

A little farther down the row is a tablet bearing the thoughtful inscription, "May the years of your life be happy and of good quality. For life without good quality is of little value, no matter how much there is of it."

In the lower right front is the bronze marker of a young woman whose life was cut tragically short. **Dominique Dunne** (1959–1982), a beautiful young actress best known for her role in *Poltergeist*, lies under a simple marker with a rose and the words "Loved by All."

It was not love but jealous rage that infused John Sweeney on Halloween eve to attack his former girlfriend. Five weeks earlier Sweeney, the head chef at Ma Maison — a Los Angeles restaurant so exclusive that it had an unlisted phone number — had attempted to strangle her after an evening out. Dunne, frightened, had broken off the relationship and ordered the locks on her house to be changed. She had refused Sweeney's entreaties for another chance.

A letter, written by the actress to Sweeney and read during his trial for murder, pointed out his obsessiveness and stated, "The whole thing has made me realize how scared I am of you and I don't mean just physically. I'm afraid of the next time you are going to have another mood swing." Yet the jury found Dominique's strangulation death to be involuntary manslaughter. They were not allowed to know about an earlier girlfriend of Sweeney's, whose nose he had broken and whose lung he had collapsed in 10 separate beatings. In what some criticized as "California justice," John Sweeney was released from prison in June 1986 after serving just three years.

Mario Castelnuovo–Tedesco (1895–1968) is farther to your left and to the front under a plain bronze marker. Born in Italy, the composer fled Mussolini's anti-Semitism and, with the help of Heifetz and Toscanini among others, entered the United States in 1939. Castelnuovo–Tedesco was enamored of Shakespeare and composed seven overtures to his plays in addition to numerous songs based on Shakespearean texts. He also composed operas, concertos, and incidental pieces. Being firmly rooted in the past, Castelnuovo–Tedesco's music broke no new ground and gained him little acclaim as an important composer. Nevertheless he had concertos premiered by Heifetz and Segovia (the Concerto in D for Guitar remains his most popular work), and his songs have been highly praised.

Two graves down from Castelnuovo–Tedesco is a marker in a style seen predominantly in the west. It is lightly carved and shows a pastoral scene of mountains and trees; above them a setting sun spreads its rays.

Move back to the fifth row and over to a prominent brown marble marker belonging to **Dorothy Stratten** (1960–1980), another victim of wrongful death at the hands of an obsessive lover. Her inscription, taken from *A Farewell to Arms*, reads:

> If people bring so much courage to this world the world has to kill them to break them, so of course it kills them . . . it kills the very good and the very gentle and the very brave impartially. If you are none of these you can be sure it will kill you too, but there will be no special hurry.
> We love you, D.R.

Dorothy Stratten was a beautiful Canadian blonde working after school in a Dairy Queen when she met her future husband, Paul Snider. Snider, who fancied himself an entrepreneur, soon realized that her innocent voluptuousness would make Dorothy the perfect *Playboy* centerfold. He began a relentless campaign to persuade her to pose nude, then sent the photographs to a California contact. Less than two days after Hugh Hefner, publisher of *Playboy*, saw the pictures, the young couple was welcomed into the Magic Kingdom.

Magazine layouts and movie roles followed. So did marriage to Snider. Dorothy was named *Playboy*'s 1980 Playmate of the Year and subsequently became involved with film director Peter Bogdanovich, who had made *Mask* and *The Last Picture Show*. Snider, out of favor at the Playboy mansion, was desperate to recover his young wife's affections. Hoping to explain to him conclusively why their relationship was over, Dorothy agreed to speak with him on August 14, 1980. The discussion at his house went badly. Within an hour Snider had raped her, tortured her on a crude machine he had devised, and fired a shotgun fatally into her head. He used the same weapon to kill himself an hour later.

Dorothy Stratten, who wrote poetry in an attempt to clarify her own feelings, was buried at Westwood. The important men in her life were present — Peter Bogdanovich, Hugh Hefner, *Playboy* photographer Mario Casilli, and her father, who had not seen her since she was four. Paul Snider's body had been returned to Canada for burial.

Along the same row but farther back is **Minnie Riperton Rudolph** (1947–1979), whose marker is inscribed, "Lovin' you is easy 'cause you're beautiful." At the bottom her marker reads: "Hers was the gift of love, a miracle of life for all the world to see and hear forever." The epitaph refers to her hit record of 1973, "Loving You." A singer with a five-and-a-half-octave range, Riperton died of cancer at 31. After a mastectomy in 1976, she became a spokeswoman for the American Cancer Society and was chosen its educational chairman in 1978.

If you move back and to your right, under the huge spreading tree you can locate **Will Durant** (1885–1981) and **Ariel Durant** (1898–1981), the historians and writers famous for their *Story of Civilization* series. Actually it was Will Durant who conceived the series in 1912 when he lay recovering from dysentery in Damascus. He had been inspired by Henry Thomas Buckle's similar but uncompleted effort in the nineteenth century. But it would be another 15 years before Durant got around to starting his first volume. The series ran to 11 thick volumes of history before its completion in 1975. In the course of the work Ariel became increasingly involved with the research and writing. By the time the seventh volume was published, she was sharing joint credit with her husband. The Durants received a Pulitzer Prize for the tenth book, *Rousseau and the Revolution*.

While the 13-year difference in their ages did not seem like much at the time of their deaths (he 96, she 83), it loomed a great deal larger at the time of the Durants' marriage which took place in New York City when Will was 28 and Ariel was 15. Ariel transported herself to her wedding by roller skating from her house in Harlem to City Hall. Their remarkable lives together were detailed in *Will and Ariel Durant: A Dual Autobiography*

Will Durant was a firm believer in change; he himself had changed from a Roman Catholic seminarian to an atheist and finally to an agnostic over the years. He emphasized the need for civilization, even during times of change, but was not optimistic about the future, which he saw threatened by a lack of civilized standards. His views on death were unorthodox. "Life might be unforgivable if it were not for death. Suppose you live forever. Not only would you be useless to everyone around you, but you'd be sick and tired of being what you are. The thought you'd not be allowed to die would be a horrible thought. Has it ever occurred to you that death is a blessing?"

This extraordinary couple died just two weeks apart; Ariel's death was kept from Will, who lay in intensive care.

Also buried near the big tree is actress **Norma Crane** (1928–1973), who played the mother, Golde, in the film version of *Fiddler on the Roof*. Her career was tragically cut short when she died of cancer at 42.

Move along the row of markers to the center of the cemetery, to the bronze marker of **Richard Nicholas Peter Conte** (1910–1975–?). The dates should give you a clue as to Conte's beliefs. In each of the four corners of his marker is a pyramid; at the top is what appears to be a tree trunk with several fat roots coming out of the bottom. Beneath it is inscribed, "Actor–Writer–Painter–Composer–Poet," followed by:

> A man of many talents and graces
> Loved by a thousand unknown faces.
> But he loved best and is loved most
> By his lover–friend–mother–child–wife
> Shirlee Colleen.
> Nicky—the master of gentle words and deeds.
> He shared so much, gave so much
> Received so little, until now when all is yours.
> Fly with joy that I may greet you
> On the wings of our friend, the bird of blue.
> May the fates be kinder in our next life
> And take us together to be at long last complete.

Conte, who died of a heart attack and paralyzing stroke after 13 days in intensive care, was the son of a New Jersey barber. He began his career on Broadway, then moved to Hollywood, where he played character roles: a Nazi spy, a captured American pilot, an amiable gangster. One of his last roles was Don Barzini in *The Godfather*. He and his wife, Colleen, had been married only two years when he died.

Also close to the center, about six rows down from the back, are **Darryl Francis Zanuck** (1902–1979) and **Virginia Fox Zanuck** (1906–1982). His large plaque has the Twentieth Century–Fox emblem in the upper left-hand corner and lists his achievements, with an emphasis on his military record. It concludes: "A man who used his imaginative creative genius to deliver inspiration through his celebrated motion pictures. He imparted a lifetime message of decency, love, patriotism, equality and hope throughout the nation and the world."

Darryl F. Zanuck was the man who gave the world Rin Tin Tin, first discovering "Rinty," then writing dog film scripts for her to star in. He was probably the only non-Jew working for Warner Brothers who, after frequently hearing, "If only you were one of us," offered to circumcise himself. Zanuck was prolific and gifted, writing eight screenplays in 1927 alone and producing more than 160 films — including such classics as *The Jazz Singer* (1927), *The Grapes of Wrath* (1946), *Miracle on 34th Street* (1947), and *All About Eve* (1950).

Zanuck, who came from Wahoo, Nebraska, was the product of an insecure childhood — a disappearing father and a mother who had many lovers and neglected Darryl — and grew into an insecure adult. His arch-enemy, Henry Fonda, suggested that his middle initial actually stood for his favorite pastime. It was true that Zanuck went through women like red lights. In later years, though married, he concentrated on serial romances, and did what he could to make stars out of the women involved. Bella Darvi, Juliette Greco, and Genevieve Gilles were three that he took further than he should have.

Zanuck eventually lost control of Twentieth Century–Fox and suffered several strokes before his death in 1979. At his funeral, following his instructions, there were no dirges or death marches. Instead, the theme from his favorite of his movies, *The Longest Day*, was played over and over.

Virginia Fox, daughter of a West Virginia coal mine owner, was no ordinary starlet. On a visit to Hollywood, she was introduced to Mack Sennett, who offered her a role in his films. Tiny, auburn-haired, and pretty, she resisted Zanuck, who insisted on marrying her in 1924. Virginia ended her film career soon after and concentrated on raising their three children. Deciding that she had signed on for life, she endured Zanuck's infidelities but did not condone them. When he left her in 1955 and moved to Europe, offering no hope of reconciliation, she waited 18 years. Sick, beaten, and in need of comfort, he finally came home.

Virginia Fox Zanuck's stone praises her achievements, though not her endurance, and ends with a poem:

> With that cheerful smile and a wave of her small hand,
> She has just wandered off into that unknown land.

So think of her faring on my dear
In the love of there as the love of here.
Think of her still as the same, I say.
She is not dead, she is just away.

To the left of the Zanucks, under a brown marker, is the second most visited resident of Westwood. The marker of Natalie Wood Wagner describes her as "Beloved daughter, sister, wife, mother and friend." It is decorated with a rose and a Russian cross. People frequently leave sugar cubes on Natalie's grave, following the custom that the ants will first eat the sugar rather than the deceased.

NATALIE WOOD (NATASHA GURDIN) *b. July 20, 1938, San Francisco; d. November 29, 1981, Catalina Island, CA.* Because she was so much a part of our lives, it is hard to accept the fact of Natalie Wood's death. She is alive every Christmas in *Miracle on 34th Street*, and some of her best-loved films — *Splendor in the Grass*, *West Side Story*, and *Love with the Proper Stranger* — still resonate in our memories. We resist believing that she died through the malevolence of a freak accident and look for other ways to explain the unthinkable.

From the beginning Natalie had what was necessary to succeed: a wonderful face, the ability to dramatize herself, and a determined mother. Maria Gurdin, recognizing little Natasha's appeal, quickly sacrificed the family to the child's career. After she and Natalie appeared as extras in *Happy Land* (1943), Maria brought the family to Los Angeles. Her daughter from an earlier marriage, Olga, was moved to her father's house; soon-to-be-born Lana was expected to duplicate Natalie's success.

At 7, Natalie played a European orphan adopted by Orson Welles in *Tomorrow Is Forever* (1945). Soon she became everyone's daughter, niece, or kid sister. To break out of the Cute Moppet syndrome, she talked her way into *Rebel without a Cause* (1955), a picture that developed an eerie mythology after co-stars James Dean and Sal Mineo died early deaths. *Rebel* earned Natalie an Academy Award nomination for Best Supporting Actress, but also helped her to receive the *Harvard Lampoon*'s award of Worst Actress of the Year four times.

As Hollywood's hottest starlet, Natalie dated everyone from Elvis Presley to Raymond Burr, both of whom she considered marrying. After declaring "understandings" with Robert Vaughn and Nicky Hilton, Natalie, at 19, became involved with Robert Wagner. She soon found "RJ" the most romantic of them all; on the first anniversary of their relationship he poured her a glass of champagne that

Natalie Wood

had at the bottom a diamond ring engraved, "Marry me?"

The wedding took place three weeks later, but it came at a time when Natalie's career was hitting a bad patch. Although she had campaigned strenuously to play the lead in Herman Wouk's *Marjorie Morningstar* (1958), both she and the picture flopped. So did *Kings Go Forth* (1959). Before she had a chance to redeem herself, Natalie was suspended by Warner Brothers for refusing to go to England to film *The Devil's Disciple* — a part that would have meant three months away from RJ. She didn't sacrifice her career a second time, however, when the opportunity came to make *Splendor in the Grass* in New York. When the filming was over, Natalie didn't sacrifice her budding relationship with Warren Beatty either.

By the time a year later when Beatty walked out of Chasen's restaurant in Los Angeles with the hat-check girl instead of Natalie, she was already deep into psychoanalysis. Since early childhood she had assumed other personalities, allowing her emotions to be dictated by the adults around her. She had little idea what her own feelings were. For eight years, five times a week, Natalie worked with a therapist, trying to make sense of her life. Although she likened the expense to the yearly budget of a third-world country, she felt the analysis was crucial.

Still, she did not escape the Hollywood complex entirely. Anxious to be loved, she had numerous affairs after her divorce from Wagner. She made a brief, unhappy marriage to Richard Gregson in 1969. With her remarriage to RJ in 1972 and the birth of her second daughter, it seemed as if her life was achieving more stability. Yet there were the peculiar stresses of the trade — gossip about RJ and Stephanie Powers in their TV show "Hart to Hart," and rumors that Natalie was attracted to Christopher Walken, her co-star in *Brainstorm*.

In the fall of 1981 the Wagners invited Walken onto their cabin cruiser, *The Splendour*, for the Thanksgiving weekend. The three went ashore on Saturday evening for dinner on Catalina Island, then returned to the boat. At 12:20 A.M. the skipper, Dennis Davern, saw that the boat's dinghy, *The Valiant*, was missing. Natalie was absent, too. Patrol boats and the Coast Guard started searching the nearby waters. At 7:44 A.M. her body was discovered floating just beneath the water in a cove one and a half miles from the *Splendour*. She was wearing a blue nightgown, a red down jacket, and heavy socks.

It was suggested that Natalie, bothered by the banging of the dinghy against the yacht, had attempted to retie it and fallen overboard, striking her head. Pulled down by her waterlogged jacket, she eventually drowned. Another theory suggested that she became furious with Wagner and left for shore. The Los Angeles County coroner, Thomas Noguchi, obscured the issue further by reporting that Robert Wagner and Christopher Walken had argued heatedly that night. Whatever happened, the scratches on her wrists and hands, presumably from the rocks in the cove, indicate that Natalie fought to save her life.

Halfway between Natalie Wood and Dominique Dunne, on the diagonal is **Donna Reed**, born Donna Belle Mullenger (1921–1986). Although she won an Academy Award for her portrayal of a prostitute in *From Here to Eternity* (1953) and was a staple on "The Donna Reed Show" from 1958 to 1966, Reed is now most often known for her role in the perennially revived *It's a Wonderful Life* (1946). In December 1985 she was hospitalized for a bleeding ulcer; during tests a malignancy was discovered, and she died the following month of pancreatic cancer.

In the front of the cemetery in the Urn Garden East rests **Sebastian Cabot** (1918–1977). Although he played in classics such as *Ivanhoe* (1952) and *Romeo and Juliet* (1954), the massive actor is better known for his persona of a pompous but likeable Englishman. He starred in the TV series "Family Affair" (1966–1970) and "Checkmate" (1959–1962).

Character actor **Victor Killian** (1891–1979) was cremated, his ashes scattered in the Rose Garden. Stereotyped as a villain in his films, Killian was well known to TV audiences as The Fernwood Flasher in the series "Mary Hartman, Mary Hartman." In a chilling coincidence, both Killian and actor Charles Wagenheim were murdered in March 1979 in separate incidents, in each case just after having finished taping an episode of "All in the Family." Victor Killian was in his living room in the Lido apartments in Hollywood watching television when he was attacked by an intruder.

Westwood, more than other small cemeteries, is a metaphor for life just off the silver screen: Disappointed hopes, murderous emotions, unhappy endings, frustrated loves. Yet the better part of the California spirit is also found here, summed up by a final epitaph from a more obscure grave — an epitaph Mark Twain used in 1896 on the grave of his beloved daughter, Olivia Susan Clemens:

> Warm summer sun shine kindly here.
> Warm western wind blow softly here.
> Green sod above, lie light, lie light.
> Good night dear heart, good night, good night.

DIRECTIONS TO WESTWOOD MEMORIAL PARK: Take Route 405 (the San Diego Freeway) to the Wiltshire Boulevard exit, then go east to Glendon Avenue. The entrance, 1218 Glendon, will be on your left.

Hollywood Memorial Park

Betting on how many leaves cover a birch, then counting them. Betting how many Buicks drive by the grave- yard in a single week, then doing the sums. Betting how many crows fly north-south as opposed to east-west in a single month, then adding them up. Such are the games of the dead.

—STEPHEN DOBYNS

THIS CEMETERY IS like an aging movie star living in Holly- wood's Garden of Allah bungalows—a little worn around the edges, but fascinating and able to tell some wonderful stories. Founded in 1899 by wheat developers I. N. Van Nuys and his father-in-law, Colonel Isaac Lankershim, the cemetery originally contained 100 acres and was the burial spot for such luminaries as Douglas Fairbanks, Sr., Cecil B. DeMille, and Rudolph Valentino. In the 1920s, however, with the rise of Forest Lawn, Hollywood Memorial began to pall. It lost 40 acres to Paramount Motion Picture Studios and gradually acquired the look of an interesting but un- tended garden.

Yet the stories remain. Many come from the stones. Others are told by security guard William P. Phillips, who startles visitors by announcing himself as Deputy Chief of Police of Hollywood. Phillips, who came to Los Angeles in 1928 as a stuntman and rode with Victor McLaglen's motor- cycle men, also has a squad carfull of cemetery jokes.

When you enter the cemetery, you will see an explicit statue of Cupid and Psyche in the distance. Stay on Pineland Avenue, then turn right onto Maple. On your right is the flat marker of **Carl "Alfalfa" Switzer** (1927–1959) with two Masonic symbols and a side view of Petey, the *Our Gang* dog. Switzer's role as the freckle-faced Little Rascal who wore suits and crooned an off-key "I'm in the Mood for Love," won him a place in American film lore. But Hollywood got out of the mood before he did. Switzer stayed around Los Angeles for the rest of his life but managed only an occasional bit part.

To support himself Switzer tended bar and worked as a hunting guide, his name making the papers occasionally for drunken fights and disorderly conduct. On January 29, 1959, he and a friend went to the home of Bud Stiltz in the San Fernando Valley to demand $50. Alfalfa had lost a valuable hunting dog belonging to Stiltz and paid out a reward of $50 to retrieve it. Now he wanted to be reimbursed. When Stiltz refused, the Little Rascal broke a glass-domed clock over his head. Switzer then pulled out a hunting knife, but Stiltz produced a pistol, and, in what a jury termed justifiable homicide, Alfalfa died at 31.

Even Petey, shown here, is not all he seemed. The black ring around his eye was painted on—sometimes on one eye, sometimes on the other.

Next to Alfalfa is his father, **G. Fred Switzer** (1905–1960), whose marker bears the notation "Switzer Method" and the image of a miniature receiver resembling a gas pump.

On the next corner, across the way, is the huge stele with a laurel wreath which commemorates General **Harrison Gray Otis** (1837–1917) and his wife **Eliza A. Otis** (1833–1904). Like Ulysses S. Grant, Otis found his metier in warfare and shone during the Civil War. But success eluded

A	Carl "Alfalfa" Switzer	M	William Desmond Taylor, Wilcox Family
B	Harrison Gray Otis		
C	George Townsend Cole	N	Peter Lorre
D	Adolphe Menjou	O	Rudolph Valentino, Peter Finch
E	John Huston	P	Barbara La Marr
F	Cecil B. DeMille	Q	Douglas Fairbanks, Sr.
G	Jayne Mansfield Memorial	R	Gene Stratton Porter
H	Virginia Rappe	S	Jesse Lasky, Darla Hood
J	Marion Davies	T	Clifton Webb
K	Tyrone Power	U	Talmadge Sisters
L	Harry Cohn	V	Bugsy Siegel

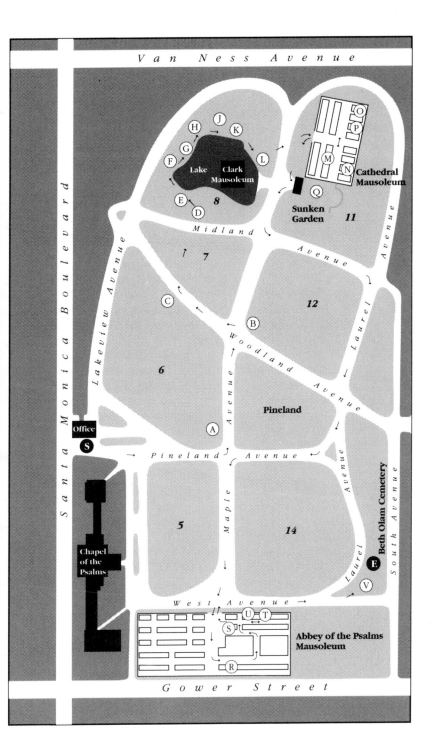

him afterward until he came to Los Angeles in 1882 and became editor and publisher of the *Los Angeles Times*. He retained the military theme, building his offices to resemble barracks, calling his employees the "phalanx" and his mansion The Bivouac. An erect, sandy-mustached man, Otis enjoyed being photographed wearing his chestful of medals.

As Los Angeles grew, Otis' real-estate holdings prospered. He was not above urging the public in editorials to favor bond issues which would further enrich Harrison Gray Otis. The most famous of these, in 1905, brought water to the San Fernando Valley where the Los Angeles Suburban Homes Syndicate (which included Otis, Henry E. Huntington, and railroad magnate E. H. Harriman) owned huge tracts.

Otis' greatest struggle was against labor unions. Firing the first salvo, he cut his printers' salaries by 20 percent, and when they protested brought in scabs from the Midwest. For a decade he battled with the International Typographers Union. Matters peaked in 1910 with an explosion at the *Times* building, killing 20 men who are also commemorated here (see below). General Otis died at 80 of heart disease, after finishing breakfast and stating, "Take away my tray; I am gone."

Set behind Otis' stele is the semi-circular monument of **Harry Chandler** (1864–1944) and **Marion Otis Chandler** (1866–1952), decorated on each side by a patriotic eagle. Harry Chandler continued everything his father-in-law had started, from running the *Los Angeles Times* and attacking unions to amassing a fortune through real estate. Though he was less militarily inclined than the General and more of a workaholic, he died at the same age of the same cause.

To the right of the Chandlers is a monument surmounted by a dark eagle or vulture, its wings furled close to its body. It commemorates the 20 employees of the *Los Angeles Times* who died in what the inscription calls "the Crime of the Century," the bombing of the newspaper's building on October 1, 1910. When James McNamara of the Ironworkers Union set a suitcase full of explosives against the wall of the building shortly after midnight, he may not have known that a crew was inside working on the morning edition. His sabotage was the culmination of two decades of bitter labor-union disputes at the *Times*. The explosion was traced to the McNamara brothers (John blew up the Llewelyn Iron Works in Pennsylvania on Christmas Eve), and they were illegally seized and brought to Los Angeles. In an historic trial covered by Lincoln Steffens, defense

Carl Bigsby

lawyer Clarence Darrow allowed James and John to plead guilty to avoid the death penalty.

The epitaph to their victims concludes, "For the score of loyal men who sleep the sleep that knows no waking, peace to their ashes! Forever green be the turf which California through all her perennial summertime will graciously lend above their cherished graves."

From the workers' memorial you can't miss the marble rocket ship that rises across the road directly ahead of you. The inscription reads, "The Atlas Pioneer in space here symbolizes the lifetime activities of **Carl Morgan Bigsby** (1898–1959). A recognized leader in many phases of the graphic arts, he too was a pioneer." The rocket is an exact replica of the Pioneer Atlas as it went into orbit December 18, 1958. **Carl Bigsby**, a local publisher with no direct connection to the space program except admiration, was "Retired by God."

In a lighter vein, **Constance W. Bigsby**'s inscription notes, "Too bad . . . we had fun."

Return to the Otis monument and continue along Woodland Avenue into the Highland section. Just beyond the large open Bible, a memorial to **J. Dabney Day** (1872–1929), there is a wonderful bronze cameo of **George Townsend Cole** (1874–1937). It shows him in three-quarter profile, mouth set in determination, necktie askew. The youngest son of Senator Cornelius Cole, one of Lincoln's confidants, George was a well-known landscape and portrait painter. He employed the then-novel technique of combining oil paints and watercolors. Suffering an attack of acute indigestion in his studio, Cole died in the arms of his companion, actor Jimmy Wolfe.

The nearby marble sculpture of a mournful young woman, face covered with her very long hair, commemorates philanthropist **Frederick W. Blanchard** (1864–1928). It appears that the statue originally had a lyre on her lap. Now only traces remain.

The next section, Number 8, glitters with stars, though in the center is a nonstar, **William A. Clark, Jr.** (1877–1934). His family mausoleum, built in 1920, sits on an island in the middle of a pond and is reached by a walkway. The frieze shows a seated nude woman who appears to be pushing back a curtain. On the right a winged hourglass is sinking out of view. On the left a beast of some kind is in pursuit. The inscription reads: *Memoria dilectorum dulcis mortis metum fugit vitae novae spem adfert celestium natura.* (The sweet memory of our beloved ones banishes the fear of death; the nature of heavenly things brings hope of new life.) The monument was designated as the most beautiful erected between 1925 and 1928 by the Architectural Society of America.

William A. Clark, Jr., a lawyer, violinist, and brilliant conversationalist, was the youngest son of Montana Senator W. A. Clark. Wealthy in his own right from mining speculation, Clark spared no expense to try and save his 23-year-old wife from "childbirth fever." Mabel Foster had given birth to their first son — known as the $1-million Baby because the Senator had promised him that gift at birth — on December 2. She died in the early hours of New Year's Day.

Clark went on to found the Los Angeles Philharmonic in 1919, though he was unable to get Rachmaninoff to conduct it as he had hoped. He donated his home and library to UCLA and started other charities. The mausoleum is filled with pieces from his art collection. Once or twice a year a tour led by cemetery expert Roger Sinclair is open to the public. Clark himself rests between his two wives.

After leaving the Clark mausoleum, turn left at the walkway and walk straight toward the road. Just past the **Mattoon** circular bench, in the third row from the road, is **Adolphe J. Menjou** (1890–1963). The plain, flat marker gives no clue that it contains Hollywood's best-dressed man. Son of a French restaurateur, Menjou began his film career in New York as an extra. Seeing that his moustache was getting him roles as a foreign nobleman, he quickly added an ascot, white spats, and a walking stick.

Menjou was nominated for an Oscar only once, for his explosive portrayal of an editor in *The Front Page* (1931), but he had parts in many well-known films: *The Three Musketeers* (1921), *A Woman of Paris* (1923), *Little Miss Marker* (1934), *A Star Is Born* (1937), and *Paths of Glory* (1957). Three years before he died of chronic hepatitis, he made his last film, *Pollyanna* (1960). Menjou also found time to join the John Birch Society and support Richard M. Nixon's unsuccessful presidential campaign of 1960.

About ten rows of markers to the right and one row down from Menjou's is the marker of **John Huston** (1906–1987) and his mother **Rhea Huston** (1881–1938). The marker is made of veined pink marble from Ireland with their names deeply engraved and incised with gold.

John Huston was the Ernest Hemingway of film making. Lusty and dramatic, he too loved storytelling, big-game hunting, and literature. He once characterized his five wives as "a schoolgirl, a gentlewoman, a motion-picture actress, a ballerina, and a crocodile." Both his daughter, actress Angelica Huston, whom he cast in *Prizzi's Honor*, and his father, Walter Huston, won Oscars under his direction.

Although he was introduced to vaudeville at an early age through his father, John Huston boxed, painted, and did some newspaper reporting before coming to Hollywood as a scriptwriter. After some misadventures and false starts, he realized his ambition to direct films with *The Maltese Falcon* in 1941. He gained further recognition with *The Treasure of the Sierra Madre* (1948), *The African Queen* (1952), and *Freud* (1962). Huston had a particular weakness for making films from literary novels and brought out *The Red Badge of Courage* (1951), *Moby Dick* (1956), *Reflections in a Golden Eye* (1967), *Wise Blood* (1979), and *Under the Volcano* (1984) with varying success. His reputation sagged in the 1960s and into the 1970s, but before he died, of acute emphysema, he had redeemed himself with such films as *Chinatown* (1974), *Prizzi's Honor* (1985), and *The Dead* (1987).

Going around the corner you will see the twin sarco-

Cecil B. DeMille

phagi of Cecil B. DeMille and **Constance Adams DeMille** (1874–1950). The only ornamentation is two urns with lids.

CECIL BLOUNT DeMILLE *b. August 12, 1881, Ashfield, MA; d. January 21, 1959, Laughlin Park, CA.* One might expect the monument of Cecil B. DeMille to be a marble bathtub or a religious frieze; its plainness belies his film extravaganzas, his talent for creating whole worlds out of nothing. When DeMille arrived in California in 1913, Hollywood was a stage set of rickety boarding houses and orange trees. Movies were considered a new toy his Eastern friends hoped DeMille would outgrow. No one would have predicted that the Massachusetts-born son of an Episcopalian clergyman and playwright would stick it out and create an empire in the sand.

Cecil B. DeMille became a movie director in the informal way things are done at the start of any enterprise. At lunch in New York City, Jesse Lasky and his brother-in-law Samuel ("Include Me Out") Goldwyn suggested making movies together. Later that afternoon, at the Lambs Club, DeMille and Lasky ran into actor Dustin Farnum, who introduced them to the author of *The Squaw Man*, and the Jesse L. Lasky Feature Play Company was born. Soon afterward DeMille left for California and set up the fledgling company in a rented barn which was grossly overpriced at $200 a week. (The barn, saved for sentimental reasons, eventually became part of the "Bonanza" TV series' set.) Their first movie, *The Squaw Man* (1913), grossed $244,700. The studio's subsequent pictures, *The Virginian* (1914) and *The Call of the North* (1914), were equally successful.

From the beginning DeMille devised stunning camera effects. In *The Virginian* he used only the pattern of shadows cast by the noose, hangman, and struggling victim to illustrate an execution. He experimented with the look of a room lit only by a match and with hand tinting which suffused outdoor scenes with a golden glow. He also created the persona of Movie Director. As a young man, with a smooth, open face and receding hairline, DeMille dressed in jodhpurs, high boots, and a flat cap. His leather puttees and his pistol were meant to ward off rattlesnakes on location. Seated above the action with several megaphones, DeMille cracked a whip whenever he was annoyed — a gesture which endeared him to no one except younger directors.

They were less quick to copy his physical daring. On location off Mexico, DeMille swam in shark-filled waters to encourage his cast to do the same, and he literally offered his naked body to snakes and scorpions in the jungle. While lighting one hundred sulphur pots on a schooner to create an "explosion" in another venture, he was thrown, burned and unconscious, into the Pacific. The young De-Mille had attended a quasimilitary academy after his father's death, in which stoic courage was regarded as the highest virtue. It was a value he cherished all his life.

It was also a value that made him take enormous risks with the lives of his actors. The director admired women such as Barbara Stanwyck, who allowed herself to be chased by an actual herd of stampeding buffalo, and Dorothy Lamour, who hung by her teeth 40 feet above ground. But he labeled Victor Mature "100% yellow" for his fears, and jeered at Cornel Wilde for acrophobia. During the chariot race in *The Ten Commandments* (1954) the horses stampeded, severely injuring four people, then charged en masse at the 30-piece Palm Court orchestra, which had been brought to provide atmosphere. More fearful of De-Mille's censure than of a herd of wild horses, the musicians continued playing bravely until they and their instruments were trampled.

DeMille, as a boy, had daydreamed about commanding armies. DeMille, as an adult, did so and became annoyed when human weakness interfered with his strategy. When a blinded Samson (Victor Mature) brought the Philistine temple crashing down, co-star Henry Wilcoxon was struck in the head by a column. As he staggered toward DeMille, blood pouring down his face, the director looked down. "Good God, Henry," he said crossly, "you look terrible; you're going to hold up production!" DeMille's wife, Constance, fared no better. When she had to lock her bedroom door for health reasons, DeMille recruited two mistresses, Julia Faye and Jeannie Macpherson. They traveled with the director and spent weekends at his ranch, Paradise.

Perhaps it had been the shocking death of his father from typhus when Cecil was 11 which made him a man of action rather than emotion. Yet toward the end of his life he tried to recapture what had been lost by reviving his childhood faith. He erected a cross at Paradise over the tombstone of an ancestor, Stamford DeMilles, and spent time there in meditation. In the last months of his life he pondered the amount of good he had brought to the world and wondered whether it was enough.

If you walk forward a few rows from the DeMille memorials, you will see the black-and-white marker of **Janet Gaynor Gregory**, born Laura Gainer (1906–1984). Although she won an Academy Award for her role in *Seventh Heaven* (1927), a World War I romance set in Paris, Janet Gaynor is largely forgotten. She retired from films in 1939 after making sentimental romances such as *Daddy Longlegs* (1931) and *The Farmer Takes a Wife* (1935).

Down by the water, next to a large bush, is the marker of Jayne Mansfield. Her memorial is a pink granite heart with the words, "We live to love you more each day" over an ivy-entwined cross, placed here by her fan club. Jayne's body is actually buried in Pennsylvania, at Fairview Cemetery in Pen Argyl, where her grandparents also lie. Although some of Jayne's close associates and her third husband, Matt Cimber, argued that she should be buried in Hollywood, her parents and second husband, Mickey Hargitay, felt that she belonged with family.

JAYNE MANSFIELD (VERA JAYNE PALMER) *b. April 19, 1933, Bryn Mawr, PA; d. June 29, 1967, New Orleans.* Jayne Mansfield and the fifties were a unique combination; the actress and her life epitomized the decade. Raised on Shirley Temple movies and promised the world by her doting mother, Jayne grew up wanting to be a movie star. She was a conventional student and became a wife and mother at 17, but at 21 she prevailed upon her husband, Paul Mansfield, to move to Los Angeles so she could try for a career.

After haunting the movie studios unsuccessfully, Jayne became convinced that publicity was the key. There was no stunt too blatant — from "losing" her bathing suit top in public, to posing under a construction sign that read "Excess Frontage Overhang" — for her to try. But although her 41-inch frontage attracted notice, Jayne was getting nowhere with the movie studios.

In 1955 her agent arranged a part for her in the Broadway show *Will Success Spoil Rock Hunter?* Jayne's role satirized a dizzy Hollywood blonde. She returned to Los Angeles more determined to become a serious actress, but could not see that accepting roles in movies such as *The Girl Can't Help It* (1957) and *Kiss Them for Me* (1957) might preclude her appearing in more serious dramas. She did not understand that food shopping in a velvet bikini with her two Chihuahuas and showing up to cut the ribbon at bowling alley openings would not make her another Kate Hepburn.

As the 1960s got underway, the few films she did make, pictures like *Panic Button* (1964) and *A Guide for the Married Man* (1967), were not successful. Jayne Mansfield was a casualty of the freewheeling 1960s. It was as if she had been peddling an exotic prescription drug that was now being sold over the counter. Free sexual expression was no longer rare. Jayne commenting, "I don't think there's a thing I welcome like my Frederick's of Hollywood catalogue," was out of sync with the new decade.

Her life off screen had deteriorated as well. After divorcing Paul Mansfield, she had married Mickey Hargitay, a former Mr. Universe. That union ended in 1964, and she married and then was divorced from Matt Cimber. Physical fights between Jayne and the various fathers of her five children were reported in the papers, as well as altercations between the men themselves. Jayne's clothing designer, Mr. Blackwell, announced, "I can't go on designing for an actress who shows off my work by either having the dresses ripped off her or wrestling on the floor with them." Jayne was also lessening her pain by drinking heavily.

Yet neither Jayne nor her latest paramour, Sam Brody (who had been reported by Jayne's 16-year-old daughter, Jayne Marie, for child abuse) were behind the wheel the night of June 28, 1967. The driver was from the Gus Stevens Supper Club in New Orleans, where Jayne had been performing. Her three middle children were asleep in the back seat. Their car became enveloped in a mist from a mosquito-spraying machine, and the driver did not see the tractor trailer in front of them before the car plowed under it. The two men were thrown out and killed instantly. Jayne was decapitated. The children survived. It was a shocking death. Sam Brody was buried at Hillside Memorial Park. Jayne, after much debate, was sent home to Pennsylvania.

Also down by the water is another unfortunate young woman, one whose death sent tremors through the fledgling film industry and cut short the careers of several stars. **Virginia Rappe** (1896–1921) lies in a grave beside the sweetheart who worshipped her memory until his death in 1946.

Probably no one will ever know what transpired in the St. Francis Hotel that Labor Day weekend. A collection of film personalities rented three suites in the San Francisco hotel and settled in to celebrate. Roscoe "Fatty" Arbuckle, who had just signed a $3-million contract with Paramount, was there, a slapstick buffoon described by one writer as "hard-drinking, likable in a sloppy good-old-boy sort of way." Virgina Rappe, whose star had faded considerably since she appeared on the cover of the sheet music for "Let Me Call You Sweetheart," was there as well.

Sometime during that weekend the two collided. Maude Demont, who procured young women for such parties and sometimes blackmailed the men afterward, claimed Fatty had dragged Virginia into a suite and violently raped her. There was also a rumor that he had violated her with a champagne bottle or a piece of ice. Other theories suggested that she had died from peritonitis after a botched abortion. In any case Virginia Rappe was taken to a hospital, where she lapsed into a coma and died of a ruptured bladder five days after the melee at the St. Francis.

In the ensuing trial Fatty's size was against him. Women all over the country looked at the man who had weighed 16 pounds at birth and shuddered. He was brought to trial on first-degree-murder charges in November. Three trials (and two hung juries) later, he was acquitted with apologies from the last jury which felt that there was nothing to link him with any crime. Nonetheless, Arbuckle's movie career was over.

Virginia Rappe was buried near the water by film director **Henry Lehrman** (1886–1946), who fashioned the rest of his life around her memory. He visited her weekly, made plans to be buried to her left, and finally joined her in 1946.

The next landmark is the large mausoleum beside the pond with the name **Douras** and a thick braided garland of leaves encircling the top. The frieze shows two angelic figures holding the name. Inside rests **Marion Davies**, born Marion Douras (1897–1961).

There is no telling what Marion Davies might have accomplished had she not met William Randolph Hearst when she was 20. The 54-year-old publisher fell in love with the actress from Brooklyn and whisked her out of Ziegfeld's Follies into what he was sure would be movie stardom. That she did not unseat Mary Pickford, or even Norma Shearer, was not due to lack of money. Hearst did not allow Marion to consider the heavily dramatic roles she was interested in, such as Sadie Thompson in *Rain*; he preferred her in happy parts — *When Knighthood Was in Flower* (1922) and *Blondie of the Follies* (1932).

They would have married had Mrs. Hearst, living in New York, consented to a divorce on any terms. She did not. Nevertheless Marion ruled Hearst Castle when she and WR were not at the Santa Monica mansion he had built for her. In his last years he spent hours watching her old films, weeping at her youth and beauty and the golden times that were no more. When Hearst died in 1951, his family had their revenge. They whisked his body away while Marion was sedated, lying in another room, and refused to tell her where the funeral would be held. Since he had left editorial and financial control of his publishing empire to her, however, Marion finally received recognition from the Hearsts that she had indeed existed as part of his life.

Ten weeks after Hearst's death, Marion married a former stuntman and sea captain, Horace Brown, allegedly the image of a younger W. R. Hearst. He was not the reincarnation of her longtime lover, however. She filed for divorce twice, but Brown was at her bedside when she died of cancer. Characteristically, she had disbelieved the diagnosis until she was forced to undergo jaw surgery three months before her death.

As you stand in front of the Douras/Davies mausoleum, to your left is the grave of **Hannah Chaplin** (1866–1928), the mother of The Little Tramp. Brought over here by Charlie from England, she fell ill and died.

To the right of the mausoleum is the memorial bench of **Tyrone Power** (1914–1958). Between bookends on the bench is a single volume showing the masks of Comedy and Tragedy. On top of the bench are the lines from *Hamlet*:

> There is a special providence in the fall of a sparrow. If it be now,'tis not to come; if it be not to come, it will be now; if it be not now, yet it will come — the readiness is all. . . . Now cracks a noble heart. Good night, sweet prince, and flights of angels sing thee to thy rest.

Tyrone Power

Tyrone Power succumbed to a heart attack at 44 while filming a duel in *Solomon and Sheba* on location in Madrid. Although he made a number of swashbucklers on the order of *The Mark of Zorro* (1940) and *Captain from Castile* (1947), the year before his death he filmed *The Sun Also Rises* and *Witness for the Prosecution*. He is also remembered by modern audiences for his role in *The Long Gray Line* (1954).

With unconscious humor, Power's *New York Times* obituary points out that "Only 100 close friends of the actor could be accommodated in the small chapel at the cemetery." His wife, Deborah Anne Power, sat in front of the open coffin, while Cesar Romero gave a eulogy. He also read the essay, "The Promises of America" by Thomas Wolfe, which Tyrone Power had been scheduled to read Thanksgiving Day to Air Force personnel stationed in Spain.

If you walk straight back from the Power memorial toward the Hollywood Cathedral Mausoleum, you will find a monument that balances Cecil B. DeMille's. The white marble sarcophagi belong to another film mogul and his family. One reads "Harry Cohn (1891–1958)" and has a star of David on top; the other, with a cross, is blank. The film executive, at his wife's request, made a deathbed conversion to Christianity

Harry Cohn was a man whose ego knew no bounds. When he was seated at his raised desk à la Mussolini, Cohn's voice could penetrate via intercom to the farthest reaches of the Columbia Pictures studios. Once when a startled listener heard an all too familiar rebuke on the system, he asked who was speaking. Cohn's voice replied, "God." And, though damned more than worshipped, God he was in that studio.

Originally a song plugger, Cohn formed C. B. C. Films with his brother Jack and Joseph Brandt. Because of their cheap productions and salaries, the outfit was known in the industry as Corned Beef and Cabbage Productions. The Cohns eventually bought out Brandt and formed Columbia Pictures and later its subsidiary, Screen Gems. The studio flourished and attracted and groomed such names as John Wayne, Kim Novak, Rita Hayworth, Glenn Ford, and Frank Capra. Over the years Columbia garnered 45 Oscars by producing such films as *Mr. Deeds Goes to Town*, *Mr. Smith Goes to Washington*, *Lost Horizon*, and *On the Waterfront*.

Cohn's ego and love of power led to famous battles with his stars and directors. He was sued by Charles Vidor for abusive treatment, although the judge ruled in Cohn's favor, citing the nature of the profession and noting that Cohn's abuse was indiscriminate and habitual. Obsessed with power, Cohn was said to have modeled the characters of Willie Stark in the film version of *All the King's Men* and Harry Brock in *Born Yesterday* on his own personality. For his funeral Columbia's Sound Stage 12 was converted to a chapel, and his coffin was placed on a raised platform. Over 1,500 people, though not necessarily all mourners, attended his funeral.

When you enter the Cathedral Mausoleum at Hollywood Memorial today, you may find yourself in the presence of thirteen 10-foot statues. They are waiting to be moved outside to the cemetery's Court of the Apostles when it is constructed. Walk past them and turn right into the second hall. On your right you will find the crypt of **William Desmond Taylor**, born William Deane–Tanner (1877–1922).

Unlike most real-life murders, William Desmond Taylor's story was filled with intrigue and red herrings. On the

morning of February 2, 1922, when the body of the aristo-
cratic-looking movie director was found neatly laid out on
his living-room floor, several factions began cover-ups. Taylor's studio, Famous Players–Lasky (later Paramount),
rushed representatives to his house. They planted love
notes and negligees and spread rumors of pornographic
pictures taken with beautiful actresses. In the wake of the
Fatty Arbuckle scandal, the studio was terrified it would
emerge that Taylor was a homosexual whose houseman,
Henry Peavey, helped procure young men for him.

Ironically, the Taylor murder helped ruin the careers of
several other stars, including Mabel Normand and 20-year-
old Mary Miles Minter, who was hotly pursuing Taylor. The
night he died, Mary had gone to his bungalow. Her mother,
Charlotte Shelby, had tracked her down there. Enter the
next faction. Despite strong evidence that Charlotte Shelby
had made good on previous threats and gunned Taylor
down, she was never indicted. The district attorney's office
took pains to present alternate scenarios — mysterious
hitchhikers, and an employee who had been forging
checks with Taylor's signature. Investigators who came too
close to Shelby and Minter were pulled off the case.

It remained for another movie director, King Vidor, to
look into the Taylor case 60 years later. Reading transcripts
of family lawsuits from the 1930s, he learned that Charlotte
Shelby had been accused by her accountant of paying off
prosecutors Thomas Woolwine and Asa Keyes (who was
later sent to San Quentin for taking bribes in other cases).
Another of Shelby's daughters, Margaret Fillmore, sued for
money she said she was owed for providing her mother
with false testimony during the Taylor investigation. By the
time Vidor found this out both women were dead. Mary
Miles Minter, long unbalanced, would say only, "My mother
killed everything I ever loved."

In the alcove directly across from Taylor, down on the
left, are the remains of the founders of Hollywood. **Horace
H. Wilcox** (d. 1891) and **Daeida Wilcox Beveridge** (d.
1914) have no doubt flipped in their crypts over what their
city has become. The Wilcoxes envisioned Hollywood as a
devoutly Christian community and gave free land to Protes-
tant churches. The sale and ingestion of liquor was prohib-
ited. Originally from Topeka, Kansas, Mrs. Wilcox named
the area Hollywood after the country estate of someone
she met on a train trip.

Farther down, in the Alcove of Reverence, in the glassed-
in area in a small compartment on the bottom row, you will
find **Peter Lorre**, born Laszlo Lowenstein (1904–1964).

No one who has seen Lorre's flat brown eyes set in pouches in a larger moon face, or heard the menacing whisper which signals a madman on the brink of losing control, will ever forget what he looks like. The actor, who studied psychology under Sigmund Freud and Alfred Adler, began his career in Fritz Lang's masterpiece *M* (1931), as a psychotic killer of little girls. He went on to play other psychopaths—an assassin in *The Man Who Knew Too Much* (1934), an insane doctor in *Mad Love* (1934), and Raskolnikov in *Crime and Punishment* (1935). When Lorre deviated slightly from type, as in the *Mr. Moto* detective films, he was less effective. Of the 75 films he made, those which have achieved cult status include *The Maltese Falcon* (1941), *Casablanca* (1942), and *The Beast with Five Fingers* (1946).

Peter Lorre suffered from high blood pressure and died of a stroke at 59. His eulogy was given by another master of the horrific genre, Vincent Price.

Walk straight across through the main lobby to the next hallway and make the third right. The fresh flowers at the end will guide you to the compartment (Number 1205) of Rudolph Valentino. In the center of the marker is a cross flanked by two bronze flower holders. Ladies in Black still keep Valentino's memory alive with flowers, messages, and something unknown in his time, heart-shaped foil balloons. The best-known Lady in Black was probably Ditra Flame, who came on the anniversaries of his death, threw away the flowers left by other Ladies, and replaced them with her own red roses while she recited poems by Valentino.

RUDOLPH VALENTINO (RODOLPHO GUGLIELMI) *b. May 6, 1895, Castellaneta, Italy; d. August 23, 1926, New York City.*

> I'm the Sheik of Araby.
> Your heart belongs to me.
> At night when you're asleep,
> Into your tent I'll creep. . . .
> The stars that shine above
> Will light our way to love.
> You'll rule the world with me,
> The Sheik of Araby!

In 1921 American women were all too ready to be ravished by the Sheik—a celluloid barbarian who lured beautiful English women into his tent, had his way with them, then tossed them out into the jungle. Valentino, with his burning eyes, haughty profile, and air of menace, was the perfect incarnation. Although he was already having doubts about the Cult of the Sheik and despised the hit song that he had inspired, it was the role that made him America's idol. For the rest of his life Valentino could go nowhere without having his clothing torn off and his hotel room looted for personal souvenirs.

His own origins, though hyped up by Hollywood, were less exotic. Rodolpho Guglielmi was born in the backward village of Castellaneta, a town so poor the villagers' teeth turned black and rotted away in their mouths. Although his family was marginally better off than most because his father was a veterinarian, the elder Guglielmi died when Rodolpho was 11. Young Rudy refused to settle down and learn a trade. After he was jailed for vagrancy and his mother locked him out, he threw rocks at the house and broke the shutters. Finally she gave in to his pleas and sent him by steerage to New York City.

Although he found the usual unskilled employment—dishwasher, grocery clerk, and gardener—at night the young Valentino practiced his ballroom dancing and conversation. He was rewarded with a job as a paid dance partner at Maxim's, though he did not plan to remain a gigolo. He improved his tango and began to tour, signing on for a show traveling to San Francisco in 1917. The show collapsed in Omaha but Valentino continued on to California.

His first break came in 1920, when *The Four Horsemen of the Apocalypse* established him as a serious actor who could duel, dance, and ride horses. *The Sheik* followed and, in 1922, *Blood and Sand*, in which as the bullfighter Juan Gallardo he gave one of the finest performances of his career. Despite his ambivalence about sheikdom, in 1926 he made *The Son of the Sheik*, spending $11,000 of his own money for Arabian burnooses, an embroidered revolver holster, and silver spurs.

Valentino, who swept women away on screen, was less successful off. Wearing a corset, he struck less than an idol's image in the flesh. His first marriage, to starlet Jean Acker in 1919, ended on his wedding night when she smiled, slammed the hotel door in his face, and told him it was "a horrible mistake." It did not prevent her from suing him for alimony on grounds of desertion 14 months later. His second marriage, in 1922 to dancer-set designer Natacha Rombova (*née* Winifred Hudnut), foundered in 1925, in part because of her attempts to choose movies for him and dominate his career.

Valentino was learning to play the field and telling fan magazines how much he was enjoying it when he was rushed to Manhattan's Polyclinic Hospital with a perforated ulcer and ruptured appendix. For seven days the world held its breath as his temperature fluctuated and then soared heavenward. Rumors grew that he had been poisoned, or shot by a jealous husband. Despite these allegations, an autopsy was never performed. Instead he was laid out at the Frank E. Campbell Funeral Church and a dignified funeral — by invitation only — was planned.

Valentino's fans were outraged. By 2:00 P.M. 20,000 people were outside the chapel demanding entry. They finally crashed in the plate-glass window and trampled floral arrangements in an effort to find their idol. More than one-hundred people were injured. When peace was restored, another fight broke out between a self-appointed honor guard of Black Shirts and the Anti–Fascist Alliance of North America. Actress Pola Negri added to the carnival atmosphere, insisting that she and Valentino had been engaged, and screaming and fainting on command for the press.

With his brother's approval, Valentino's body was brought by train to Los Angeles, where blueprints for a monument at Hollywood Memorial were drawn up by architect Matlock Price. These plans included a large statue of Valentino as the Sheik, set in a semicircle of Roman columns. At the base of each column would be bas reliefs of Valentino in his six greatest films: *The Four Horsemen*, *The Sheik*, *Monsieur Beaucaire*, *Blood and Sand*, *The Eagle* and, of course, *Son of Sheik*. In the meantime he was placed in a vault that had been purchased by **June Mathis Balboni**. After she died tragically in a fire and Valentino's monument was still not built, he was moved into her husband's more modest crypt. A few years later, Albert Guglielmi quietly purchased the vault from Sylvano Balboni, making sure that his brother would, at least, have a roof over his head.

Across the way from Valentino and nearer the entrance in Vault 1224 is **Peter Finch** (1916–1977), who collapsed with a massive heart attack in the lobby of the Beverly Hills Hotel. His vault reads, "Distinguished actor, loving husband and father. Forever in our hearts." Although he made many films in Australia and England and won the British Film Award several times, Finch is best known for movies which became popular in America such as *The Nun's Story* (1959) and *Sunday Bloody Sunday* (1971). He was posthumously awarded an Oscar for Best Actor for his portrayal of Howard Beale, a crazed TV commentator, in *Network* (1976).

In the next alcove, Vault 1308, by the window and second from the bottom, is that of **Barbara La Marr**, born Reatha Watson (1896–1926). Her epitaph reads, "With God in the joy and beauty of youth." Barbara La Marr was a beautiful brunette whose career in silent pictures was cut short after three years by alcoholism and a nervous breakdown. She died at 30 of anorexia.

Returning outside, visit the magnificent sunken garden of Douglas Fairbanks, Sr. Here a long rectangular reflecting pool mirrors the classical Greek architecture. The center piece, fronted by the raised tomb, bears a cameo profile and is framed by a laurel wreath.

DOUGLAS FAIRBANKS, SR. (DOUGLAS ULMAN) *b. May 23, 1883, Denver; d. December 12, 1939, Santa Monica.* Douglas Fairbanks, Sr., who popularized the California tan with his bronzed complexion, liked to claim that he was so dark at birth his mother refused to show him to neighbors. "Oh, I don't want to disturb him now—he's asleep, and I'd rather not." Eventually Doug had to come out of the bedroom. When he did, he distinguished himself, at 3, by climbing trees, scaling roofs, and swinging from one branch to another. The son of his mother's brief third marriage, he lived with the consequences of an unhappy mother and absent father. (In later years Charles Ulman, a former lawyer turned heavy drinker, would sheepishly show up backstage for handouts; his son never turned him away.)

When Fairbanks first joined the theater at 17, however, there was nothing to share. He received his first notice for playing Laertes in *Hamlet*: "Mr. Warde's supporting company was bad, but worst of all was Douglas Fairbanks." Detouring briefly into a semester at Harvard, a job on Wall Street, and a period working his way through Europe, Fairbanks was soon drawn back to the footlights. His first success was in *The Man of the Hour* (1908), and he continued a respectable stage career until he was lured to Hollywood in 1916.

At Triangle Pictures, Fairbanks was assigned to D. W. Griffith, who was not pleased. "He's got the face of a cantaloupe and can't act," the director complained. Fairbanks' instinct for comedy and his preternatural energy unnerved Griffith—the actor killed time during one rehearsal break by walking up and down a staircase on his hands. Over Griffith's protests, an Anita Loos vehicle Fairbanks had selected, *His Picture in the Papers* (1916), was filmed and distributed. The public was enthralled. Fairbanks continued to please them with *The Mark of Zorro* (1920) and *The Three Musketeers* (1921).

There was no physical feat the exuberant actor would not attempt, from shinnying up a drainpipe to leaping into the sea from the top of the mast. Learning to use an Australian stock whip, in one picture alone he employed it to disarm a swordsman, capture a wild bull, and scale a castle's walls as well as put out a candle and slice in two an unwanted marriage contract.

Fairbanks had already done that in real life, of course, shedding his first wife, Beth Sully, to marry Mary Pickford (see Forest Lawn Glendale: Tour One). Ensconced in their estate, Pickfair, Fairbanks developed a taste for royalty which was increasingly reflected in his films—in *Robin Hood* (1922) he played the disguised nobleman with a sense of noblesse oblige, creating a gulf between himself and the poor that had not been there before. By 1930, however, he found that despite visitors like Babe Ruth, Conan Doyle, Lord Mountbatten, and King George of England, the genteel ambiance of Pickfair was smothering him.

One problem, of course, was age. Just as Mary Pickford was permanently imprisoned in childhood by her long golden curls and tiny size, Fairbanks had selected a persona that was eternally daring, eternally young. He could not put on a business suit and play character roles. Even at 41, swarthy and bare chested, white teeth gleaming, he had looked wonderful in *The Thief of Baghdad* (1924). But now doctors were warning him that he was muscle-bound and if he didn't cut down on his activity he would suffer serious circulatory problems. The spectre of aging was not helped by his son, Douglas Fairbanks, Jr., launching *his* career.

Fairbanks turned to acting out his previous adventures in real life, traveling to India, Cambodia, and Japan, hunting on safari and climbing mountains. He made a travelogue, *Around the World in Eighty Minutes* (1931), which was little more than a glorified home movie. But he would not stay home any longer. And Mary, the First Lady of Hollywood, would not leave Pickfair. So they did a two-step, moving toward reconciliation and then backing away. In the end there was too much anger for either to call a halt to the divorce decree. A month after the divorce, on March 7, 1935, Fairbanks married Lady Sylvia Ashley.

The couple traveled, but came home in September 1939 at the approach of World War II. Two months later, a day after attending a USC–UCLA football game, Douglas Fairbanks, Sr., died of a heart attack. He was laid out in an ornately carved bed in his Santa Monica home, in front of a

Douglas Fairbanks, Sr.

window facing the Pacific Ocean. As visitors came and went, the actor's 150-pound mastiff, Marco Polo, lay by his bed whining and refusing to move. Mary Pickford, accompanying her new husband, Buddy Rogers, on a tour with his orchestra in Chicago, sent condolences but did not come to the funeral.

Our final stop in Hollywood Memorial is the Abbey of the Psalms, down Maple Avenue. Currently under construction, the mausoleum has a proposed facade based on Psalm 23, which begins, "The Lord is my Shepherd, I shall not want." Twenty-eight marble statues, 11 feet high, are planned by sculptor Nisson Tregor to illustrate various aspects of the psalm.

Enter through the older main entrance. As you come in, in Vault 117 on your left is writer **Gene Stratton Porter**, *née* Geneva Grace Stratton (1863–1924). On her plaque is a quill symbolizing her profession. Although her novels might be laughed off the bookshelf today for their innocence and idealized characters, *Freckles* (1904) and *A Girl of the Limberlost* (1911) were extremely popular in the early twentieth century. Also an ornithologist who wrote nature studies, Porter founded a film company in Los Angeles two years before she died.

Right next to her is actress **Renée Adorée**, born Jeanne de la Fonte (1898–1933), a French actress with circus acrobatic experience. Her films were rarely more than B pictures. The exception was King Vidor's *The Big Parade* (1925).

In the Sanctuary of Light, in the extreme left hallway, is **Jesse Lasky** (1880–1958). His epitaph reads, "Beloved son of California who in 1913 headed the company that produced the first feature-length film made in Hollywood. His greatness never lacked simplicity. Carry the song along the passage, you the soul of all there is in glory forevermore." The plaque has the masks of Comedy and Tragedy and is circled by a reel of film.

Like Peter Finch and Clifton Webb in the next corridor, Jesse Lasky collapsed in the Beverly Hills Hotel. He had just concluded a lecture on his book, *I Blow My Own Horn*, which detailed his career from his first attempts as a cornet player for German–American picnics to his success as a film producer. Along the way he was involved in the Alaska gold rush and the promotion of such acts as the Lasky Quintette — four female cellists and a male bass playing romantic music from inside a giant seashell. Lasky, his brother-in-law Samuel Goldfish (later Goldwyn), and Cecil B. DeMille teamed up to produce *The Squaw Man* (1913).

Three years later Lasky joined Adolph Zukor to create what eventually became Paramount Pictures. When it went into receivership in 1932, Lasky began producing independently. He was responsible for *Sergeant York* (1941), *Rhapsody in Blue* (1945), and *The Great Caruso* (1951), but freely admitted his two greatest mistakes: turning down Irving Berlin's *Alexander's Ragtime Band* and failing to recognize the potential of vaudeville moppet Frances Gumm (a.k.a. Judy Garland).

Also in the Sanctuary of Light, in Crypt G4, is **Darla Hood** (1931–1979), the darkhaired charmer in *Our Gang*. In later years she did the voiceover of the mermaid in Chicken of the Sea tuna commercials and was also the voice for a line of talking dolls.

Clifton Webb (1889–1966) is in the Sanctuary of Peace, the third section on the left. His marker has an urn and an eternal flame. Webb, who never married — preferring to squire around his mother, Maybelle, with whom he had, according to Oscar Levant, an "adhesive" relationship, achieved stardom late. It wasn't until *Sitting Pretty* (1947), in which he played the dyspeptic professor, Mr. Belvedere, forced to play nursemaid to a bunch of miserable brats, that he struck a responsive note in American hearts. Webb's other notable films include *Cheaper by the Dozen* (1950), *Titanic* (1953), and *Satan Never Sleeps* (1962). Besides being nominated three times for an Academy Award, he is also credited with introducing into American fashion the double-breasted vest, the white mess coat dinner jacket, and the red carnation as boutonniere.

Webb's spirit is restless. He is said to haunt this corridor of the mausoleum as well as his former Beverly Hills home. After his mother died in the house in 1960, Webb was certain he saw her ghost as well as that of actress Grace Moore, who had previously lived there and died in a plane crash.

In the last alcove, the Shrine of Eternal Glory, to the left, is the vault of **Harry Ross** (1896–1974) whose vault describes him simply as "Makeup Artist."

Norma Talmadge (1897–1957), along with her sisters **Constance** (1899–1974) and **Natalie** (1897–1969), have their own alcove located in the Sanctuary of Eternal Love. Inside is a marbleized pink-and-gray bench and a stylized stained-glass window of Jesus and two worshipping angels.

As a star of numerous silent films, Norma Talmadge earned over $5 million between 1922 and 1930. During that time she was married to movie mogul Joseph M. Schenck, and the couple was characterized by Anita Loos as "looking like Snow White and an overgrown dwarf." She left him for actor Gilbert Roland but actually married Georgie Jessel in 1934. Five years later they too were divorced. Norma last married the physician who had been supplying her with the drugs to which she had become addicted.

Constance, a pretty and gifted comedienne of the silent movies, drifted away from movies with the advent of sound. She married four times but lapsed into alcoholism and died alone albeit wealthy. She left the bulk of her over $1 million to her nephews, Bobby and Jimmy Keaton.

Natalie married Buster Keaton and starred with him in several of his films. She lacked, however, the flair and personality of her sisters and did not aggressively pursue a career. Divorced from Keaton in 1933, she raised their two sons, frequently without much financial help and without any paternal contact for eight years at one stretch. She too became alcoholic and with age grew increasingly reclusive, dying alone in her Santa Monica apartment.

The most unusual epitaph in Hollywood Memorial is said to belong to actress **Joan Hackett** (1934–1983), in the Sanctuary of Trust: "Go away, I'm asleep."

BETH OLAM CEMETERY

In Beth Olam Cemetery, which adjoins Hollywood Memorial, is Hollywood's favorite gangster. **Benjamin "Bugsy" Siegel** (1906–1947) rests in the mausoleum behind a marker which does not have the nickname he detested. It is an open book with the words, "In Loving Memory from the Family."

Growing up in the Williamsburg section of Brooklyn, Siegel sidestepped the respectability which led his brother to become a physician and made his money bootlegging. When Prohibition ended, he headed for Los Angeles and moved into the same neighborhood as Anita Louise and Sonia Henie. He was considered by some to be as handsome as his friend George Raft and certainly more vain. Bugsy, who had secret aspirations toward stardom, slept with cold cream and a chin strap.

Once he was settled in Holmby Hills, Siegel returned to gambling. He was investigated by the IRS and indicted for the gunning down of Big Greenie Greenbaum, but the indictment was mysteriously withdrawn. In the end he was done in by his own greed. Obsessed with building the most glamorous casino in the world, Bugsy sank his money and that of fellow gangsters into the Flamingo in Las Vegas. The nightclub went $6 million into debt amid rumors that Siegel had been skimming off money and hiding it in Switzerland. His fellow mobsters decided to teach him a lesson. On June 21, 1947, nine shots were fired at Bugsy through the window of his mistress' house, killing him instantly.

Ironically Bugsy's casino, now the Flamingo Hilton, had begun to thrive. His prize rose garden is maintained with a plaque reminding people that Bugsy was an accomplished gardener. It suggests that his "secret formula to keep his roses so beautiful and richly red" might be none other than Frankie Giannattasio, Mad Dog Neville, and Big Howie Dennis, all of whom disappeared without a trace. The ground around Beth Olam mausoleum does not give evidence of any special fertilizer.

DIRECTIONS TO HOLLYWOOD PARK MEMORIAL CEMETERY: Take Route 101 (Hollywood Freeway) to the Santa Monica Boulevard exit and go west. The cemetery is on your left at 6000 Santa Monica Boulevard, between Gower Street and Van Ness Avenue.

CHAPTER 3

Forest Lawn Glendale

TOUR ONE

I met a Californian who would
Talk California—a state so blessed,
He said, in climate, none had ever died there
A natural death

—ROBERT FROST

IN A TOWN where the pink and purple Frederick's of Hollywood building has a museum devoted to the Bra, a town which sports the fanciest McDonald's facade in the country, replicating classic works of art isn't such a strange idea. While it is odd to see Michelangelo's David standing like a visiting ghost in Southern California, and Boston's Old North Church surrounded by palm trees, the museums and stained glass make the cemetery that contains them more interesting. When Herbert Eaton took over the struggling cemetery in 1913 and made it into Forest Lawn, he began to amass what has become the largest collection of marble statuary in America.

Yet Forest Lawn's real riches are the personalities buried here. They constitute an attraction the cemetery prefers to downplay, but most of the stars buried here played to the crowd when they were living, and it is difficult to believe that in death they would want the applause to end. With that in mind, Forest Lawn is included in this book even though some of the gardens and mausoleums are private. If you are fortunate enough to know a property owner with a key, you can visit them all. If not, we are providing a literary key so you will know what lies behind the walls.

Forest Lawn Glendale breaks down naturally into three main areas: the outdoor gardens, including the Columbarium of Honor; the lower outdoor sections such as Whispering Pines; the Freedom Mausoleum and the Great Mausoleum. We will cover Forest Lawn Glendale in the next three chapters. In this chapter we will deal with the outdoor gardens. To orient yourself, go to the Freedom Mausoleum. In the garden to your left as you face the mausoleum is one of Hollywood's most enigmatic giants. A little mermaid sits on a rock in front of a wall giving his name and dates.

WALTER ELIAS DISNEY *b. December 5, 1901, Chicago; d. December 15, 1966, Los Angeles.* When Walt Disney was operated on for a cancerous left lung, he arranged for his doctors to save it. At the time he was investigating cryogenesis — a method of freeze-drying bodies so that they can be resurrected in a later century — and he knew that he would need all his parts. Yet that seems to be as far as the project went; as tempting as it is to imagine Disney springing to life and introducing Mickey to another century, the best evidence suggests that his ashes are here in the family vault.

Disney, at 65, was not anxious to leave. He had long before abandoned the making of cartoons and moved into creating entire worlds. With Disneyland and Walt Disney World operating successfully, he was rushing to complete EPCOT in Orlando. But Walt Disney had been rushing all his life. As a boy he was rousted out at 3:30 A.M. to deliver newspapers for his financially unsuccessful father. Because he and his brother Roy were paid nothing, Walt secretly developed a second route without telling his father and took a candy-store job during lunchtime recess.

Stationed in France during World War I, Disney attempted to launch a freelance cartooning career through the mail. He failed, but he earned extra money by decorating trucks and helmets for other Doughboys. When he came home, he found work at the Kansas City Film Ad Company, learning the infant art of animation. He teamed up with another animator, Ub Iwerks, to form their own company. The partners soon realized that to succeed they would have to head west to California.

Disney's first cartoon animal was a cuddly charmer named Oswald the Rabbit; his second was Mortimer — soon to be called Mickey — Mouse. The mouse's first cartoon, "Plane Crazy," was silent, but by "Steamboat Willie" (1928) he had added a musical track in which Mickey and Minnie, running wild in a barnyard, play a cow's-tooth xylophone and a nursing-sow bagpipe, then crank a goat's

Forest Lawn Glendale, Tour One

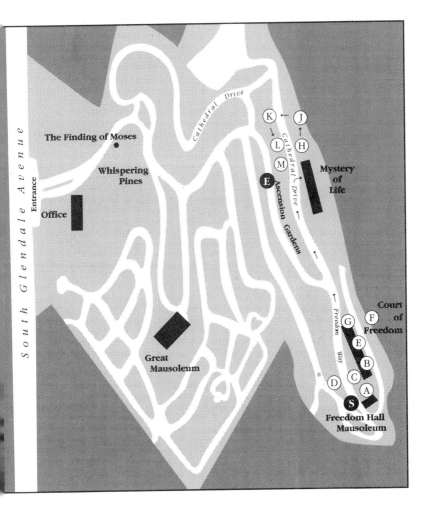

A	Walt Disney	H	Humphrey Bogart, Atwater Kent,
B	Errol Flynn		Kathryn Kuhlman
C	Spencer Tracy	J	Mary Pickford, Terry Allen Kath
D	Lilli Palmer	K	Mitchell Ayres
E	Robert Taylor, Clifford Odets	L	Ted Knight
F	George Cukor, Sam Cooke	M	Ethel Waters
G	Casey Stengel		

tail to get "Turkey in the Straw." He next moved into Technicolor with "Flowers and Trees" (1931), the first Disney picture to win an Oscar. Indeed, winning an Academy Award for the Best Cartoon of the Year was soon an annual event. In 1937 *Snow White*, Disney's first feature-length cartoon, emerged as a box-office success.

Disney never varied the pattern that made him so successful — driving himself and his employees mercilessly, borrowing money, cutting back on his own salary, plunging into debt and financial crisis. His more conservative brother Roy tried frantically to block the very things which helped create the Disney empire: use of Technicolor, full-length cartoon features, Disneyland. Walt's wife, Lillian, added her own advice. "There's something so nasty about dwarfs," she told him when he was excited about making *Snow White*. And, later, "But why do you want to build an amusement park? They're so dirty!"

Only once, in 1931, did worries about the future drive Disney to a breakdown. The studio was in debt, and in six years of trying he had not fathered a child. (Roy had a new baby son.) Lillian found Walt collapsed in the bedroom after he had taken an overdose of sleeping pills. A vacation helped to restore his equilibrium, as did the birth of his daughter, Diane, in 1933, and the success of *The Three Little Pigs*.

Except for allowing him to indulge in the miniature locomotive that ran through his estate and which constituted the main form of entertainment for visitors (he took guests for rides and planned spectacular crashes), financial security changed Walt very little. He never stopped rushing, although he became less avuncular and more of a bully. One associate pointed out that Disney looked at people as if he was seeing "something very small and very ugly at the back of your skull." His word was absolute; his smile increasingly rare. He growled at one reporter, "I don't have depressed moods, and I don't want to have any. I'm happy, just very, very happy."

But, of course, it was the classic stance of the entrepreneur who has met his challenges courageously, put aside transient pleasures, and now finds that despite his hard work he will not be allowed to go on forever. Enter cryogenesis. It did not seem fair to Disney that a man who had been called the most famous person in the twentieth century would not get another chance to shine in 2400.

If you enter the Garden of Everlasting Peace, against the far wall you will see a bronze statue of a woman with her hands folded across herself, looking away. Beneath her is the marker for **Errol Flynn** (1909–1959), inscribed "In memory of our father from his loving children," which was placed there in 1979. There is a simple leaf design around the top with the initial F.

Although it was rumored that Errol Flynn took six bottles of whiskey to the grave with him, such provision was probably superfluous; Flynn had probably imbibed enough in life to keep him well preserved. In fact one of Hollywood's greatest pranks revolved around Flynn and his alcoholic companion, John Barrymore. Imposing himself as a house guest against Flynn's generosity and admiration during his final days, Barrymore was little moved to do anything but drink. So unmoved, in fact, that he simply urinated on the plate-glass windows while enjoying the view. Flynn, ever tolerant, kept pouring until his friend died a few months later.

In mourning Barrymore, Flynn and his friends headed for a tavern to reminisce and drown their sorrow. Before the night was over, several of the mourners had slipped off to the funeral home, bribed the undertaker, headed back to Flynn's with Barrymore's body, propped it in his favorite chair, and waited for the host to arrive. When the drunken Flynn turned on the lights and saw his pale, puffy, resurrected friend, he let out a "delirious scream." Recovering quickly, he treated the pranksters to another round but refused to help them return the body.

Such shenanigans were typical of Flynn, whose real life equaled the swashbuckling adventures of his movies. Born in Tasmania, he was educated in Paris, London, Sydney, and Ireland. He took on many jobs including journalist, sailor, novelist, and fighter, before he and his sailboat were discovered off New Guinea by a film crew. Flynn liked the limelight and returned to England for acting lessons. His breakthrough came in the movie *Captain Blood* (1935). After that he was typecast as the spirited leader of small heroic bands of adventurers. In real life Flynn's roguish adventures brought him into court on more than one occasion for charges of assault or statutory rape. Seemingly always acquitted, he would declare with suave solemnity his complete faith in the American system of justice.

In a garden to the right of the George Washington statue is Spencer Tracy. The marker says only "Tracy" and has a marble bench surrounded by beautiful plantings.

SPENCER TRACY *b. April 5, 1900, Milwaukee; d. June 10, 1967, Beverly Hills.* Spencer Tracy was not a happy man. He drank too much and too often. He became obsessed with death and had an explosive temper. Intensely private, he was given as a young man, not unlike certain stars of the present, to fighting photographers and breaking their cameras. Whatever the nature of his demons, it's clear that he never exorcised them. Despite all this Tracy was loved by his friends, admired by his fans, and was one of the greatest actors in the history of film.

Tracy's tempestuous Milwaukee childhood was a clear indicator of things to come. He majored in fights, expulsions, failed grades, and new schools. Only late in high school, at the Jesuit Marquette Academy under the influence of his friend Bill O'Brien (later to be better known as Pat O'Brien) did he show any academic aptitude. After service in the Navy, Tracy attended Ripon College in Wisconsin. There he took to the theater and with his clipped, forceful tones quickly became a leading man.

After two years, stagestruck and successful, he was off to New York for drama school. Hooking up with Pat O'Brien again, he obtained bit parts on and off Broadway. He also met and married an actress, Louise Treadwell, and by 1924 was father to John Tracy. Tracy was already given to bouts of depression, and his son's deafness only furthered his gloom, his guilt, and his remove from his family. Meanwhile, however, his career was beginning to flourish. He auditioned for George M. Cohan and captivated the grizzled stage veteran ("Tracy, you're the best godamned actor I've ever seen."). With Cohan Tracy enjoyed successes such as *The Baby Cyclone* but in lean times had to fall back on touring stock companies.

In 1930 Hollywood was raiding Broadway, where Tracy was playing a prisoner in *The Last Mile*. John Ford, scouting for Fox, overlooked Tracy the first night but was captivated by the play and returned the following evening. This time he was caught by Tracy's strong performance. When he returned a third time it was solely to see Tracy. After the play Ford went backstage to meet Tracy, and by the evening's end the two Irishmen were well on their way into the wee hours and a long friendship.

Tracy was soon in Hollywood with a contract from Fox and a start (along with Bogart) in a prison movie, *Up the River*. Known as a sturdy, masculine type who could act with great intensity, Tracy was never considered handsome by the studio and therefore lacked a glamorous image. Nevertheless he slowly moved into the first ranks of stardom, capped by his back-to-back Best Actor Oscars for *Captains Courageous* and *Boy's Town*.

Tracy was a director's dream come true. He studied his craft and his parts and knew his lines in their entirety before rehearsals began. Frequently he knew the other parts before his fellow actors did. Above all he was a natural, an actor who rarely required a second take, whose instincts and skill brought him the right reaction to virtually any situation.

Tracy's personal life fared less well. Although he had learned better how to deal with his son, his marriage had seriously deteriorated. Bouts of drinking, affairs (most notably with Loretta Young), a fiercely guarded privacy, and bellicosity became his trademarks. He spent less and less time at home although, because of his Catholic faith, he and Louise never divorced. Rather than dissolving, however, the relationship evolved into one of friendship.

In 1941 Tracy was teamed up with Katherine Hepburn in *Woman of the Year*. Not only was a great film partnership born, but a fabled romance was begun. It seemed an odd match: Hepburn, tall, outspoken, aristocratic, individualistically feminist, and Tracy, stocky, reserved, traditional, down to earth. But they admired each other's character, and they respected each other's talent. Quickly drawn to each other, the relationship seemed never to falter. It was at once Hollywood's best known and least discussed affair. Their strength of character, obvious devotion to one another, and obsessive privacy removed all titillation, and even the worst of the gossip sheets left them alone.

Tracy and Hepburn teamed up in nine films but are best remembered for their intelligent romantic comedies, *Woman of the Year*, *Adam's Rib*, and *Pat and Mike*, where they struggled for romance with subterfuge and disarming honesty and humor. They acted apart as well, with Tracy performing some of his most memorable roles in *Bad Day at Black Rock*, *The Old Man and the Sea*, *The Last Hurrah*, *Inherit the Wind*, and his favorite, *Judgment at Nuremberg*.

By the early 1960s Tracy had been off alcohol for years, but his heart was not good, and he looked far older than his years. He made *It's a Mad, Mad, Mad, Mad World* in 1963 and then went into seclusion for four years. With Hepburn he would take long walks in the hills where they would fly kites together.

In 1967 Stanley Kramer convinced Tracy to take a leading role opposite Hepburn in *Guess Who's Coming to Dinner*. Unable to obtain insurance against Tracy's health, Kramer took full responsibility for the risk. He shortened Tracy's work day and tried to ease him through. Three months later the shooting was finished, and Tracy had turned in another fine and convincing performance. He was ecstatic.

George Washington memorial

Wanting to go out as Ted Williams had done, with a home run, he had succeeded. Making a rare phone call, he crowed to Garson Kanin, "Did you hear me, Jasper? I finished the picture." Two weeks later he died of a heart attack in the early morning.

Nearby in the grassy area is director **Frank Borzage** (1893–1962), who several times directed Tracy, and who won the first Oscar given to a director for his movie *Seventh Heaven* (1927). Around the corner in the Sanctuary of Affection is a well-known newspaper editor from the *Los Angeles Times*, **Agness Underwood** (1902–1984).

Before walking to the opposite end of Freedom Court to visit a baseball great, cross the road. Opposite the tree-trunk receptacle is the marker of **Lilli Palmer–Thompson**, born Lilli Peiser (1914–1986). First married to Rex Harrison, she is here as the "Unique wife of Carlos Thompson–Palmer with whom she keeps their pact, 'Forever beyond,' and their creed, 'To die is but to pass from one room to another.' " Carlos Thompson, an actor in his own right, began as a matinee idol in Argentina. Lilli Palmer began her career as one of Austria's leading actresses but made the bulk of her films in England, including *Thunder Rock* (1942) and *The Rake's Progress* (1945).

Also in this area is **Samuel Laird Cregar** (1914–1944), who gave a creepy rendition of Jack the Ripper in the original version of *The Lodger* (1944). Plagued with a weight problem, the 28-year-old actor had gone from three hundred to two hundred pounds but required a stomach operation because of complications. While recuperating, Cregar suffered a fatal heart attack.

To your right as you walk toward the statue of Immortality is the private Garden of Honor. Inside, in the Columbarium of the Evening Star, is **Joan Blondell** (1906–1979), a comedienne often cast as a Depression-style gold digger in films such as *Gold Diggers of 1933* and *Footlight Parade* (1933). Although she was married to some industry greats, including Mike Todd and Dick Powell, she was never driven to succeed in films. Two of her best roles were in *He Was Her Man* (1934) and *A Tree Grows in Brooklyn* (1945). Joan is located directly above the statue of a woman holding flowers standing under a shell.

To the side of the Greek statue is **Robert Taylor**, born Spangler Arlington Brugh (1911–1969). His plaque reads, "A lifetime to go." Robert Taylor was a durable, untemperamental actor, featured in movies from 1934 to 1968. Unfortunately most of his films were forgettable. The exceptions were *Magnificent Obsession* (1935), *A Yank at Oxford* (1938), and *Bataan* (1943). Taylor, who was married to Barbara Stanwyck and Ursula Thiess, was better known to modern audiences for his role in the TV series "The Detectives." After his death from lung cancer, he was eulogized at Forest Lawn's Church of the Recessional by Ronald Reagan.

In the Columbarium of Honor is **Jerry Wald** (1911–1962), an exuberant writer and producer who was said to be the original for Sammy Glick in *What Makes Sammy Run?*, Budd Schulberg's novel of life in Hollywood. Finally, in the base of the classical marble statue you see when you enter, is **Clarence Brown** (1890–1987), the director, who died of kidney failure at 97. Best known for films such as *National Velvet* (1944) and *The Yearling* (1946), he was nominated for an Academy Award six times. Don't ask.

Also in this area is **Clifford Odets** (1906–1963). When he died, Cary Grant and Zsa Zsa Gabor were among the mourners. Danny Kaye gave the eulogy, praising the deceased as a man "with a completely humane faculty for sorrow and humor." Dinah Shore sent flowers. Yet it is doubtful that any of this would have cheered up the playwright. His best plays, *Waiting for Lefty* (1935) and *Awake and Sing* (1935), had been written at the beginning of his career, and two of his later works that were successful, *Golden Boy* (1937) and *The Country Girl* (1950), he professed to dislike. In between were many failures, either at the box office or with the critics.

A shy, intense man who championed left-wing causes, Odets wrote plays of social protest that combined poetic style with realistic vitality. He blamed "maternity" (having to raise his two motherless children) on his decreased output but often told friends that he should have been a composer instead of a playwright. When he died at 57 of stomach ulcers complicated by cancer, he did not go easily. From his deathbed he tried to effect a reconciliation with his father, insisted that his psychotherapist marry him (she wouldn't), and, on occasion, would raise himself up in bed to shout, "Clifford Odets, you have so much to do! I may fool you all . . . you know, I may live. . . . Then perhaps Clifford Odets will do something to redeem the last sixteen wasted years." His son described his death as, "This mountain blown to dust in two weeks."

Charlotte Shelby, the mother of Mary Miles Minter, was originally buried outside the Columbarium of Honor. But Mary had Charlotte and her sister, Margaret, removed and their remains scattered, as she was herself. Mary was an adorable 17-year-old with long blonde curls when the murder of William Desmond Taylor ended her movie career. In the fallout from the investigation, it was revealed that she had been passionately pursuing the director. The overbearing Charlotte Shelby was suggested as a suspect in the murder but was never questioned by police. William Desmond Taylor and his story are buried in Hollywood Memorial Park Cemetery.

Several other interesting personalities are located here. The touching plaque of figure skating champion **Dona Lee Carrier** (1940–1961) has the medal of the US World Championships 1961, a flag and a skate blade through it. It explains that she was "Gold Medalist and member of the U.S. Figure Skating Team representing the United States in world competition to be held in Prague. She perished at the peak of her career with all her teammates in the Sabina Airlines crash in Brussels, Belgium."

Dona Carrier's marker also has testimonial quotes, perhaps from newspapers: "Like a cup of gold on the ice."

"Her grace and sweet spiritual fragrance touched many lives." "Her loveliness glowed from within." There is also the Bible verse, "I will come again, and receive you unto Myself." John 14:3.

To Carrier's right is the unmarked garden of **George Cukor** (1899–1983), director of such classics as *Little Women* (1933), *The Philadelphia Story* (1940), and *Gaslight* (1944). He received an Oscar for *My Fair Lady* in 1964. As the discoverer of Katherine Hepburn, Cukor collaborated happily with her for nearly 50 years, marred only by the time when she spilled ice cream on a valuable dress during the filming of *Little Women*, after he had warned her to be careful. When she laughed, he slapped her and called her an amateur.

Nearby is **Sam Cooke** (1930–1964). He has a popular plaque showing a couple in classic dress standing together looking over to a mountain, with the Bible verse from Song of Solomon 2:17, "Until the day break and the shadows flee away."

Sam Cooke, who began by singing gospel music, reached national acclaim in 1957 with his recording of his brother's song, "You Send Me." He went on to write his own hits, including "Cupid," "Chain Gang," and "Bring It on Home to Me," and married his high-school sweetheart, Barbara Campbell. Cooke also owned his own record company, developing such stars as Lou Rawls and Little Richard.

What happened the night of December 10, 1964, is still a matter of conjecture. It appears that Cooke picked up a 22-year-old woman at a restaurant, took her to a rundown Los Angeles motel and forced himself on her. When she escaped from the room, he broke into the manager's office looking for his date, then turned his anger on the manager, Bertha Lee Franklin. They struggled, and she shot him three times with a pistol she kept for protection, then hit him repeatedly with a stick until he died. The jury found her actions justifiable homicide. Cooke's friends, who knew him as charming and refined, believed the killing had been a setup — though by whom and why was never made clear.

To the left of the Statue of Immortality is a plaque on the wall to Charles Dillon "Casey" Stengel. On the bottom is a quote, "There comes a time in every man's life, and I've had plenty of them." On top is Casey's cameo portrait over two crossed bats; it appears to be carved and painted. The eulogy starts, "For over sixty years one of America's folk heroes who contributed immensely to the lore and language of our national pastime, baseball."

CHARLES DILLON "CASEY" STENGEL *b. July 30, 1890, Kansas City, MO; d. September 29, 1975, Glendale.* Listening to Casey Stengel talk was like reading James Joyce. His language, "Stengelese," was marked by stream-of-consciousness, broken sentences, run-on sentences, free association, comedy. It rambled, digressed, turned back on itself, and no one, not even Casey, was sure where it was headed. It was a random ride through the complexities of Casey's mind and memory.

Casey was the youngest of three children and grew up in a close-knit family of modest means. He had Irish ancestry on his mother's side and German on his father's. Though intelligent, Casey did not do well in school. Instead his visits to vaudeville stirred his natural gift for mimicry, first used against his fellow students who recited Shakespeare. Among those students was William Powell with whom Casey also played basketball. It was at athletics that Casey starred. At five feet, eight inches, and 170 pounds, he played fullback and captained the football team, and was the star of the city's champion basketball team.

Baseball was his real love, however. Throughout his career he was a scrappy, aggressive player who worked hard to sharpen his less-than-spectacular gifts. He was a crowd pleaser; a well-liked troublemaker who often fought and who held out for better contracts. Because of his uncertain progress Casey almost quit baseball for dental school. He signed with the Brooklyn Dodgers, however, and by mid-September 1912, was with the parent club. He arrived in big-league style, with a new suit and a new suitcase, and went four for four with three stolen bases. He also acquired his nickname, "Casey," for K C or Kansas City.

Casey's hitting was erratic, but his fielding improved to the point where the papers referred to Stengel's "daily sensational catch." Playing for the Dodgers, Pirates, Phillies, Giants, and Braves, he had his moments of glory. His home run off Grover Alexander took the spirit out of the Phillies as the Dodgers moved past and to the pennant in 1916. In 1922 he had his finest year batting .368 with John McGraw's Giants. In 1923, near the end of his career and playing with injuries, he hit two game-winning home runs in the World Series, including an inside-the-park homer in which Casey heroically gimped and puffed around the bases.

Casey also began to make his legend. Placing a captured sparrow under his cap, he went to bat. Upon reaching the plate he acknowledged the crowd's usual applause by doffing his hat and setting the bird free. The fans and the press

loved it. He also thumbed his nose and blew kisses to the Yankees while rounding the bases after hitting a World Series home run off them. Contrary to popular belief, however, it was not Stengel who dropped a grapefruit from a plane to a waiting Wilbert Robinson, who was expecting a baseball on the mound below. The glory for that act goes to Frank Kelley.

Ending his career in 1925, Casey started managing in the minors. He was a fine student of the game and an admirer of the great John McGraw, and by 1934 he was managing the Dodgers. When he came to the Yankees in 1949 he was still viewed as a clown and faced an imposing team of stars led by the disdainful Joe DiMaggio. It took Casey the season to prove himself. Winning the World Series helped his confidence, and by 1950 the Yankees were Casey's team. He used the platooning he had learned from McGraw and set up instructional schools for the minor-league players. And he was not afraid to bench the fading DiMaggio. The Yankees won five straight pennants and World Series (1949–1953), something that no one, not even the great McGraw, had ever done. When Casey left the Yankees in

1960, he had won another five pennants and two more World Series.

And then bathos. Casey became the first manager of the New York Mets (1962–1965), the worst team in baseball history. His career went from the sublime to the ridiculous and then back again when the mandatory five-year retirement rule was waived and he was elected to the Hall of Fame in 1966. He was justifiably proud and on all subsequent autographs he added Hall of Fame after his name.

Casey had long been a legend. His speech, his winks, his big ears, his mugging for the cameras. He was the "Old Perfessor." After retirement he still followed the game and the banquet circuit, but the last years were tough. His wife, Edna, suffered a series of small strokes which left her incapacitated. Then Casey was diagnosed with lymphatic cancer. In the hospital, watching a game about to begin, he stood "one last time" for the national anthem. Fittingly, he died the day after the season ended.

Just outside Casey Stengel's wall is the monument of **Dan Dailey** (1915–1978). Dailey, an accomplished actor as well as a song-and-dance man, died of severe anemia after a fall during a performance of *The Odd Couple*.

Inside the open mausoleum, in the last section beyond Casey Stengel's tablet, is another former athlete, **Johnny Mack Brown** (1904–1974). His name is on a small bronze plaque. Brown first came to national attention when he caught two touchdown passes for the University of Alabama in the 1926 Rose Bowl. Soon after, he began making films. Although he was featured in *Our Dancing Daughters* (1928), the film that made Joan Crawford a star, he soon turned to Saturday-matinee westerns. Helped by his horse, Reno, he made over two hundred movies.

The next work of art of interest is in the adjoining section behind the statue of David. It is known as the "Mystery of Life" and shows eighteen marble figures engaged in various enterprises.

In the private garden to the left of this statuary group are a number of interesting personalities. The first monument is to **Earl Carroll** (d. 1948) with the epitaph, "In life we weep at the thought of death. Perhaps in death we weep at the thought of life." It has a beautiful winged bronze statue standing nearby. Carroll, whose theater on Sunset Boulevard was famous for its slogan, "Through these portals pass the most beautiful girls in the world," was killed in a plane crash. His companion, **Beryl Wallace**, who died with him, is also said to be buried here.

Going left and up the steps and then to your right, look

for the plain plaque against the wall, in memory of **Atwater Kent** (1873–1949). His marble sarcophagus is below. Kent is one of America's unsung heroes. While still a teenager in Vermont, he made the first outboard motor, then went on to invent a portable meter to test dry-cell batteries. He revolutionized the automobile industry with a one-spark electric ignition and in 1923 began manufacturing radios. When radios were in enough homes to make it worthwhile, he gave listeners the "Atwater Kent Hour," a Sunday-night program of classical music.

In the garden section near the Columbarium of Sunlight is **Harvey S. Mudd** (1888–1955). His garden is decorated with a dark bronze oriental statue of a woman holding a flower bud. Mudd, a mining engineer and president of Cyprus Mines Corporation, is best known for his contributions to education. A trustee of the California Institute of Technology, which has a school named after him, Mudd was also the founder of the Southern California Symphony Association.

This garden is a combination of individual walled-in plots, outdoor mausoleums, and grassy center areas. In the ground in the center is evangelist **Kathryn Kuhlman** (d. 1976). Her marker states, "I believe in miracles because I believe in God." Practicing that creed, Kuhlman, an attractive red-haired woman who dressed in white, toured the country for 25 years, holding prayer and healing services. A Johns Hopkins doctor often appeared with her to attest to the genuineness of the healings. Miss Kuhlman always kept her age a secret; she was believed to be in her early sixties when she died while recuperating from open-heart surgery.

Several other, less well known personalities are also in this area. Bandleader **Abe Lyman**'s (1899–1957) marker says, "Goodbye my love. I'll see you later." As leader of The Californians and a songwriter, Lyman is credited with such hits as "I Cried for You" and "What Can I Say, Dear, After I Say I'm Sorry?"

Over to the right is **Warner Baxter** (1893–1951), best known in his role as the Cisco Kid, for which he won an Oscar in 1929. He was also the guy in *42nd Street* (1933) who encouraged the understudy to "go out on stage a kid, and come back a star." Three weeks before he died, Baxter underwent a lobotomy to alleviate the pain of arthritis.

In the ground in the back is **S. Z. Sakall** (1883–1955), familiar to *Casablanca* (1942) aficionados as the rotund waiter at Rick's Place. Beside him is dapper comedian **Charlie Ruggles** (1886–1971) and his director brother

Wesley Ruggles (1889–1972). Before he moved to the other side of the camera, Wesley was one of the original Keystone Kops.

In the last columbarium on your left, on the right wall beneath a statue of a woman under a seashell, is Humphrey Bogart. He has a small marker the size of a coaster, with a vase to the right.

HUMPHREY BOGART *b. December 25, 1899, New York City; d. January 14, 1957, Los Angeles.* Not all movie stars scramble out of poverty to become famous. Some, like Humphrey Bogart, begin life on Park Avenue. He was the firstborn son of a Manhattan doctor, and his suffragette mother was a well-known illustrator who studied with Whistler in Paris. The "Maud Humphrey baby" was as famous as the Gerber's years later. When not being sketched by his mother, young Bogie attended private schools. His education at Phillips Academy, Andover, Massachusetts, ended when he was expelled for failing five subjects and committing various infractions.

A week after leaving Andover, young Bogart joined the Navy for the end of the war. When he was transporting another seaman to Portsmouth Naval Prison in New Hampshire, the prisoner smashed Bogart across the mouth with his handcuffs and tried to flee. Bogart shot and wounded him but was left with a permanent scar on the right side of his upper lip. Allegedly the wound caused his slight lisp as well.

After his discharge Bogart decided to become an actor. Early reviews described him as giving a "rather trenchant exhibition of bad acting" or, simply, as "inadequate." He ping-ponged back and forth between Broadway and Hollywood. By the time he had had his first success as escaped killer Duke Mantee in the Robert Sherwood play *The Petrified Forest* (1935), Bogart had been an actor for 13 years. His success in the movie version the next year further typecast him as a criminal. It wasn't until he was offered the part of Sam Spade in *The Maltese Falcon* (1941), followed by that of Rick in *Casablanca* (1942), that he got back on the right side of the law. Incredibly, *The Maltese Falcon* was his 43rd movie.

Bogart was taking a long time to find himself personally as well as professionally. His first marriage, to an actress 10 years older who had pursued him, was undertaken half-heartedly. It ended after a year. His next union, to actress Mary Philips, could not survive their separate careers. Number three, Mayo Methot, was a blend of Zelda Fitzgerald and Tugboat Annie, but Bogie was rather proud of their altercations. During their seven years together she pushed him off a dock, threw a Thanksgiving turkey at his head, and stabbed him with a kitchen knife. He nicknamed her Sluggy and hit her back.

In the end, Mayo's irrational jealousy, exacerbated by alcoholism, was too much. When Bogart met 20-year-old Lauren Bacall (Betty Perske) and co-starred with her in *To Have and Have Not* (1945), Mayo's suspicions were finally justified. Though she promised to stop drinking and harassed Bacall with phone calls ("Listen, you little bitch, who's going to wash his socks?"), Mayo bowed to the inevitable. Bogart and Bacall married quickly and never looked back. Their next picture together was *The Big Sleep* (1946), followed by *Dark Passage* (1947), and *Key Largo* (1948). It was for *African Queen* with Katharine Hepburn, however, that he won an Academy Award in 1952. His role as Captain Queeg in *The Caine Mutiny* two years later brought him another nomination, though not an Oscar.

Without Mayo to fight with, Bogart took on the larger world. Fortified by Drambuie, he insulted everyone from his studio head, Jack Warner, to John Steinbeck ("Hemingway tells me he doesn't think you're all that good a writer.") and Lucius Beebe ("We have a bet at our table. Are you or aren't you a homosexual?"). Perhaps he was trying to live up to his tough-guy screen image, to counteract the image of the gently raised doctor's son and the "Maud Humphrey baby." But few of his confrontations ever reached physical violence. Once, after goading a writer into stepping outside "where we'll settle this right here and now," he put his arm around the man's shoulder and suggested, "Let's put on ladies' hats and go back and make 'em all laugh."

Liquor, as well as cigarettes, had other effects. In early 1956 Bogart's esophagus and the cancer encircling it were cut away. He spent nearly a year more at home, holding court but getting weaker, until one Sunday morning he slipped into a coma and was gone. While the brief memorial service at All Saints Episcopal Church was being held, he was cremated at Forest Lawn. The gold whistle that Bacall gave Bogie to commemorate the line from *To Have and Have Not* ("If you want me, just whistle. You know how to whistle, don't you, Steve? You just put your lips together and blow.") was with him.

On the other side of Bogart is a memorial to the brawny Irishman **Victor McLaglen** (1886–1959). Before beginning his acting career, McLaglen spent time as a wheat farmer, gold prospector, professional boxer, South Seas pearl diver, and captain in World War I. *What Price Glory?* (1926) brought him fame, but his masterful acting job in *The Informer* (1935) gave him an Oscar. McLaglen died at 72 from congestive heart failure.

Near Victor McLaglen is **Judy Canova** (1913–1983) whose plaque reads, "Love and laughter." The mention of laughter is appropriate, as the hayseed comedienne specialized in hillbilly humor and raucous yodeling. Canova's pictures had names on the order of *Hit the Hay* (1945) and *Singin' in the Corn* (1946). Her husband, **Leon "Zeke" Canova** (1898–1980) is designated as "One who loved."

In the corner garden on the right is **Buddy Adler** (1908–1960) whose epitaph reads, "From Here to Eternity," and **Anita Louise Adler Berger** (1915–1970), with "Love surrounds her beauty." Buddy Adler was head of production at Twentieth Century–Fox when he died at 51 of lung cancer; his film *From Here to Eternity* (1953) won nine Academy Awards, including Best Picture. Anita Louise, a delicate, pretty blonde, preferred costume roles such as Titania in *A Midsummer Night's Dream* (1935) and the title role in *Marie Antoinette* (1938). But she stepped out of costume long enough to become the "Post Toasties girl" on cereal boxes, and "Paper Doll of the Salvage Campaign" during World War II. It is probable that she selected Buddy Adler's epitaph, as she was married to him when he died.

Also on the right side of the garden, closest to the entrance, is a marble monument showing a classically dressed group consisting of three women and four small children. Actually two of the women are distinctly barebreasted with the most prominent leaning on a cornucopia. Another is blowing on a goat's horn while the third has her ear cupped as if trying to hear the sound. The babes seem happy to be clambering about this scene of plenty. Just below fly two doves. It is in memory of Mary Pickford Rogers (d. 1979), America's Sweetheart. Functional as well as decorative, the arched section with the birds pulls open to receive ashes; the nameplate section opens for coffins. Mary's brother Jack and sister Lottie, as well as their mother, Charlotte Smith, are also buried here.

Close by is **Ivan Lebedeff** (1899–1953), designated as "Beloved husband of Versa and Mary's devoted friend." Lebedeff, who died at 52 of a heart attack, was a Russian actor brought to America by D. W. Griffith to appear in *Sorrows of Satan* (1927). He also wrote the novels *Legion of Dishonor* and *Brothers*.

MARY PICKFORD (GLADYS MARIE SMITH) *b. April 9, 1893, Toronto; d. May 29, 1979, Santa Monica*. Mary Pick-

Mother and child

ford, the vest-pocket beauty with the waist-long blonde curls, tried many times to grow up. She felt that she could not go on playing Rebecca of Sunny Brook Farm indefinitely. But every time she attempted a more mature role, her fans protested. Always a shrewd businesswoman, Pickford gave in. She was 28 when she played a convincing 9-year-old, Little Lord Fauntleroy.

Mary had very little childhood herself. She was 4 when her father, who ran a fruit and candy concession on a Lake Ontario steamboat, was hit in the head by a dangling pulley and died from a blood clot on the brain. Left with two children even younger than Mary, Charlotte Smith was talked into putting them on stage. From then on Mary was the family's main support.

It was a precarious existence. To get Little Mary, directors also had to find parts for Little Jack, Little Lottie, and a buxom matron with no acting experience. Not every theater manager was willing to do so. In time the family split up professionally, and at 13 Mary took a role in a David Belasco theater production, *The Warrens of Virginia* (1908). She enjoyed the part and considered it a comedown when she was reduced the next year to signing on with the movies.

At Biograph Studios Pickford made dozens of silent short features with titles like "Her First Biscuits" (1909) and "A Lucky Toothache" (1910). She played scrubwomen, Mexican teenagers, and choir singers. Because director D. W. Griffith was a strong believer in anonymity for his troupe, it took several years for Mary to get any billing at all. Film producers were afraid — rightly so, as it happened — that individualizing actors would lead to salary increases over the standard $5 a day. By the time Mary left Biograph for a brief fling on the stage, she was making $175 a week.

After *A Good Little Devil* (1912) Mary returned to the movies, but with Adolph Zukor's Famous Players at $500 weekly, a sum Griffith was not willing to match. It was as the child-woman in *Tess of the Storm Country* (1914) that Pickford found her perfect role. From then on her films were actively sought out by the American public. Pressure from Mother Charlotte and Mary raised her salary to $4,000 per week. Money was always important to Pickford, who tended to hold onto it when she had it. In the early days she would walk miles to avoid breaking a dollar bill; later on she was dunned by dressmakers and butchers for her snail-like pace in paying her bills.

Pickford eventually realized she was carrying Famous Players in the same way she had supported her family, and in 1918 left to start her own unit. In 1919 she founded United Artists with Douglas Fairbanks, Charlie Chaplin, and her old mentor, D. W. Griffith. By producing their own pictures, they could reap the profits themselves. Despite the dire warning that "the lunatics had taken over the asylum," Mary's first UA film, *Pollyanna* (1920), was one of her best. Her sensitive, spirited portrayal of the 10-year-old orphan helped make her what the *Chicago Tribune* called "the most beloved face in the world." Though she was only five feet tall, the furniture on her sets was built one-third larger than normal to further the illusion of her youth.

It was a measure of Mary's credibility that during this time she cut loose her first husband, Owen Moore, and married the recently divorced Douglas Fairbanks without disturbing her illusion of innocence. Moore, a cranky alcoholic actor 10 years older than Mary, threatened to shoot "that climbing monkey." But he accepted a cash settlement, and Pickford went to Nevada for her decree.

It was the joining of two dynasties. The Fairbankses' domestic castle in Beverly Hills, Pickfair, was more publicized than the White House. Every detail of their lives was generously shared with the public, from the color of their bathroom towels to the fact that they snuggled up to watch movies and munch popcorn in the evenings. Guests who joined them were served Ovaltine and fruit at 11:00 P.M., signaling that the party was over. Although British and European royalty ate there happily on solid-gold plates, not everybody relished an invitation. The sedate atmosphere, perhaps overemphasized to tone down the scandal of the principals' divorces, put some people to sleep.

In 15 years it was all over. Fairbanks himself had gotten bored with Pickfair and was resolving his midlife crisis by constant travel and adventure. Mary responded by burrowing in further. Neither would compromise to try and regain what had been lost. They were divorced in 1935. By then Mary's wonderful curls were gone, clipped in front of a coven of photographers, and she had retired from acting after making *Secrets* (1932).

In 1965 Pickford, married to younger actor, Buddy Rogers, retired from living as well. She went to bed and, except for secret nocturnal creepings around the house, never got up again. Her butler brought up her meals, whiskey, and a newspaper which, on Buddy Rogers' orders, had any upsetting stories clipped out. Visitors spoke to her by downstairs' phones. For 12 years, until she died of a stroke at 86, America's Sweetheart hid out in a sad attempt to please her "public." "People remember me most as a little girl with long golden curls," she said. "I don't want them to see me as a little old lady."

In the private garden to the left of this one is **Terry Allen Kath** (1946–1978), identified as "Composer, Guitarist, Singer . . . The memories of love he left on earth all the world has shared. Rare and gifted, a gentle man whose riches were a symphony of songs for young and old because he cared." The marker is decorated with music notes.

Kath was the lead singer and guitarist for the rock group Chicago and had played bass for Jimmy and the Gentlemen. The day of his death, he spent the afternoon drinking and socializing at the home of a friend. When the party was breaking up, Kath pulled an automatic pistol from his pocket and began playing with it. Asked to stop twirling the gun, Kath answered, "Don't worry, it's not loaded. See?" He put the gun to his temple and pulled the trigger, killing himself instantly.

Directly across the way and slightly back is English actress **Merle Oberon Wolders**, born Estelle O'Brien Merle Thompson (1917–1979). She is seen chiefly these days in revivals of *Wuthering Heights* (1939).

Outside, left of the Court of the Christus and halfway up the hill on the left, is bandleader **Mitchell Ayres** (1909–1969), who was run down by a car while crossing a street in Las Vegas. A companion, Betty Phillips, was injured seriously. Ayres, in Las Vegas as music director for Connie Stevens, had also worked with Perry Como and Guy Lombardo. In the 1940s he had his own dance band, Fashions in Music.

On the left side of Ascension Garden, as soon as you come in and to your right, is **Ted Knight** (1923–1986) whose marker bears the bronze faces of Comedy and Tragedy. It gives his real name, Theodore C. Konopka, and on the bottom says, "Bye, Guy." Ted Knight, who won five bronze stars in World War II, is best known for his Emmy-winning performance as the pompous announcer on "The Mary Tyler Moore Show." Knight died from complications following surgery to remove a urinary tract growth.

Farther down the lawn is **Robert Alda**, born Alphonso Giuseppe Giovanni Roberto D'Abruzzo (1914–1986). Although perhaps now best remembered for being Alan Alda's father and for his guest appearances on "M*A*S*H," the elder Alda had a fine career in his own right. He starred in the original Broadway cast of *Guys and Dolls* as Sky Masterson, the smooth-talking gambler and lover. For his vivid portrayal he gathered up most of the dramatic awards in 1950, including the Tony, Drama Critics Circle, and Donaldson. In addition to his work on Broadway, Alda made many movies, the most notable being his portrayal of George Gershwin in *Rhapsody in Blue* (1945).

In the center of Ascension Garden, in the row beside the sidewalk and near the statue of the woman with a child, is **Ethel Waters** (1896–1977). Buried under a marker with the epitaph, "His Eye is on the Sparrow," Miss Waters epitomized the patient suffering of her race. She was born into poverty, stealing food to keep alive, and found work as a chambermaid in a small Philadelphia hotel. After appearing in an amateur show, Miss Waters began her career as a blues singer, appearing as Sweet Mama Stringbean and specializing in a rendition of the "St. Louis Blues."

In the 1920s, once again Ethel Waters, she appeared in Harlem nightclubs and several of the black-and-tan shows on Broadway, such as *Africana* (1927) and *Rhapsody in Black* (1931). In 1950 she played her most famous Broadway role as the warm, maternal cook in *Member of the Wedding*, into whose welcoming lap children of all ages — including the play's author Carson McCullers herself — yearned to throw themselves. By then she had ballooned to three hundred pounds and was fighting diabetes.

Although Waters had come to dislike singing, she consented to do so in the Billy Graham campaigns and in Richard Nixon's White House. Her epitaph, also the title of her autobiography, is from the hymn whose chorus goes:

> I sing because I'm happy,
> I sing because I'm free.
> His eye is on the sparrow,
> And I know he watches me.

Across the road below, in the Eventide section, is **Ralph M. Byrd** (1909–1952), best known for his film role as *Dick Tracy* (1938). Also in this area is **Suzan Ball Long** (1933–1955), whose epitaph reads, "Love attends you on your new adventure." If courage and spirit alone could have kept Suzan Ball alive she would not have died at 22. A knee injury during a dance rehearsal triggered a malignancy that eventually resulted in the amputation of her right leg. Three months later she married actor Richard Long, appeared in a TV drama, and made the film *Chief Crazy Horse*. Despite treatment, the cancer spread to her lungs.

Forest Lawn Glendale

TOUR TWO

Time proved the representation false. Oh, the tangle of human life! How dimly as yet we see.
— THEODORE DREISER

THE SECOND TOUR begins outside the Great Mausoleum, shown on the map. Down the hill and to the left you will see the family monument of **Joe E. Brown** (1891–1973). It shows a classically dressed man and woman with their three small children, the smallest held aloft on the father's shoulders. It was originally erected as a memorial to Brown's son, Captain **Don Evan Brown**, Commander 1st Squadron, 6th ferrying group, Air Transport Command, Army Air Force, Long Beach. "Killed in line of duty October 8, 1942, Palm Springs, CA."

Joe E. Brown's marker reads, "Beloved husband, understanding father, cherished friend. His courage in the face of trouble, his modesty in the rewards of triumph won the love and esteem of people all over the world. His personal integrity and devotion to all people reflected the love of the Saviour into whose hands his life was given." Joe E. Brown is better remembered for his elastic features and clown-sized mouth than for any particular film role.

Located on the periphery of the Great Mausoleum are several other notable monuments. Character actor **Wallace Beery** (1885–1949), whose epitaph reads, "No man is indispensable but some are irreplaceable," is in the Vale of Memory. He won an Academy Award for *The Champ* (1931) and recognition as Long John Silver in *Treasure Island* (1934).

Walking up the front lawn toward the Great Mausoleum

you will see an elaborate monument worthy of a fascinating woman. This long, low-lying monument is guarded in front by a heavy chain supported by four bollards. Facing each other from either end are two kneeling angels with bowed heads. Between them the long, slightly raised stone bears the name of:

AIMEE SEMPLE McPHERSON *b. 1890, Ingersoll, Ontario; d. September 27, 1944, Oakland, CA.* Although little Aimee Kennedy marched in Salvation Army parades and wore a banner which designated her "God's Little Child," as a teenager she had different aspirations. Born to straight-laced Calvinistic parents on an obscure Canadian farm, she planned a career as the second Sarah Bernhardt. Then at 18 she met Robert Semple, a Pentecostal preacher. Her conversion was immediate, helped by his Scottish burr and clear brown eyes. Embracing faith as wholeheartedly as she had her other passions, she married him. But their life as missionaries in China was not to be. In 1910, while Aimee was carrying their first child, Roberta, her husband contracted malaria and died.

Aimee was desolate. She waited in China for Roberta to be born, then brought her to her mother's new apartment in New York City. For the next year and a half, mired in depression, she ignored her baby and her mother's platitudes. Then one night she ran out of the apartment and picked up the man who became her next husband: Harry "Mack" McPherson. But Mack was not the answer. Aimee's melancholia returned after the honeymoon. When their son, Rolf, was born, she threatened to kill herself and Mack if her life did not improve.

It began to improve when Aimee decided she had a mission to preach. As she soon found out, she had the gift for it. Her sense of drama returned; her early arrogance was mellowed into compassion and humor. When Mack decided a tent preacher's life wasn't for him, the beautiful Titian-haired Aimee barely noticed. In a matter of weeks she and her mother, Minnie, had taken the children and were headed for California in a new Gospel Automobile — an Oldsmobile which demanded in gold letters, "Where will you spend Eternity?"

By the end of a six-week campaign, Aimee was preaching to 4,000 people nightly in the Los Angeles Philharmonic Hall, billed as the "Lady Evangelist." Through Minnie's careful financial strategies, Aimee's church, Angelus Temple, opened in January 1923. The temple, which seated 5,300, featured tiered seats, a 30-foot golden organ, and a mural of Jesus with His hand outstretched toward Aimee.

Forest Lawn Glendale, Tour Two

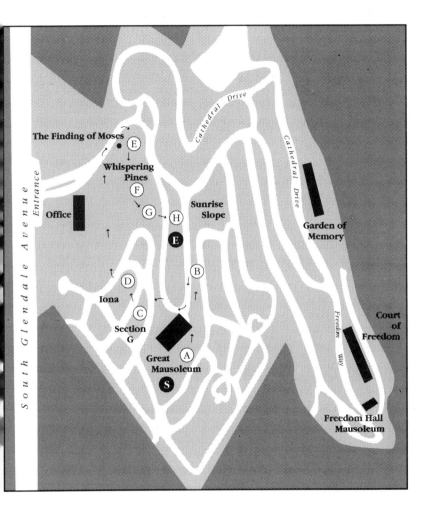

A   Joe E. Brown
B   Aimee Semple McPherson
C   L. Frank Baum
D   Eli P. Clark, Moses A. Sherman
E   Rosetta Duncan
F   Theodore Dreiser, Jackie Oakie
G   Tom Mix
H   Lawrence Tibbett

Soon she was standing beneath it, giving altar call after altar call and exhorting her ushers to, "Jump to it! Clear the one-way street to *Jesus*!" as people flocked down the aisles.

Within a year, radio station KFSG (Kalling Four Square Gospel) was broadcasting from the third floor of the Temple, reaching from San Diego to Seattle. It was all a thrilling success. Masses of people were finding Jesus, and some were even being healed. Aimee's voice was broadcast daily on her own program. The passionate Aimee, a true believer, was communicating her enthusiasm to others. Nevertheless she felt something was missing in her own life. Mack had divorced her, and Robert was just a memory.

She began to find what she craved in her radio engineer, Ken Ormiston. Escaping Minnie's watchful eye, the couple slipped away for a European vacation until someone—perhaps Ormiston's wife—leaked the story to the press. Aimee returned with little harm done, but less than a month later, on May 18, 1926, the Lady Evangelist was missing and presumed drowned. Only an enraged Minnie suspected the truth. Though she fervently prayed that Aimee's drowned corpse would bob up at Ocean Park Beach—death was better than disgrace—she knew in her heart that her headstrong daughter had disappeared once more with Ken Ormiston.

On June 23, tired of hiding out and remaining anonymous, Aimee reappeared in Agua Prieta, Arizona, with a fantastic tale of how she had been kidnapped. No one believed her story more firmly than Aimee and her followers. Indeed, no one else believed it at all. Aimee and Ken had been seen together during her disappearance by numerous people and the proof Aimee offered appeared bogus. She and Minnie were indicted for perjury and for manufacturing evidence. Yet by the time it came to trial, most antagonistic witnesses had mysteriously changed their stories in Aimee's favor. She and her mother were never convicted.

The ministry continued, but with less joy. Aimee split with Minnie, and then with her grown daughter, Roberta. Nobody cared when she married singer David Hutton and divorced him several years later. Despite a great revival that swept Angelus Temple in the late 1930s, Aimee's enthusiasms were elsewhere. She increasingly dwelt on her life in China with Robert and how different it would have been if he had lived. Perhaps that was what was in her mind when, at 52, she absentmindedly took an overdose of Seconal and died.

In one of the oldest parts of Forest Lawn, Section G, is the large granite marker of **L. Frank Baum** (1856–1919) and his wife, **Maud Gage Baum** (1861–1953). Although Baum wrote 13 other books about his fictional country, none ever topped *The Wonderful Wizard of Oz* (1900). With its profits he brought his family to Hollywood and installed them in Ozcot, along with several hundred birds in an aviary. His last words — "Now we can cross the shifting sands." — no doubt referred to the areas around Oz which were entirely desert.

To the left of Baum, in the Iona section, you can see an impressive monument showing a kneeling woman looking heavenward with two praying children. **Eli P. Clark** (1847–1931), his wife, **Lucy** (1851–1942), and her brother General **Moses A. Sherman** (1853–1932) are interred here. Sherman and Clark owned extensive real estate and built up a number of railways which eventually became part of the Southern Pacific Company. General Sherman received his rank from serving as Adjutant General of the Arizona National Guard in 1881.

The last section we will be visiting is Whispering Pines. Walk from Iona across the Cathedral Drive and orient yourself at the fountain showing Moses being discovered in the bulrushes. Memorials to several almost-forgotten names are located just around it. The marker to **Rosetta Duncan** (1901–1959) is inscribed: "Rememb'ring. One of the world-famed Duncan sisters of musical comedy success 'Topsy and Eva.' One blessed with a great talent to evoke laughter and pathos. The immortal compositions with her sister Vivian will long be remembered. Established forever in our hearts."

As half of a vaudeville team, Rosetta, in blackface, played Topsy, while her sister was Little Eva. The *Uncle Tom's Cabin* routine became a revue in 1923 and toured the United States and London. The sisters continued with films and occasional club appearances until Rosetta was fatally injured in an automobile accident. The reference to the song "Rememb'ring" may refer to the lines, "When one is gone, and one is left to carry on." When **Vivian Duncan** died in 1986 she was buried in the Cathedral Slope section of Forest Lawn.

Close to the road are **Jane Darwell**, a.k.a. Patti Woodard (1879–1967), whose last character role was as the Bird Woman in *Mary Poppins*, and **Susan Peters**, born Suzanne Carnahan (1921–1952). Susan Peters was on the threshold of a promising career when, as she was hunting with her husband, actor Richard Quine, her rifle discharged acci-

dentally. It lodged a bullet in her spine. She continued her career from a wheelchair, appearing on stage in the role of invalids, such as Amanda in *The Glass Menagerie* and Elizabeth Barrett Browning in *The Barretts of Wimpole Street*. She also had her own TV show, "Miss Susan," the saga of a wheelchair-bound lawyer. But her struggle was difficult. When the actress died, her doctor blamed her death in part on having lost the will to live.

Halfway up the hill in location Number 1570 is **Lurene Tuttle** (1907–1986). Her marker reads, "Loving mother, grandmother, great-grandmother and friend." On the early radio series "Sam Spade," Tuttle played every female, from the young secretary to old ladies. She also played Mother in the "Life with Father" TV show from 1953 to 1955.

A number of personalities are located on the crest of the hill. Theodore Dreiser rests in Plot 1132 under a marker with a shell-and-leaf design. The inscription reads: "Oh, space! Change! Toward which we run so gladly or from which we retreat in terror — yet the promise is to bear us in itself forever. Oh what is this that knows the road I came."

HERMAN THEODORE DREISER *b. August 27, 1871, Terre Haute, IN, d. December 28, 1945, Hollywood.* Moving almost every year, Theodore Dreiser experienced a Midwestern childhood marked by desperate poverty, by a father's Catholic fervor that grew increasingly fatalistic with his failures and increasingly impotent in its effect on his children as they grew older, by a mother whose charm and gritty instinct for survival kept the family afloat but who played her self-pity off on the children to create sentimentally devoted sons. Even as a young boy Theo would stroke and weep over his mother's poorly shod feet.

The girls wore make-up and were coquettish. The older boys were frequently in trouble, even Paul, who leapt to early fame with his sentimental ballads written under the altered name of Dresser. While the ungainly, unattractive Theo remained introverted and shy, he nevertheless fled the hopeless conditions at home for Chicago while not yet 16. He found he was only intermittently able to support himself, and his escape failed. Yet his academic promise saved him. Like a *deus ex machina* his former teacher, Mildred Fielding, also now in Chicago, sought him out, persuaded him to go to Indiana University, and bore the entire expense of his first year.

Attracted to and inspired by the intellectual climate of college, Dreiser, a social misfit nevertheless, left after the year. That fall his seriously ill mother died in his arms while his father reacted with hysterics, and the priest refused to give absolution. With his beloved mother gone, Dreiser, alone more than ever, burned to express himself and managed to gain experience if little money as a reporter. Later hooking up with Paul in New York, he wrote the chorus and first verse to one of Paul's best remembered songs, "On the Banks of the Wabash." More important, Dreiser moved under the sway of Spencer and Darwin and took a great interest in the mass of humanity he observed and encountered daily. Always wild, undisciplined, and inaccurate, his stories and poems contained enough power and eloquence to attract magazines, although diligent and substantial editing was required.

In 1900 Doubleday published *Sister Carrie* but did so only because Dreiser would not let them out of their contract. Although the novel got a tremendous push by Frank Norris, the publisher found its degree of social realism offensive and immoral. Most American reviewers agreed, and the unpromoted book failed to sell out its first printing.

Dreiser took the disappointment hard. Now married, he left his wife behind in Missouri and returned to New York, where he worked on his next novel, *Jennie Gerhardt*. His depression worsened and with it his living conditions. Impoverished and living in a squalid apartment, Dreiser felt a compulsion to walk in a circle, and he drifted in and out of hallucinatory states in which his doppelganger, a silent philosopher, observed the tall, self-centered writer. Only his brother Paul's intervention pulled Dreiser out of his despair.

If Dreiser's decline was precipitous, his resurrection was no less spectacular. Moving from one editing job to another, he gained prestige, money, and the company of H. L. Mencken, whose work he accepted for publication. Dreiser and Mencken's friendship was mutual admiration based on their contempt for the reserve of American literature and manners. With success also came love affairs. No surprise, certainly, for Dreiser was promiscuous throughout his life. Despite his looks and his hang-dog mien, he could pour on the charm and held a great sexual magnetism for women. In 1919 he met Helen Richardson, who became his long-suffering but steadfast companion and eventual second wife.

With structure imposed on him by his publisher, Horace Liveright, Dreiser achieved his greatest success and renown with *An American Tragedy* in 1926. In his later years his output declined, although he remained an influential literary presence. Dreiser's antisocial attitudes seemed at times pugnacious and even deliberate. Frequently rude and boorish, he was viewed as a naive, platitudinous lowbrow by his intellectual acquaintances. Indeed Dreiser wrote better when he described rather than philosophized. His erratic mind and mouth, seldom disengaged, caused his offer of support to be long shunned by the Communist Party, which feared his loud intemperate outpourings.

Yet he had character. He believed in his social realism, and he believed in the strength and accuracy of his portrayals. Dreiser's novels paved the way in loosening the straitlaced hold that the censors had on American literature. He fought against the censors, took up the cause of miners, and supported the Spanish Loyalists. Always contradictory, he also grew increasingly anti-Semitic and supported Germany over Britain in World War II.

Even as an old man Dreiser pursued large, eternal issues. He continued to be outspoken, but as his health failed he grew morose and tearful, and described himself as "the loneliest man in the world." His self-centeredness had cost him his dearest friendships. With Helen holding his hands he passed away into death that Dreiser saw as "a wooly fog that blocks one's course and quenches all."

Next to Dreiser is his wife **Helen** (1894–1955), whose epitaph on her marker is the lines to a sonnet she wrote, "To a Poet":

> If I did touch the margin of your soul
> In its swift moving earthly seeming plight,
> And but beheld its burnished aureole

That shed a brilliance to the inner sight,
And opened up the windows of the mind
To rarer beauties far than most men feel;
Then I have sung the lark's sweet song designed
To fuse our senses with celestial seal
As once on grassy sward we lay enthralled;
But moved as quickened spirits to the birth
Of other joys to which our hearts were called:
To ride melodic wings above the earth
Where you, the song and I are now afloat
In that one crystal clear immortal note.

Her signature is below.

Helen did indeed touch the margin of Dreiser's soul; how much more deeply she or anyone else could have touched is doubtful. Giving up a promising film career, she remained available to him, the one constant person in his life, even though it cost her numerous and flagrant rejections. When Dreiser's eye had been captured by another woman, he made no attempts to cover up his admiration and many times left Helen, his Babu, for varying lengths of time. As the author and Helen were companions for 26 years, most people, including several intimate friends, assumed they had married early on. Dreiser, however, dodged marriage as long as he could, and it was not until his first wife died in 1942 that Helen had a clear path. Even then it took more than another year and a half before she could legalize her name.

Realizing that his lack of loyalty had cost him dearly, Dreiser tried to make it up to Helen in their last months together. "Teddy flooded me with his love," she wrote. It was no small consolation.

To the left of the Dreisers is **Nonnie Doolittle** (d. 1965), wife of Jimmy. She is eulogized as having "lived with Jimmy in harmony, love, and true companionship. The world is a better place because of her life, brief alas as it was. She will leave in the hearts and minds of all us who knew and loved her a shining graciousness and everlasting memory."

Nonnie Doolittle, who died at 40 of a heart attack, appeared in opera productions as Nonnie Franklin. Her husband was not Jimmy Doolittle, the flying general, but Jimmy Doolittle, the theater impresario.

To the right of the Dreisers are a trio of comic actors and one retired cowboy. The first of these, Louis Delany Offield, a.k.a. **Jack Oakie** (1903–1978), has a reminder of his trademark on his marker:

In a simple double take
Thou hast more than voice e'er spake.
When you hear laughter, that wonderful sound,
You know that Jack Oakie's around

Not far away is **Andy Clyde** (1892–1967), who found his niche as the grizzled, good-natured dimwit. He is probably best known as Hopalong Cassidy's sidekick, California. Clyde is here with his sister-in-law **Fay Holden**, born Fay Hammerton (1894–1973), who is described as "Resting with those she loved." Her most famous role was as the mother in the series of Andy Hardy movies.

The third member of the trio is **Edward Everett Horton** (1886–1970), who made movies for nearly 50 years. He also played an Indian chief on "F Troop" during the 1960s.

The cowboy, closest to marker Number 986, is **Tom Mix** (1880–1940). His grave marker has his signature and a replica of his belt buckle, with his initials TM combined to look like a brand. Allegedly the original belt buckle, which spelled TOM MIX in diamonds, was buried with him. Mix, who died in an automobile crash, was a United States marshal before he began starring in the four hundred westerns that made his name (and that of Ralston cereal) a household word. In the radio series, however, Tom Mix never played himself.

If you continue down the hill to ground marker Number 794 you can find singer **Lawrence Tibbett** (1896–1960). "Beloved in life, in memory." Because Lawrence Tibbett's great-aunt and uncle planted the first navel orange tree in California, it can be said that his family was firmly rooted in the state long before his birth. When Tibbett was just 7 his father, a deputy sheriff in Bakersfield, was shot and killed while pursuing the notorious Wild Jim McKinney.

Tibbett later lived in Los Angeles, where he studied voice and music. In 1922 he moved to New York to pursue his vocal lessons and to audition with the Met. His start was not auspicious, as he failed his first audition. Although he succeeded the second time, he was signed only to a one-year contract and was kept on for a second year only because he agreed to forgo a raise over his current $60 per week. Midway through his second year, however, Tibbett changed the course of future negotiations when, on short notice, he played the part of Ford in Verdi's *Falstaff*. His second act monologue brought down the house in one of the wildest and longest displays of audience approval in Metropolitan history. For 15 minutes the audience let the young baritone hear its appreciation. Only when Tibbett made a solo bow was the music allowed to continue.

Tibbett quickly became a Met favorite and drew enthusiastic responses from the audiences throughout his career. With over 70 roles to his credit, he not only starred in the standard repertoire but also premiered many new works.

Several of these new operas remained in the Met's schedule on the basis of Tibbett's authoritative performances. Most notable of these was his performance in the title role in Louis Gruenberg's *The Emperor Jones*. Tibbett possessed a beautiful baritone, even throughout its range and bronzelike in its tone. Studying his parts with care, he brought a great sense of character and drama to his singing.

Tibbett's career did not stop with opera. He also performed in movies such as *Rogue Song* (an Academy Award nomination) and *New Moon*, both in 1930, and he sang on Broadway. He was a fine exponent of less operatic songs as well, as his idiomatic performance of "On the Road to Mandalay" attests. Tibbett also enthusiastically pushed to have opera sung in English and recorded several of the more famous arias in his native language in hopes of demonstrating its validity in English as well as drawing a wider audience to opera.

Musical interests aside, Tibbett was a staunch believer in labor unions. He helped to form the American Guild of Musical Artists in 1937, became its first president, and played a similar role with the American Federation of Radio Artists.

Performing as a replacement for Ezio Pinza in *Fanny*, Tibbett took his final bow in 1956. In retirement he made his home in Manhattan. He died two days after undergoing surgery for an old head injury.

Although the prayer for world peace and prosperity on Marker 1689 makes it appear that Madame **Alla Nazimova** (1879–1945) was a religious cult figure, she was actually a Russian actress who made a number of American films. She was also the focus of a lesbian cult for many years.

Finally, in this area is **Gus Kahn** (1886–1941), a lyricist whose best-known songs were "Mammy," "My Blue Heaven," and "Whoopee." In his spare time he was Groucho Marx's father-in-law.

C H A P T E R   5

Forest Lawn Glendale

TOUR THREE

*Now, my usefulness over,
the weight of your death
in a handful of ashes
drags at my mind.*

— EDWIN HONIG

THE GREAT MAUSOLEUM, standing on Westminster Road,
resembles a large brown castle. Its squared-off turrets and
arched windows have a forbidding look — appropriate,
since it is not open to the general public. Inside the castle
there are two main areas of interest. One is through Holly
Terrace on the second floor. The other is on the ground
floor behind the Last Supper window. If you know a property owner and are invited onto the second floor through
Holly Terrace, these are some of the personalities you will
find:

In the Columbarium of the Dawn on the right wall is a
bright bronze marker against a rose setting. It reads simply

Dear God,
    Thanks.
        Ed Wynn

Ed Wynn, born Isaiah Edwin Leopold (1886–1966), had
a lifelong affair with hats. As a child he entertained everyone (except his father) by putting on headgear and mim-
icking customers at his father's millinery business in Philadelphia. When he entered vaudeville, one of his most
successful acts was billed "The Boy with the Funny Hats."
At the height of his career he owned eight hundred, along
with three hundred coats which he used to portray differ-

ent characters. By the 1950s, however, Ed found that his jokes were growing threadbare: the 11-foot pole he had invented for people who wouldn't touch someone with a 10-foot pole; the typewriter carriage designed to move as he ate corn on the cob; the nervous giggle that earned him his sobriquet, The Perfect Fool. With his son Keenan's encouragement, Wynn switched to more serious film roles. He was nominated for an Academy Award for his role as Mr. Dussel, the dentist in *The Diary of Anne Frank* (1959).

Just above Ed is **Keenan Wynn** (1916–1986), who survived two plane crashes and four car accidents, and totalled a motorcycle and a speedboat to die in bed. Francis Xavier Aloysius James Jeremiah Keenan Wynn followed his grandfather, Frank, a Shakespearean actor, and his father into the theater. For a long time he was known simply as Ed Wynn's son, and indeed he made his debut as such when his father presented him as an infant to a Winter Garden audience. Gradually Keenan emerged into his own spotlight, playing supporting roles. Among his best-known performances were the macho paratrooper in *Dr. Strangelove* (1963), the fight handler in *Requiem for a Heavyweight*, and the comic rendition of "Brush up Your Shakespeare" in *Kiss Me Kate* (1953).

In the open corridor near Ed Wynn is **John Anson Ford** (1883–1983) whose epitaph is "Public service, humanitarian." As a member of the Los Angeles Board of Supervisors, Ford helped clean up LA politics, opposed the internment of Japanese Californians during World War II, and developed county parks and cultural facilities.

In an outside corridor, to the left of the Hall of Inspiration, is the plain marker of W. C. Fields.

W. C. FIELDS (WILLIAM CLAUDE DUKENFIELD) *b. January 29, 1880, Philadelphia; d. December 25, 1946, Pasadena*. W. C. Fields was nobody's fool. He grew up too tough for that. Like a boy out of Dickens, he suffered through a childhood of poverty and the physical abuse of his religious and ever-disapproving father. At 9 he was already practicing juggling with his father's vegetables. Obsessed with the idea of fame, he practiced through long hours, tears of frustration, and bloodied limbs with a discipline and persistence that he likened to that of Mozart or Kreisler.

Fields sought escape. Whether he left home at 11 or just made himself scarce, he did turn to the streets — to thievery, hustling, fights, cold nights, and brushes with the law. His frequent fights took their toll on his nose, that mangled, bulbous glory that subsequent drinking only enhanced and reddened. And his living conditions brought on respiratory infections which damaged his voice. Fortunately his juggling skills became expert, and by 1900 Fields was getting rave reviews across the country and in Europe. Now, bearing a modicum of confidence, he married his assistant, Harriet Hughes.

Unfortunately Fields' difficult personality was already firmly cast. The couple, now with a son, Bill, Jr., soon became estranged. According to Fields' later mistress, Carlotta Monti, "They have said he was crotchety, castigating, had a jaundiced eye, was larcenous, suspicious, shifty, erratic, frugal, and mercenary. I can only confirm these accusations." And she left out bigoted. During this time Fields also started to drink, a habit which would become the bane of his existence.

Meanwhile his juggling act continued with great success, and he started adding comic asides and ad libs. In 1915 he made a marvelously comic movie debut in *Pool Sharks* but returned to vaudeville for 10 more years before starring as Eustace McGargle in D. W. Griffith's *Sally of the Sawdust*. Signing with Paramount, he made a series of movies with poor box-office returns and was eventually let go.

Fields bided his time while the talkies made their headway, then moved to Hollywood and badgered producers for a year before he was taken back by Paramount. Unlike those of other silent stars, Fields' voice proved to be an asset. His hoarse drawl became a colorful part of his persona, a character who was not so much created as transferred from Fields' real life. All his natural antipathies were on display. Constantly at war with the world, bedeviled by shrewish wives and bratty kids, he demonstrated that sentimentality was a hoax and that cynicism prevailed. There was no room in his world for the glowing sunsets of fairytale endings. He was out to show that the world revolves around the maxim "Never give a sucker an even break."

During the early thirties, Fields produced four short comedies, "The Dentist," "The Barber Shop," "The Pharmacist," and "The Fatal Glass of Beer"—classics all. He moved on to three films with Baby LeRoy but, feeling upstaged by the toddler, a jealous and perhaps paranoid Fields took revenge one day by filling the baby's bottle with gin and then announcing, when Baby LeRoy couldn't stand, that "The kid's no trooper."

Not much later it was Fields who proved to be no trooper. Consuming over two bottles a day, he experienced hallucinations and insomnia for over two years and required rest in a sanitarium to recover. His movie career appeared to be over, but he resurrected himself with the help of Edgar Bergen and Charlie McCarthy in *You Can't Cheat an Honest Man*, and then moved on, in 1940, to his two greatest movies, *My Little Chickadee* and *The Bank Dick*, the former's script having been written by Fields and his co-star, Mae West.

Once again his health caught up with him. Still drinking, and suffering from consumption, Fields no longer had the strength to perform. For much of his adult life he had been enamored with the works of Dickens, finding inspiration in the comic names and being able to identify with the horrors of Oliver Twist's childhood and the scrimping of Scrooge. By 1946 Fields, like Scrooge, was lying in bed on Christmas eve awaiting a visit from "the fellow in the bright nightgown." For Fields there was only one spirit to come and no hope or wish for redemption. That would be too sentimental. Whether out of defiance or mockery, he died on Christmas Day, the day he hated most.

Across the way from Fields is **Henry Travers** (1874–1965), best known as the angel who badgered James Stewart in *It's a Wonderful Life* (1946).

In the Sanctuary of Courage, beneath a statue of a youth coaxing a bird to come to him, is **Charles W. Nash** (1864–1948). Those who remember kneading the yellow pellet through white blobs of oleomargarine will also remember Nash cars. Charles Nash, who was first in partnership with David D. Buick and then the president of General Motors, broke away to start his own company. It merged with Kelvinator in 1937 and was successfully turning out automobiles, refrigerators, and electric ranges at the time of Nash's death.

In the Sanctuary of the Holy Spirit is the memorial of **Hermione Gingold** (1897–1987), whose vault simply gives her name, dates, and the inscription "Actress." Gingold, who began her career as a child actress with Noel Coward, played some fine roles, including the courtesan grandmother in *Gigi* (1958) and the mayor's wife in *The Music Man* (1962). But she also shone off stage as a comedienne. One of her most memorable comments came on a television talk show when she was asked if her latest husband was dead. "That's a matter of opinion," she answered.

There is usually an overflow of flowers around the Sanctuary of Golden Slumber. It is the final resting place of **Paramhansa Yogananda** (1893–1952). Those who read comic books in the fifties will remember a persistent ad in the back of comic books for *The Autobiography of a Yogi*. The ad showed a pencil sketch of the long-haired guru. Unlike many of his successors, however, Yogananda was not first an ambitious boy in New York but a genuine monk who came to California from Calcutta in 1920. His type of meditation, kriya yoga, attracted several hundred thousand to what became his Self-Realization Fellowship.

Yogananda himself could subordinate his body to his mind (for example, he could slow his pulse in one wrist but not the other) — so much so that when he died at a banquet for the Indian Ambassador at the Biltmore Hotel in Los Angeles, his followers said he had deliberately chosen that moment to exit. The rumor, allegedly confirmed by Forest Lawn personnel, was that his body was so devoid of impurities that it showed no signs of decay for three weeks.

In the Sanctuary of Sacred Promise, in a large marble drawer to the left, is **William Boyd** (1895–1972). His better-known persona, Hopalong Cassidy, is mentioned on the vault. Boyd, whose hair turned its distinctive silver-white when he was 21, made numerous Hoppy films between 1935 and 1948. In the alcove with Boyd is singer **Gene Austin** (1900–1972), who popularized the song "My Blue Heaven." His inscription points out:

> There's a new blue heaven in the sky,
> Where loving friends will never die.

Across the way is composer **Max Steiner** (1888–1971), whose prolific output of film scores included *Gone with the Wind* (1939), *Casablanca* (1942), and *The Big Sleep* (1946). He won Academy Awards for *The Informer* (1935), *Now Voyager* (1942), and *Since You Went Away* (1944).

Inside the Sanctuary of Twilight are two musicians. One, **Isham Jones** (1894–1956), is designated "Inspired bandleader and composer." The inscription continues, " 'I'll See You in my Dreams' was his song and he will always remain in the dreams of those who love him." The song, Jones' first hit, was written in 1923. The former mule driver in the coal mines had a number of other successes, including "It Had To Be You," "Indiana Moon," "Swinging down the Lane," and "I Can't Believe It's True."

The other musician here is the diminutive titan of the keyboard, **Josef Hofmann** (1876–1957). Born in Cracow, Poland, Hofmann was a true prodigy who began playing in public at the age of 6 and who made his sensational New York debut at 11. The critics and the public went wild. Fortunately for young Hofmann, so did the Society for the Prevention of Cruelty to Children. Concerned over the boy's heavy schedule (52 concerts in 10 weeks while travelling between Boston and Baltimore) the society issued a complaint. The exploitation came to an end when the philanthropist Alfred J. Corning put up $50,000 for the boy and his management on the condition that he not play publicly again until he was 18.

As an adult Hofmann was the envy of his peers. His tone, his shadings, his clarity were all of the highest level, and he played with passion and aristocratic grace. Following Busoni, he was, along with Rachmaninoff, one of the first modernists. Gone were the sentimental phrasings and sloppy passages of so many of the Romantics. He believed in textual accuracy, an idea that was implanted in him by his teacher, the great Anton Rubinstein. Nevertheless, Hofmann's musical insights were so strong and original that he rarely ever played a piece the same way twice. Whatever his approach, the results made musical sense.

Hofmann was a short, solidly built man with small hands which made his technical feats seem all the more amazing. To make himself more comfortable he had a piano made to order with the keys ever so slightly shaved in width so as to better accommodate his hands. While his sight reading was just ordinary, his ear was so extraordinarily acute that he could identify a tuning fork that was barely out of pitch. He was also able to perfectly reproduce a fiendishly difficult Godowsky transcription after hearing the composer play it just three times and never having seen the text.

Little of Hofmann's playing has been retained on recordings. A pity, for we are deprived of the full pleasures of listening to one of greatest of all pianists, a man who put technique at the service of art, a man who combined passion and intelligence, a man whose sparing but savage attacks at the piano could sound like "the roar of an enraged lion."

Yet another musician, **Alfred Newman** (1901–1970), is in the Sanctuary of Eternal Prayer. He is designated "Musician in Heaven," with the epitaph

> He will take him in his arms,
> He will lift him up on high,
> He will show him all the charms
> Of his mansions in the sky.
> He will let him hear the songs
> That the angel voices sing.
> He will be where he belongs
> In the chorus of the King.

While he was a musician on earth, Newman composed scores for more than 250 films, winning Academy Awards for seven of them, including *Alexander's Ragtime Band* (1938), *With a Song in My Heart* (1952), and *Love Is a Many-Splendored Thing* (1955).

Opposite the door to the Sanctuary of Harmony is a beautiful stained-glass window showing a woman in her study with a book open, a globe nearby, and the biblical injunction, "Wisdom is the principal thing. Get wisdom, and with all thy getting, get understanding." It is dedicated to **Marian E. Lemerett**, about whom nothing else is known.

Just down the hall in the Corridor of Mercy is the original Tonto, **Chief Thundercloud**, a.k.a. Victor Daniels (1899–1955). His crypt has his signature on it in brass.

If you detour upstairs briefly to the third floor, you will find, at the top of the steps in a small vault, **Jim Davis** (1915–1981), who played Jock Ewing, the crusty patriarch of that generation of vipers found on "Dallas."

You may also want to take a quick trip downstairs. On the landing is the sarcophagus of a comedian who achieved fame through one tagline: "Wanna buy a duck?" **Joe Penner** (1904–1941) died of a heart attack in his sleep at 37.

Downstairs is **Grant Withers** (1905–1959), who eloped with 17-year-old Loretta Young in 1930, then made a film with her, *Too Young To Marry*, in 1931. They were divorced by the time the actor died of a sleeping-pill overdose. Another suicide rests nearby in the Columbarium of Security. **Clara Blandick** (1881–1962), Auntie Em in *The Wizard of Oz*, carried her role's no-nonsense approach into death. At 81, suffering from arthritis, she dressed up in a blue gown, made up her face, then lay down and pulled a plastic bag over her head.

Finally, in an unmarked vault behind a vase, lurks **Lon Chaney** (1883–1930). Chaney, the son of deaf-mute parents, first supported himself as a Pike's Peak guide in his native Colorado. After an unspectacular beginning as a singer-dancer and movie walk-on, Chaney found his niche in playing grotesque roles. He devised his own scars for *The Road to Mandalay* (1926) and elaborate make-up for *The Hunchback of Notre Dame* (1923) and *The Phantom of the Opera* (1925). He invented a way of throwing his shoulder out of joint which left him permanently lame. In *Tell It to the Marines* (1926), one of the few films in which he wore no make-up at all, an unknowing critic complained that he didn't look "natural," that one of the lines on his face was out of place.

Chaney had recently completed *The Unholy Three*, in which he used five different voices as well as his disguises, when the fact that he had lung cancer became known. Weakened by pneumonia earlier in the year, he was severely anemic; even so, he was considered on the way to recovery when he hemorrhaged unexpectedly and died at 46.

As you leave the Great Mausoleum, you will see a wonderful plaque to **Otis A. Pritchett**, Civil Engineer. It has a bas relief of the Panama Canal and motifs of many organizations on it. Pritchett's epitaph reads, "Dearly beloved husband, thoroughly trained in civil engineering, a world traveler."

To complete your tour, go outside and follow the signs to the entrance for the Last Supper Window. Across the road you will see the monument to **Jean Hersholt** (1886–1956), a name familiar to viewers of the Academy Awards. There is a long eulogy honoring him as "Actor, Cultural Leader, Humanitarian." The statue is of Klods Hans "inspired by the Hans Christian Andersen tale of the boy who went forth into the world to win a princess and a kingdom." Evard Erikson's sculpture shows a boy in a tennis hat riding a goat and waving a dead bird over his head.

Jean Hersholt had a long and happy career in films, a longevity he attributed to never becoming a star. He was nevertheless honored at the end of his life with awards, tributes, and honorary degrees. In 1948 the King of Denmark knighted him. Although ranked as one of the great silent-film character actors, Hersholt gained recognition in the 1930s in various doctor roles, beginning with *The Country Doctor*, in which he played the Dionne quintuplets' physician. He went on to create the *Dr. Christian* series of films.

The Hans Christian Andersen statue marks Hersholt's other great interest, as owner of the world's largest collection of Andersen memorabilia. He also translated many of Andersen's fairy tales into English.

The Last Supper Window is one of Forest Lawn's most appealing works of art, a combination of block mosaic and skillfully painted faces. It is certainly in better shape than the original painting by Leonardo da Vinci in Milan, whose egg tempera has been exposed to bombing and centuries of weather. For those interested, there is a dramatic narrative about the window, given at scheduled intervals.

Seven notable people are honored right under the window. The most easily recognized of these, probably because the presidential heads on Mt. Rushmore are depicted in bronze on his plaque, is **Gutzon Borglum** (1867–1941). The titanic heads of Washington, Lincoln, Jefferson, and Theodore Roosevelt are, of course, his most famous undertaking; the figures, if complete and to scale, would be 465 feet tall. Begun by Borglum in 1927 when the sculptor was already 60, the work was nearly finished when he died of a heart attack after gallbladder surgery.

Gutzon Borglum was born in Idaho and studied sculpture in Paris under Auguste Rodin. After his return to America, his first commission was in 1901, the statue of Lincoln in the rotunda of the Capitol in Washington, DC. Other works followed, but his first mammoth sculpture was planned for the face of Stone Mountain, Georgia, and was to show Robert E. Lee, Jefferson Davis, Stonewall Jackson, and 1,200 other Confederate figures. Conflicts developed among members of the committee that had ordered the work and between the tempestuous sculptor and the committee, and Borglum was fired—not before destroying all the models of the memorial, however. He was indicted for "larceny and malicious mischief," but the charges were withdrawn when he agreed to complete the memorial after finishing Mt. Rushmore.

Two composers are similarly honored beneath the Last

Supper Window. **Carrie Jacobs Bond** (1862–1946), a self-taught musician, wrote the music and lyrics for over 175 songs. When "I Love You Truly" became as much of a staple at weddings as Lohengrin and rice, her fortune was made. She invested it in an estate called The End of the Road. Bond's marker shows a piano in a concert hall.

Rudolf Friml (1879–1972) has a piano on his marker as well, though he is sitting behind his. One of the great composers of operetta, Friml wrote *Indian Love Call* and was thus responsible for one of the now most parodied scenes in movie history, that of Jeanette MacDonald and Nelson Eddy crooning the song under the western Canadian sky. But Friml was a serious composer who enjoyed tremendous popularity in his prime. From the late 1930s on, however, he increasingly fell victim to a changing musical taste which harbored little room for his sentimental, star-struck melodies.

Friml was born "in the Prague of the Austro–Hungarian Empire, operetta-land itself." He studied composition with Dvořák at the Prague Conservatory and developed considerable skills at the piano as well. Moving to the United States in 1906, he premiered his own Piano Concerto with Walter Damrosch and the New York Symphony. When Victor Herbert had a falling out with the diva Emma Trentini, Friml was called in to compose the star's next show. Around the same time he collaborated with Otto Harbach to produce *The Firefly*. The show was a smash hit and Friml was on his way. *The Vagabond King* (1925) was his biggest hit. Several of his shows later enjoyed revivals as films.

Spry, clever, and remarkably fit, Friml rejoiced in music, and in his longevity. He started his day by standing on his head for 10 minutes and ended it by having his wife walk barefoot up and down his back. In between he would practice or play the piano for four to six hours per day. He never grew tired of music's charms. "I'm so full of music that if I don't sit down and let some of it flow I think I would burst from the pressure. Music is a gift of God for everyone. It can bring so much happiness and so much peace," Friml declared.

Also under the Last Supper Window are scientist **Robert Andrews Millikan** (1868–1953) who won the Nobel Prize in Physics in 1923 for his work on electrons and on the photoelectric effect; California educator **Rufus B. Von Kleinsmid**, and Forest Lawn artist **Jan Styka**.

Finally, Forest Lawn's founder, **Herbert Eaton** (1881–1966), is honored by a bronze cameo showing what he has created. He and his family are actually buried in the private room to your right which has "Eaton" over the door. Herbert Eaton, a pleasant-faced, bespectacled man, has probably come in for more satire than he deserves. Just because he put a fig leaf on *his* statue of Michelangelo's David and gave his cemetery sections names like Lullabyland and Inspiration Slope is no reason to poke fun. A more serious indictment of Eaton would be that in his Builder's Creed for Memorials at Forest Lawn he bans "misshapen monuments and other customary signs of death"—the very lifeblood of serious cemetery buffs.

Herbert Eaton began life in Missouri as a mining engineer, then came to California to put some other ideas into practice. After taking over a small cemetery in 1913, he developed something new for those times—a "Before Need Plan" in which a family purchased a plot and memorial in advance, so that at the time of death everything was in place. During the 1930s, by lobbying for permission for cemeteries to have their own mortuaries, Eaton paved the way for funerary one-stop shopping. At Forest Lawn the body is embalmed, displayed in a Slumberroom, surrounded by tributes purchased in the Forest Lawn Flower Shop, eulogized in one of the on-site churches, and then buried—without ever having to be driven "through crowded city streets under the stares of curious onlookers."

As you face the stained-glass window, the entryway to the right leads to the Sanctuary of Trust in which are interred Carole Lombard and Clark Gable side by side. Their white marble wall crypts have brass plates bearing only their names and dates. On the other side of Carole is her mother, Elizabeth Peters, who died in a plane crash with Carole. A dabbler in astrology and numerology, Mrs. Peters predicted that their flight from Indianapolis to Burbank would be ill-fated. They took it anyway.

CLARK GABLE *b. February 1, 1901, Cadiz, OH; d. November 16, 1960, Los Angeles.* Oldtime movie stars were different from ordinary people. Able to indulge their wildest whims, they lived as if there would be no tomorrow. In Clark Gable's world, there often wasn't. Co-star Jean Harlow, whom Clark called Baby, collapsed and died of uremic poisoning at 26. MGM vice-president Irving Thalberg contracted a fatal case of pneumonia at 37. During a wild game of hide-and-seek, Primmie, David Niven's 25-year-old wife, opened the wrong door and fell down a flight of stairs, dying of a concussion. Most devastating to Gable, his wife, Carole Lombard, perished in a plane crash at age 33.

The pattern of loss began at 10 months for Clark Gable, when his mother died. His father left him with his maternal uncle and aunt, then ripped him away from them when he had found a stepmother for Clark, who was 2. Jennie Dunlap doted on the boy, encouraging him to read the classics and play the French horn, but he was wary of forming an attachment to her. Turning his back on the culture she offered, he began working the local oil rigs with his father. Yet over the shrill squeal of the oilfield's whistle, Clark heard the theater's whisper. The tall, ham-handed 21-year-old joined an acting workshop. Though he demonstrated a complete lack of ability, provoking audience laughter when he was playing serious roles, Clark Gable was taken seriously by Josephine Dillon, a tiny, thin-lipped acting coach 40 years old to his 23.

Dillon introduced him to Shakespeare's plays and taught him how to enter a room and speak his lines. She coached him intensively, like a gardener focusing all her attention on one flower. In gratitude, Clark married her. Yet even when he started becoming successful, she could not stop critiquing his performance. Clark finally rebelled while on tour, sending home a dozen new silk shirts, given him by an admirer, for Josephine to launder. The admirer was not his second wife, socialite Ria Langham, but he met her within the year. She was also 17 years his senior. Their union began with Clark's "stark and stunning" performance as a death row inmate in *The Last Mile* in 1930 and lasted through the films *Painted Desert*, *The Easiest Way*, *Red Dust*, and *It Happened One Night* — for which he won an Oscar in 1934.

By then he was creating a personality drawn from the roles he played, a Clark Gable who was at once boyish and sensual, humorous yet strong. Few women could resist him, and he didn't expect them to. Ironically, the role that captured his screen essence so completely, that of Rhett Butler in *Gone with the Wind*, was one he strongly resisted, insisting he would not speak with a Southern accent. He finally capitulated, only because he needed the money to divorce Ria and pursue his next wife, Carole Lombard.

Although she was younger than Gable and a glamorous actress in her own right, Carole knew the kind of mothering he needed. They called each other Ma and Pa and settled into a ranch they had redesigned to their whims. They loved and fought hard. Carole screamed at Clark for the flings he seemed unable to resist and tried to produce the baby they both wanted. By all accounts they were blissfully happy, entertaining each other with zany jokes and playing at ranching—until the war-bond junket from which she did not return alive.

It was the most devastating loss of Clark's life. A private man, he only cried in public twice. Once, under coercion, in *Gone with the Wind*. And again at the launching of the Liberty ship, *Carole Lombard*, which Irene Dunne christened with champagne. After Carole's death, his drinking raged out of control. In 1942 Gable joined the Air Force and was assigned to a heavy bombardment group in England. Not caring if he died, he returned unscathed.

Despite his recklessness and wild motorcycle rides, he continued to escape. In 1960 he was happily married to Kay Spreckels, who was pregnant with his first child. He had just completed *The Misfits* with Montgomery Clift and Marilyn Monroe, a role he was pleased with. Working around the ranch, he began experiencing severe chest pains. These were confirmed as a coronary thrombosis. Over the next few days Gable seemed to rally. He enjoyed a telegram from President Eisenhower—"BE A GOOD BOY, CLARK, AND DO AS THE DOCTORS TELL YOU TO DO."—and listened to his baby's heartbeat. On November 16 at 10:50 P.M., Gable turned the page of a magazine he was reading, and fell back. The King was dead.

Carole Lombard (1908–1942) was discovered for the movies as a tomboy living in Los Angeles. High-spirited and given to practical jokes, she was featured in films from age 17. Most were predictable comedies, with *No Man of Her Own* (1932), *My Man Godfrey* (1936), and *They Knew What They Wanted* (1940) better than average. Lombard, always forthright about what she wanted, was married and divorced from Dick Powell, involved with singer Russ Columbo before his tragic death, and finally married to Clark Gable. She was so anxious to get back to him from her war-bond drive in Indiana that instead of using her train ticket home she boarded a TWA DC–3 instead.

Ironically, the war that she had just been supporting was indirectly responsible for her death. Warning beacons outside Las Vegas had been blacked out for fear of Japanese bombers. The plane strayed off course and crashed into a cliff near Potosi Mountain. The star's charred body and those of the other passengers were retrieved from the snow-capped mountains by mules pulling stretchers. In a will Lombard made two years before she died, she requested that her body be clothed in white and that she be placed in a "modestly-priced crypt" in Forest Lawn. She was interred in a white gown created by the designer Irene.

Also in this alcove is **David O. Selznick** (1902–1965). David was a true child of Hollywood, the son of producer Lewis Selznick, a man whose behavior was so erratic that confederates like Louis B. Mayer squeezed him out of the business. Raised to get even, a young and bumptious David fought his way quickly through MGM, Paramount, and RKO to establish his own production company. His first film was based on a book his father had read to him as a child, *Little Lord Fauntleroy* (1936).

Selznick, used to ordering people around, was always surprised when anyone objected. His psychoanalyst, Dr. May Romm, terminated him after a year of Selznick's sleeping through their sessions in her office, then showing up at her door at midnight. His wife, Irene, daughter of Louis B. Mayer, sat up one night in bed and announced, "The jig's up," explaining that she was leaving him. Ingrid Bergman "quit" after their first meeting when he demanded she change her name and have her teeth and eyebrows fixed. (On first seeing her he said, "God! Take your shoes off!" in reference to her height of five feet, eight inches.)

Unlike Selznick's wife, Bergman stayed with him, as did Vivian Leigh, Gregory Peck, Katherine Hepburn, Cary Grant, and Joseph Cotton. They put up with his brashness and demands because of the fine pictures he made. Selznick was responsible for *A Star Is Born* (1937), *Intermezzo* (1939), *Gone with the Wind* (1939), *Rebecca* (1940), *Duel in the Sun* (1946), and *Tender Is the Night* (1962), to name only a few. One of his discoveries, who not only stayed with him but married him in 1949, was Jennifer Jones. He was still liquidating his assets to purchase suitable vehicles for her when he collapsed of a heart attack in his lawyer's office and died.

Across the main hall in the Sanctuary of Vespers is **Russ Columbo** (1908–1934), a singer and Valentino look-alike whose own composition, "Prisoner of Love," became his trademark. He was one of Hollywood's most sought-after bachelors and was about to become engaged to Carole Lombard the afternoon he visited his best friend, Lansing Brown. As they were looking at Brown's antique gun collection, a dueling pistol that Brown was fooling with fired a slug that shattered Columbo's left eye and pierced his skull. The singer lost consciousness and died two hours later.

Nearby in the main hall is the marble statue commemorating the Dolly Sisters, identical twins **Yansci "Jenny" Dolly** (1892–1941) and **Roszika "Rosie" Dolly** (1892–1970). Between 1911 and 1927 the Dolly sisters were the stars of several continents. Beginning as a team in the Ziegfeld Follies, they starred in many Broadway and London musical productions. After their retirement at 35, they frequented gambling casinos on the French Riviera. Jenny, who was disfigured in a 1933 automobile accident, at last hung herself from a cord attached to a curtain rod. Rosie, married three times, died of a heart attack.

Around the next corner from the Dollys is the Sanctuary of Benediction. Here a number of personalities keep one another company. One is **Sid Grauman** (1874–1950), who became famous for collecting handprints and footprints in the walk of his Chinese Theater in Hollywood — stretching a point for Joe E. Brown's mouth and Betty Grable's leg. Allegedly the custom began in 1927 when Norma Talmadge accidentally stepped into freshly laid cement outside Grauman's Chinese.

The most striking room in this alcove belongs to Jean Harlow. Outside is her name and an iron gate. The interior is made of multicolored European marble and was purchased by William Powell for Jean for $25,000. For many years, Powell had white roses placed daily on her crypt; the white gardenia placed in her hand when she was buried, with its unsigned sentiment, "Good night, my dearest darling," was thought to have been placed there by Powell as well.

JEAN HARLOW (HARLEAN CARPENTIER) *b. June 3, 1911, Kansas City, KA; d. June 7, 1937, Los Angeles.* Although no murder charges were filed when Jean Harlow died, cases might have been brought against two different people. The condition which killed her began at the hands of her second husband, Paul Bern, and ended when her mother refused to get medical help. In between, the plucky blonde actress ignored the physical signs of danger and kept moving on the treadmill she had set up for herself.

The Baby, as she was always called, was an early bloomer. At 15 she was interred in a conservative girls boarding school; she escaped by eloping and telling a justice of the peace that she was 19. The "groom" was hustled back east and Jean sent home to Kansas City. But it was the end of her schooldays. That summer Jean, her mother, Mama Jean, and stepfather, Marino Bello, set off for Los Angeles.

Jean was the only one to find work. It came in bit parts and crowd scenes, but agent Arthur Landau noticed her on the set of a Laurel and Hardy comedy and worked to get better parts for her. Her main assets were her white-blonde hair and the breasts which she fondled as if they were her children. Never an actress, she developed a persona which came across on the screen: gruff, outspoken, yet as democratic as a waitress in a diner. Her wit came from the lines studio writers created for her to use with reporters ("Would you steal a husband, Miss Harlow?" "Wouldn't that be like shoplifting in a secondhand store?"), but after a while she was able to create her own rejoinders.

Harlow's first few movies cast her as a gun moll or tramp with a heart of gold. The critics were unimpressed. It wasn't until 1933 that her acting, in films such as *Hold Your Man* and *Dinner at Eight*, started to garner praise. In *Bombshell* she played an actress whose life reflected her own, but in *Wife vs. Secretary* (1935), she had the quieter, more sympathetic role of the working girl.

Outside the studio, Harlow's life was chaotic. Although emotionally tied to her mother and stepfather, she raged at the way they exploited her. She was still the only one in the family working. Mama Jean insisted on household help they could not afford, and Bello spent more money on extravagances for himself than Jean was making. He also offered to introduce her to the physical ecstasy of the parts she was acting out on screen and threatened her with a sword sheathed inside a wooden cane.

By contrast the quiet stability of Paul Bern seemed attractive. The slight, 42-year-old Bern was an MGM studio executive known as the Little Father Confessor. He had a grim secret of his own, however. Bern's sex organs had never developed, and he was hoping that the Platinum Venus would be able to work her magic on him. It did not happen. On their wedding night she ridiculed him, and he beat her savagely on the back with a cane, permanently damaging her kidneys. Two months later, sick of pretending to the world what a happy couple they were, Bern shot himself fatally in the head.

The irony of being the nation's sex goddess on the screen and celibate off it wasn't lost on Jean. She succumbed to a few anonymous one-night stands before marrying another older man, cameraman Harold Rosson, a year later. Despite their protestations (" 'We will be happy always,' they choroused."), they separated six months later. By then Jean was beginning her final romance, with actor William Powell.

At that point Jean took a step she had long contemplated: She engaged a private detective to trail Marino Bello and report on his infidelities. That would finally get him out of her mother's life and her own. The action had dire consequences. Missing her husband, Mama Jean shrieked that she hated Jean for taking everything from her. "But

when the time comes," she added prophetically, "I won't have to wave a magic wand to take everything from you!"

The time came when Harlow collapsed on the set of *Saratoga* and was sent home. Her mother, adhering to the principles of Christian Science, refused to let any doctors treat her for several days. By the time Arthur Landau and Louis B. Mayer forced her to hospitalize Jean, it was too late. Suffering from an inflamed gallbladder and failing kidneys, the actress died the next day.

Nearby is **Irving Thalberg** (1899–1936) whose private mausoleum cost $50,000, twice the price of Jean Harlow's. Thalberg, a boy wonder who became production head at Universal Studios at 20 and creative director of MGM at 24, was immortalized by F. Scott Fitzgerald as The Last Tycoon. He was notorious for keeping writers and actors waiting until he needed them. Bored with waiting for Thalberg, the Marx brothers once stripped naked, lit a fire in his office fireplace, and roasted potatoes. Upon Thalberg's return they became instant friends. Although Thalberg's health had been delicate for a long time, people were shocked when he died of pneumonia at 37.

Thalberg's widow, actress **Norma Shearer** (1900–1983), outlived him by close to fifty years before joining him here. Her best films — *The Student Prince* (1927), *The Divorcée*

(1929) for which she won an Academy Award, and *Strange Interlude* (1931) — were made before Thalberg's death and her remarriage to ski instructor Martin Arrouge in 1942. The actress died of bronchial pneumonia.

All the way at the end of the hall, in a small niche, is **Jack Carson** (1910–1963), who died of cancer the same day as his close friend, Dick Powell. Nearby is **Theda Bara**, born Theodosia Goodman (1890–1955). Theda Bara's star loomed brightly and briefly as the first on-screen vamp, aided by studio hype that made her the daughter of an eastern ruler whose name was an anagram for "Arab death." Her career began with *The Two Orphans* (1915) and ended with a self-satire, *Madame Mystery* (1926). Also here is **Laverne Andrews** (1913–1967), the oldest of the three singing Andrews Sisters.

The rest of our tour is back in the Freedom Mausoleum, at the back of the cemetery on Arlington Road. Enter the foyer and turn right. Halfway down on your left is Heritage Hall. You will notice first the dark bronze bust of **Alan Ladd** (1913–1964), slightly smaller than life size, done by Lia DiLeo. The plaque is inscribed with the Edgar A. Guest poem "Success":

> I hold no dream of fortune vast,
> Nor seek undying fame.
> I do not ask when life is past that many know my name.
> I may not own the skill to rise to glory's topmost height,
> Nor win a place among the wise,
> But I can keep the right.
> And I can live my life on earth
> Contented to the end,
> If but a few shall know my worth
> And proudly call me friend.

Ladd's vault, bearing his autograph and the inscription "Beloved Husband and Father," is to the right of the plaque. Alan Ladd, who made the trenchcoat his personal symbol, found recognition as a killer with a cold smile in *This Gun for Hire* (1941). He continued to play killers but made his reputation as an actor in *Shane* (1953). The whole world knew that the five-foot-five-inch actor often stood on a box to kiss his leading ladies, a fact no one minded. But Ladd was himself a conflicted man. A self-inflicted gunshot wound in 1962 failed to kill him, but an overdose of sedatives and alcohol 14 months later had the desired effect.

Right below Alan Ladd is **Clara Bow** (1907–1965) whose vault points out that she was "Hollywood's 'It' Girl." Clara, born in Brooklyn, was the child of a doting father and a crazed mother. She once woke to feel the steel point of a butcher knife at her throat and endured several hours of religious tirade and threats from her mother. Clara never slept through the night again. At 16 she won *Motion Picture* magazine's talent contest and escaped to Hollywood to become the consummate Jazz Baby; her bobbed red hair and tiny body inspired women everywhere to discard their underwear and paint their lips in a bee-sting pout.

Clara's movies were by-and-large forgettable, but her high spirits kept America enthralled. Her career fell apart in 1930 when Clara discovered that her secretary had been sharing her bank account as well as her clothes and boyfriends. Clara fired her, and the secretary, Daisy DeVoe, retaliated by going public with details of how the "It" Girl was enjoying herself with everyone from Gary Cooper to Bela Lugosi. The world learned that Coach Howard Jones had posted a notice in the USC locker room that "Clara Bow is off limits to all members of this football team." Venereal diseases and Mexican abortions were sordidly revealed, and it was found that Clara had violated the morals clause in her film contract.

Through it all, cowboy film star, **Rex Bell**, born George F. Beldam (1903–1962), stood quietly by and married her. Clara retired to his Nevada ranch, where she dyed the cows red to match her hair. In time she ballooned to nearly two hundred pounds and raised two sons. Developing some of her own mother's characteristics, she turned reclusive and died of a heart attack in 1965 — but not before she confided in a friend, "It wasn't ever like I thought it was going to be. It was always a disappointment to me."

Rex Bell went on to become lieutenant governor of Nevada. In 1962, when he was running for governor, he collapsed and died of a heart attack.

Above the Bells is Nat King Cole.

NAT KING COLE (NATHANIEL ADAMS COLES) *b. March 17, 1919, Montgomery, AL; d. February 15, 1965, Santa Monica*. Nat King Cole, born to the Rev. Edward Coles and his wife, Perlina, came north to Chicago when he was 4. In trying to escape poverty, they could not leave behind the caste system which went from white to light-skinned bourgeois black down to dark black and poor. All his life Cole smarted under the humiliation delivered to him as a child by a light-skinned black woman on a public bus: "You're black, and you stink, and you can never wash it off." Cole bathed two or three times a day but could never cleanse the deeply burrowed hurt and shame.

Cole first displayed his musical talents when he banged out "Yes, We Have No Bananas" on the family piano at age

4. Such talent prompted lessons, and Cole learned the classics from Bach to Rachmaninoff as a supplement to the music he heard and copied from the radio and neighborhood jazz clubs. His greatest influence was Earl Hines. When he couldn't catch the rhythm by listening in the alleyway behind the club where Hines was playing, Nat plucked up his courage, entered, and asked the master.

When Nat started playing with his brother Eddie, the boys dropped the *s* at the end of their name. By the time Nat was 17 he was graduated from high school, married, and touring with a small jazz group. The beat-up pianos he met along the way forced him to alter his style of playing and helped him to break away from being an Earl Hines copy. In 1937 Cole formed the King Cole Trio with guitarist Oscar Moore and bassist Wesley Price. Pioneering chamber jazz, the group became a great success. Cole was recognized as one of the premier jazz pianists of his day and was an important influence on younger pianists for years to come.

During this time he also began to sing, at first for variety and then by request. Through the 1940s the trio started to record hits; first "Sweet Lorraine," then Cole's own novelty song based on his father's sermons, "Straighten Up and Fly Right," and finally "The Christmas Song." Then in 1947 a strange, bearded man named Eden Ahbez unrolled himself from his sleeping bag under the first *L* in the HOLLYWOOD sign on Mt. Lee overlooking Los Angeles and appeared before Cole, offering him two songs. Cole rejected the first, "I'm a Real Gone Yogi," but fell for the second, "Nature Boy." It became one of his biggest hits and put Cole firmly before the public.

While Cole's career was reaching new heights, he met a young singer named Maria Hawkins. Cole fell in love, soon divorced Nadine, his first wife, and married Maria. More than just beautiful, the light-skinned Maria was raised in the privileged environment of her aunt, Dr. Charlotte Hawkins Brown. Used to servants, a private Pullman car, and visitors such as Eleanor Roosevelt and W. E. B. DuBois, she came from a background far more sophisticated than her new husband's. This was a mixed blessing. More adept than he at business and social matters, Maria took charge in these areas with Nat's at least tacit approval. Unfortunately, by some accounts, such authority was at the expense of Nat's "overpaid" partners, some of his friends, and the distancing of himself from his parents who were well below Maria's social standing.

After their marriage the Coles bought a house in white

Beverly Hills and quickly aroused racist sentiment and the hasty formation of a "concerned property owners" group. The Coles prevailed, however, and moved in. It was not, of course, Cole's only brush with racism. Like all black entertainers, he knew the facts of segregated audiences, performers, and lodgings; he knew clubs where he could perform but could not eat or gamble. While Cole was a generous supporter of the NAACP and an admirer and friend of Paul Robeson's throughout the latter's travails, he was not an activist. Believing he could best express his humanity through performance, he forsook boycotts. It was an unpopular stance at the time, one which caused many black activists to label Cole an Uncle Tom. If this were not enough, Cole fell into trouble with the IRS, which took an unusually harsh stance with regard to paybacks. Was their attitude racially motivated? There is no hard evidence of a vendetta, but there were certainly those who took pleasure in seeing a successful black taken down a notch or two.

To pay off his debt Cole played the club circuit in Las Vegas and increased his salary to $12,500 per week in 1954, but the hard work and tension took their toll and, that same year, Cole had half of his stomach removed due to bleeding ulcers. The following year he disbanded his trio and was performing with full orchestra. The hits continued: "Lush Life," "Mona Lisa," "Tenderly," "Je Vous Aime Beaucoup." Cole also turned to Hollywood and took roles in several movies.

Racial problems continued to trouble him, however. In 1956 he was attacked by four white men while performing in his hometown of Birmingham. That same year he became the first black entertainer to host his own television show, but the show folded the following year when it proved impossible to attract a national sponsor. "Madison Avenue is afraid of the dark," said Cole.

Cole remained popular until his death. He was the first black singer to gain popularity with romantic pop songs, an area long dominated by white singers. Barely covering two octaves, his voice was a limited instrument. According to Billy Eckstine, "Cole took a style and made a voice of it." What his voice lacked in range and strength, however, it made up for in its husky, intimate quality. With flawless diction he caressed the words and phrases in a way that let no one doubt the sincerity of his feeling.

Cole died in 1965 of lung cancer. While lying in the hospital, he was deluged with half a million cards and letters. Incredulously he smiled and asked, "Is all that for me?" It was, and one can be sure that as long as there are kids from 1 to 92 to hear Nat King Cole, he will continue to have a legion of admiring fans.

Two well-known women rest in this area; they were both born in 1906, and they died of heart attacks within a year of each other.

Jeanette MacDonald (1906–1965) is chiefly remembered for the movie operettas she filmed with Nelson Eddy, such as *Naughty Marietta* (1935), *Rose Marie* (1936), and *The Girl of the Golden West* (1938). She was brought out of retirement to sing "Ah, Sweet Mystery of Life" at Louis B. Mayer's funeral in 1957.

It was hard to know where **Gracie Allen** (1906–1964) the actress ended and Gracie Allen the private personality began. The Gracie Allen who delivered such lines as "My uncle eats concrete. Mother asked him to stay for dinner, but he said he was going to eat up the street," also shortened the lamp cords in her house because she figured it would save on electricity and put salt in the pepper shakers so that if she ever got mixed up there would be no harm done. It didn't help matters that her professional partner, George Burns, was also her husband. Although Gracie made an occasional comedy film and painted surrealistically, her scatterbrained humor is what lives on.

Walk to the opposite end of the first floor, past the main entrance, to reach the Columbarium of Victory. On the back wall just above the **Levi** plaque rests **Dorothy Jean Dandridge** (1922–1965). Dorothy accomplished many firsts in her life: first black woman to sing at the Waldorf-Astoria's Empire Room, first to be photographed for the cover of *Life* magazine, first black to be nominated for an Academy Award for Best Actress. Her role in *Carmen Jones* (1954) didn't win her the Oscar, but it enhanced her reputation and led to roles in *Island in the Sun* (1957) and *Porgy and Bess* (1959).

Yet prestige could not rescue Dorothy's drowning personal life. She gave birth to a brain-damaged child, Harolyn, for which she blamed herself. After her marriage ended, she had a series of disappointing affairs and another disastrous union. Each failure increased her dependence on tranquilizers and champagne. The day before she died she had completed negotiations for two more films and had lined up singing engagements in several countries. Her longtime agent, Earl Mills, found her body on the bathroom floor. Death was diagnosed as caused by either a bone-marrow embolism due to a small fracture in her ankle, or from an overdose of Tofranil, a drug found in her bloodstream. Perhaps the true answer was in her autobiography, *Everything and Nothing*, which had been published a short time before.

At the very end of the hall, in the Sanctuary of Commandments, in the first row three spaces up, is **Clara Ward** (1924–1973) and her mother, evangelist **Gertrude M. Ward** (1901–1981). Clara Ward first sang with her mother and her sister Willa in black churches until their appearance in 1957 at the Newport Jazz Festival. Concerts and TV appearances followed until her life was cut short at 48 by a stroke.

Take a quick detour into the basement for a group of old-timers. One can almost imagine them sitting around smoking cigars and cracking jokes about the old days. In the Sanctuary of Gratitude, on the right side, third row, is **Francis X. Bushman** (1883–1966), here designated "King of the Movies." Indeed, between 1911 and 1918 he was known as "the handsomest man in the world" and starred in over four hundred films. He didn't lose his looks, but competition from Rudolph Valentino and Wallace Reid, and the revelation that he had five children and a wife back in Virginia who was suing him for divorce, greatly diminished his fantasy appeal. Bushman made a comeback in radio and TV, however. He was recovering from a fall in his bathroom when he slipped and fell against a kitchen cabinet while getting a cup of coffee. He died on the same day as Rudolph Valentino, 40 years later.

Nearby in the Sanctuary of Worship is **Chico Marx** (1886–1961). Chico, who was named Leonard at birth, was the Marx with the pointed hat who played the piano and spoke with an Italian accent. He stayed with the group after brothers Gummo and Zeppo had dropped out. In direct contrast to his carefree movie persona, his private life was marked by womanizing, divorce, habitual lying, and compulsive gambling. Chico was simply unable to stop gambling. He even seemed to be deliberately bad at it, a knowing sucker, and at times owed notorious gangsters considerable sums of money. Despite the efforts and subterfuge of Groucho and Harpo, the considerable fortune that Chico had amassed through the movies was eventually squandered and Chico died penniless. The Marx Brothers' zany films include *Animal Crackers* (1930), *Monkey Business* (1931), *Duck Soup* (1933), *A Night at the Opera* (1935), and *A Night in Casablanca* (1946), all considered classics.

Another member of a popular comedy group, **Larry Fine** (1902–1975) is in the Sanctuary of Liberation, four rows in on the bottom. Better recognized as the frizzy-haired member of the Three Stooges, Fine joined Moe and Curly Howard to make more than two hundred short films which were re-popularized by television. So imitated was their routine of stooging—slapping each other on the forehead—that health officials feared children copying it would cause brain damage. Always amiable, the Stooges eliminated the business from future pictures.

Also In Forest Lawn Glendale

Actress **Minta Durfee Arbuckle** (1889–1975), who never stopped believing in her husband Fatty's innocence. **Bob Burns** (1893–1956), the actor who achieved fame by inventing an instrument, the Bazooka, which made a flatulent sound. The famous army antitank weapon was named after it. **Michael Curtiz** (1888–1962), director of *Life with Father* (1947), *White Christmas* (1954), and *Casablanca* (1943) which brought him an Oscar. **George G. "Buddy" DeSylva** (1896–1950), the lyricist who gave the world "April Showers," "Varsity Drag," "Look for the Silver Lining," and "You're the Cream in My Coffee." **Lloyd C. Douglas** (1877–1951), physician and author of the best-selling novels, *The Robe*, *Magnificent Obsession*, and *The Big Fisherman*, which were all made into films. **Marie Dressler** (1869–1934), who made roles like Tugboat Annie (1933) her own. **Sydney Greenstreet** (1879–1954), stage and character actor, best known for roles in *The Maltese Falcon* (1941) and *Casablanca* (1943). **Marlin Hurt** (1906–1946), a white male who played Beulah, the black maid on "Fibber McGee and Molly" (1945), before he collapsed and died at 40. **Bert Kalmar** (1884–1947), the lyricist who wrote "Three Little Words" and "Who's Sorry Now?" **Marie McDonald** (1923–1965), a model turned actress, nicknamed The Body. **Fifi D'Orsay** (1904–1983), Canadian leading lady during the 1930s. **Franklin Pangborn** (1889–1958), most frequently typecast as a disconcerted hotel clerk. **Dimitri Tiomkin** (1899–1979), the Russian composer who garnered Oscars for his scores for *High Noon* (1952), *The High and the Mighty* (1954), and *The Old Man and the Sea* (1958). **Richard Whiting** (1891–1938), the composer of "Till We Meet Again" and "Beyond the Blue Horizon." **William Wyler** (1902–1981), the director who helped form the Committee for the First Amendment to oppose the House Un-American Activities Committee investigations. He won Academy Awards for *Mrs. Miniver* (1942) and *The Best Years of Our Lives* (1946). **Joe Yule** (1894–1950), vaudevillian and Mickey Rooney's father.

DIRECTIONS TO FOREST LAWN GLENDALE: Take Route 5 (Golden State Freeway) and exit east at Glendale Boulevard. Turn right onto Forest, then left onto Glendale Avenue. The entrance is at 1712 South Glendale Avenue.

Oriental grave

Forest Lawn Hollywood Hills

This is my last song.
My flag at half-mast song.
It's the work of a brain with a
circuit of blown-out fuses,
While I'm trying in vain to in-
voke my used-up muses.
Now it's all that remains of my
dried-up creative juices;
My call-Forest-Lawn song.
My swan song.

                 —DAVE FRISHBERG

FOREST LAWN HOLLYWOOD HILLS is the second-largest cemetery in the system established by Hubert Eaton. Yet it cannot quite escape the feeling of being after the fact. If Forest
Lawn Glendale were a bookstore, Hollywood Hills would
be the sale annex. There is a reason that Walt Disney, Clark
Gable, and Mary Pickford are buried in Glendale, and Liberace and Ernie Kovacs are at rest here. Yet that same unpre-
tentiousness and smaller size makes Forest Lawn Hollywood Hills a friendlier and more manageable place to visit.
The artifacts and reconstructions here are all Early American, from Boston's Old North Church to a recreation of
poet Henry Wadsworth Longfellow's study.

    To start your tour, take Memorial Drive from the main
entrance, continuing straight until you see the statue of
George Washington on your left. This 60-foot statue, created by sculptor Thomas Ball, was first exhibited at the
Chicago World's Fair in 1893. Ball, an accomplished singer
as well as a sculptor, also created the sculpture of Daniel
Webster in Central Park, New York.

George Washington facing Old North Church   *113*

On the right lawn beside the wall, seven markers in, is the memorial of Buster Keaton.

JOSEPH FRANK KEATON *b. October 4, 1895, Pickway, KA; d. February 1, 1966, Woodland Hills, CA*. The Great Stone Face was just that by the time he was 4, when he was earning $10 per week and starring in his parents' vaudeville act. He had broken in at 9 months by crawling onto the stage to great applause. By then he had already been given his nickname by no less than Harry Houdini, who toured with the Keatons. When the 6-month-old baby fell down a flight of stairs, Houdini rushed over, found that the infant was laughing, and remarked, "That was some buster your baby took!" The word appealed to Joe, Sr., and it stuck with his son.

Buster's unsmiling nature was driven into him as a young child. In the family act his job was to get underfoot of his father. The penalty was to be kicked and hurled around the stage like a somber rag doll. For years the family dodged child-abuse complaints by demonstrating that Buster had no bruises and by dressing him up in whiskers and a suit and passing him off as a midget. Buster learned early on how to take a kick and how to fall, and he developed acrobatic skills. But the violence of the act grew too real as his father sank into alcoholism. Buster paid the price on stage and at home.

By 1917 the Keaton act had broken up, but in a chance encounter with Fatty Arbuckle, a Keaton admirer, Buster was offered a role in Fatty's next movie. The scripts were no more than bare outlines, which left the actors great

A	Buster Keaton	**L**	Fritz Lang
B	Stan Laurel	**M**	Buddy Cole, Pete King
C	Rex Ingram	**N**	Roy Disney
D	Marty Feldman	**O**	Smiley Burnette, Jack Webb
E	Charles Laughton, Clyde Beatty	**P**	Horace Heidt
F	Liberace	**Q**	Godfrey Cambridge
G	Freddy Prinze, George Raft	**R**	Ozzie Nelson
H	Andy Gibb, Harry F. Mills	**S**	Esther Phillips
J	Ruth St. Denis	**T**	Gabby Hayes
K	Ernie Kovacs		

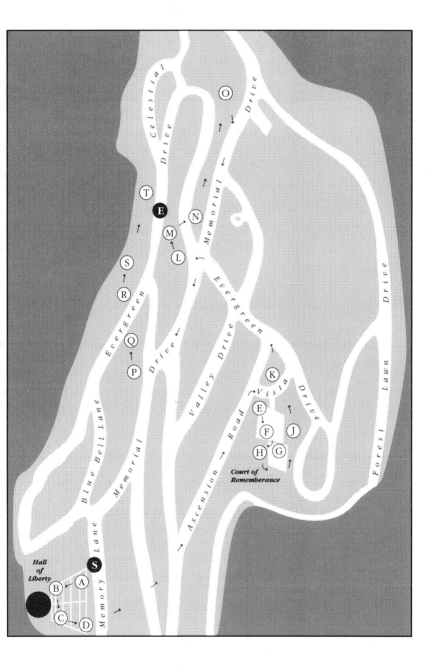

freedom and range in improvising. Buster was in his milieu, and he shone. In 1920 his own two-reeler, *One Week*, was a huge hit and already showed Keaton in classic battle with the mechanized world.

More films quickly followed. So did marriage. With his handsome features, his acrobat's strength and build, and his success, Buster was more than just eligible. He chose Natalie Talmadge, the pretty but quiet sister of Constance and Norma Talmadge, two of the era's biggest stars. The match was less than perfect. Buster was dependent on affection and organization. He needed help just to get dressed in the morning. Natalie was too passive to support him. Buster was lively, interested, and involved; Natalie was quiet and home-loving. Still they appeared to be an affectionate couple, and soon there were two sons. The relationship slid after that, however, as the passive Natalie gave in to her strong-minded, and perhaps jealous, family's demands that there be no more children. Natalie took a bedroom of her own, and Buster took to other women, bridge, and drinking.

Buster's reputation gathered momentum with *The Boat*, wherein his yacht, *Damfino*, is launched and promptly sinks to the bottom. Keaton remains on deck, stoically never budging until only his famous pork-pie hat is seen floating away. Success followed with *Sherlock Jr.*, which gave full range to Keaton's athletic skills and his penchant for daredevil stunts, and continued with one of the movies' greatest comedies, *The Navigator*. Oddly, *The General* (1926), now considered Keaton's classic, was a failure and led to the financial reins being pulled in.

These movies established Keaton as one of the great comics and formed the basis for his legend today. He never played for sentiment. As James Agee stated, "There was in his comedy a freezing whisper not of pathos but of melancholia. . . . Even a smile was as deafeningly out of key as a yell. In a way his pictures are like a transcendent juggling act in which it seems that the whole universe is in exquisite flying motion and the one point of repose is the juggler's effortless, uninterested face." Is it any wonder that Keaton held great appeal for surrealists and existentialists alike?

The advent of talkies hurt Keaton's career, for his best talents lay with improvisation and mime. His drinking and reticence hurt him even more. He was unable to ever express any hurt or pain, even to his closest friends. By 1933 he was divorced, drinking a bottle a day, and nearing bankruptcy. His second marriage was mercifully short-lived. By 1935, however, he had sobered up and caught on with MGM. Work improved, but Keaton's real lifesaver was his marriage to Eleanor Norris, an attractive 21-year-old dancer, in 1940. She realized his needs and fulfilled them. She organized his life, budgeted his money, and, most of all, gave him the love he so desperately needed.

In the late 1940s, and for many years after, Keaton achieved great popularity with his mime for the Cirque Medrano in Paris. He also played brilliantly with Chaplin in *Limelight* (1952), appeared in many cameo roles, and starred, still with stone face and pork-pie hat, in Samuel Beckett's odd *Film* (1964).

In October 1965, Keaton, now in the midst of a growing interest in all his work, was diagnosed as having lung cancer. Refusing new work, he attempted to rest, but in three months one of our greatest comedians was gone.

Continue up several flights of stairs to the last wall on the right. On it is a plaque to **Stan Laurel**, born Arthur Stanley Jefferson (1890–1965), which reads, "Master of Comedy. His genius in the art of humor brought gladness to the world he loved." Below him in the ground is **Ida K. Laurel** who died in 1980. Her inscription: "Beloved wife." Ida was the partner in Stan's eighth marriage. (His second, third, and seventh weddings were to Virginia Rogers.)

Stan Laurel was the thin one of the Laurel and Hardy team, the one with the scrunched-up, weepy eyes and the plaintive, pleading voice. He was the one who took the deliberate abuse of his oversized partner and returned it through accident and mishap. Despite his passivity, shyness, and uncoordinated ways, he usually came out on top.

Laurel and Hardy, the boys in the bowlers, were the greatest comedy team in cinematic history. Their slapstick routines left their admiring audiences weak with laughter in the 1920s and 1930s and can do the same today. Through over two hundred films they successfully spanned the transition from the silent era to the talkies. Although they requested written scripts, the studios, noting their success, refused and left the men to improvise. This they did, with comic inventiveness amounting to genius. According to Laurel, "It was damned fine fun and damned hard work."

Arthur Stanley Jefferson was born into a theatrical family in Ulverson, England. Learning the craft of comedy in his youth, he came to this country in 1920 and first teamed with Hardy in 1926. Their relationship was basically work-centered, and they never suffered from any serious disputes. Off stage Oliver was more apt to party or play golf.

Of himself Stan observed, "You know my hobby—and I married them all." One of his four wives agreed: "Stan's a good boy really, but he has a marrying complex."

Laurel and Hardy made their last movie together in 1949. After a diabetic stroke in 1955, Laurel lived quietly in Santa Monica and refused public appearances after Hardy's death in 1957. His funeral was attended by over 350 friends including Buster Keaton and cast members from his many films. The Laurel and Hardy theme, "The Cuckoo Song," was played at a dirgelike tempo in the background while Dick Van Dyke told those present of Laurel's comic genius, "He just wanted to make you laugh, and he did."

To the left of Stan Laurel is **Ray Bidwell Collins** (1889–1965), whose marker reminds the world that he was Lieutenant Tragg on "Perry Mason." Also in this garden, closer to the road, is William Talman (1915–1968), whose marker does *not* point out that as District Attorney Hamilton Berger on the same show he never won a case.

The other marble plaque on the wall with Stan Laurel is to **Borden Chase** (1900–1971). It reads, "Writer–Patriot. 'You have to help people when they need help.' His philosophy of life and work." Chase was actually an author and screenwriter with a colorful past. From his experiences in digging the Holland Tunnel in Manhattan, he wrote the novel *Sandhog* and accompanied it to Hollywood, where it was made into the movie *Under Pressure*. Chase stayed on to write western screenplays.

On the other side, in the last row of markers by the garden wall, is **Rex Ingram** (1895–1969), whose marker refers to his most famous role, in *Green Pastures*: "De Lawd–Remembered always." Ingram, who was born on the riverboat *Robert E. Lee* in Cairo, Illinois, headed for Hollywood in 1919 with his Phi Beta Kappa key, an MD degree, and no intention of becoming an actor. He was crossing the street when a talent scout persuaded him to accept a role in two early Tarzan movies.

Ingram's favorite role was as *Emperor Jones* in the play by Eugene O'Neill, though the part most identified with him was that of De Lawd God Jehovah in *Green Pastures*. Ingram was not always as pious in real life as this role might suggest. He was incarcerated in New Jersey for chronic speeding and arrested twice for assault in Harlem. In 1949 he served nine months in jail for transporting a 15-year-old girl across state lines for immoral purposes.

Ingram's scrapes with the law did not curtail his career, however. He appeared in an all-black production of *Waiting for Godot* (1957) and in *God's Little Acre* (1959), then switched to such television shows as "I Spy," "Gunsmoke," and "Playhouse 90."

In the front of the second garden, near the wall, is the marker of **Marty Feldman** (1934–1982), who died unexpectedly of a heart attack at 48. An appearance that other men might have taken as a disaster—protruding walleyes, prominent nose and chin, and a mop of curls—Feldman parlayed into comedy, first in Britain with John Cleese, then in Mel Brooks films. Feldman delighted audiences with his portrayal of Igor in *Young Frankenstein* (1973), and in *The Adventure of Sherlock Holmes' Smarter Brother* (1975) and *Silent Movie* (1976). In later years he directed movies as well.

Feldman's epitaph, written by his wife, reads, "He made us laugh, he took my pain away."

Two more personalities are buried in the open ground. Actor **Benjamin Sherman "Scatman" Crothers** (1910–1986), best known as the old musician in *The Shining*, and for his role in the TV series "Chico and the Man," is in Plot 454. **Bruce Wayne** (1933–1986), "Dean of America's Traffic Reporters" is in the Garden of Heritage. He was the first traffic reporter to use a helicopter.

Take Memorial Lane, following it to the right until you turn left into Ascension Road to the Courts of Remembrance. Go up the steps and make the first right. The black marble insert halfway down the aisle and three rows up is the vault of **Charles Laughton** (1899–1962). Laughton, who never fully recovered from being gassed in World War I, died of cancer of the spine at 63. But his war injuries did not prevent him from having a rich career as a character actor. Laughton's plump, expressive face seemed suited to whatever role he played: Nero, Captain Bligh, or King Lear. In 1933 he won an Academy Award for his lusty portrayal of the King in *The Private Life of Henry VIII*. Laughton's widow, the actress Elsa Lanchester, died recently; her ashes were scattered at sea.

Against the back wall and three positions over is a crypt marker with some character. Circus man **Clyde Beatty** (1909–1965) is commemorated by a bronze plate with his signature and a seated lion on top. It is inscribed, "Forever enshrined in our hearts."

Clyde Beatty, the greatest wild-animal trainer in the world, could make his lions and tigers leap to their perches but could not always keep them there. It was the question of whether or not his charges would attack him that kept circus goers spellbound. Over one hundred times his audiences saw Beatty get mauled by animals who were bored with the same old routine. Those who missed the actual attacks could see the scars and claw tracks across his face and read about his near escapes in the books he wrote such as *The Big Cage*.

Unlike his French counterpart, Jean Pezon, who became lionized in his pet Brutus' stomach, Beatty died quietly of natural causes.

On the left side of this area, opposite from Clyde Beatty, is a cluster of lesser-known names. Marker 341, against the wall, is that of composer **Albert Hay Malotte** (1895–1964) who wrote "The Lord's Prayer" and the score to Disney's *Lady and the Tramp*.

To your left, in the Columbarium of Remembrance, is **Ernest Loring "Red" Nichols** (1905–1965), cornetist and leader of the jazz group, Red Nichols and His Five Pennies. The group, which usually numbered closer to 14, was the spawning ground for Glenn Miller, Tommy and Jimmy Dorsey, Benny Goodman, Gene Krupa, Jack Teagarden, Joe Venuti, and many others. Always casual about numbers, Nichols started out with a seven-man band called The Syncopated Five. In 1959 Danny Kaye played the lead in *The Five Pennies*, a movie based on Red Nichols' life.

In the side wall, Vault 61274 is that of **Marie Wilson**, born Katherine Elizabeth White (1916–1972), the classic dumb blonde who brought the role of My Friend Irma to radio, movies, and TV. On the back wall, in a plainer vault bearing only his name, is Marty Melcher (1914–1968). Married to Doris Day, he also acted as her agent, business manager, and promoter. He had just finished co-producing *With Six You Get Egg Roll* when he died of a stroke at 54.

On the wall opposite Melcher, in Crypt 60987, is bandleader **Art Kassel** (1896–1965). In the center of his crypt is a small stylized castle to commemorate his band, Kassels in the Air.

Walk all the way to the back of the Courts of Remembrance. On the right is the large white sarcophagus of the **Liberace family**. On top a classical statue of a woman holds flowers and looks into the distance. Below her is **Frances** (1891–1980) "Our Beloved Mom"; **George** (1911–1983); and **Liberace**. In the center of the sarcophagus is a wrought-iron piano candelabrum with Liberace's signature, which was created by the pianist himself.

WLADZIU VALENTINO LIBERACE *b. May 16, 1919, Milwaukee; d. February 4, 1987, Palm Springs.*

Well, look me over! I don't dress like this to go unnoticed.

As the surviving brother of a twin who was born skeletal and "under the veil" (suffocated by a film of placenta), young Wladziu himself weighed a robust 13 pounds. His lust for life was evident from the start. Wladziu, called Walter, began piano lessons at 4 and showed enough aptitude to be granted a scholarship to the Wisconsin College of Music. By the time he was a teenager, the major interests of his life were in place: music, cooking (his corn muffins were prized by his classmates), and dressing up. Walter usually won first prize for originality on high-school Character Days, coming as Haile Selassie, Yankee Doodle, or Greta Garbo.

Just as his father, who was trained in the classical French horn, couldn't find work, Walter soon found there was little money in the concert hall. While still a teenager he found jobs in places such as Little Nick's beer hall, and gradually he developed a new piano technique. "Three Little Fishes" would emerge from an elegant Chopinesque introduction, and a Beethoven sonata might be followed by an audience-participation rendition of "Chopsticks." When he began accepting engagements in New York and Los Angeles, Walter took a cue from fellow countryman Paderewski and shortened his name to Liberace. His friends called him Lee.

In 1949 Liberace underwent a career re-evaluation. True, he had played for President Truman and was featured in

Liberace

the movie *South Sea Sinner* (1949). But appearing in hotels and supper clubs was not making him the star he wanted to be. He read Claude M. Bristol's *The Magic of Believing*, a book based on the principles of creative visualization, and was entranced. Applying some of the techniques, Liberace had his teeth capped, began to dress more lavishly, and contracted for his own TV show. Enter the golden candelabra and decorated pianos. The Liberace era had begun.

Liberace's appearance in Madison Square Garden in 1954 was one of the high points of his career. He was described by one writer as "A poem in white tie, tails, white shoes, and pancake make-up. Auditorium beside itself. . . . Cries of joy! Great happiness! Liberace smiling like a well-fed baby." Recostumed in gold lamé by the climax, he enthralled 15,000 fans with renditions of "Claire de Lune," "Beer Barrel Polka," and a Mexican number in which his brother George shook the maracas. For his performance at the Garden, Liberace earned $138,000—the highest amount ever paid a pianist for a single performance, according to the *Guiness Book of World Records*.

Through it all Liberace kept the personality that had won

him friends all his life. Never aggressive, he was warm, charming, and hopeful. He loved not only his mother, Frances, but his associates and friends and enjoyed surprising everyone with gifts. He was attracted to kitsch but able to laugh with those who made fun of his piano-shaped bed, Marie Antoinette room done entirely in red, and sequined hot-pants outfits.

It was the piano-shaped bed that got him in trouble, however. From the start of his career, Liberace had publicly denied his homosexuality, even "writing" a fan-magazine article about his three engagements. He won a libel suit against a British writer, Cassandra (William Connor), in 1956 for referring to him as "fruit-flavored" among other descriptions. But in private Lee surrounded himself with what his mother disapprovingly termed his "hillbillies." The palimony suit brought in 1982 by former companion Scott Thorson was difficult to explain. Ironically, Liberace won it on the grounds that their agreement "amounted to prostitution and such contracts are illegal and unenforceable."

The most serious by-product of Liberace's sexual preference, however, did not come to light until after his death. There were some hints before that. Seeing a particular look to his face, his longtime friend, Phyllis Diller, suspected AIDS. The performer's lack of energy and pronounced weight loss could only be attributed to a watermelon diet for so long. Yet when he died in Palm Springs, the disease was not reported by his doctors as the cause of death. It was only at the insistence of Riverside County Coroner Raymond Carillo that Liberace's body was retrieved from Forest Lawn and autopsied. The cover-up, if that's what it was, was at Liberace's request. It is poignant he did not realize that knowing he was a victim of AIDS would not have made people love him any less.

To the right of Liberace, in Vault 3405, is **T. Marvin Hatley** (1905–1986) whose claim to fame is listed on his marker: "Composer of the Laurel and Hardy theme song." He follows the lead of **Haven Gillespie** (1888–1975) nearby, whose "Santa Claus Is Coming to Town" is mentioned on his grave. Gillespie wrote over six hundred songs, including "That Lucky Old Sun" and "Breezing Along with the Breeze."

Behind Liberace, in the Sanctuary of Light, look for a statue of a woman with a naked toddler. Nearby is the vault of **George Raft** (1895–1980). Raft, best known for his gangster roles, had the grim, chiseled features of the comic-strip detective Dick Tracy and a wardrobe which defied belief: elevator shoes, purple shirts with yellow ties, and his standard white tie on black shirt. After a youthful career as pool-room hustler, dance-hall gigolo, and prizefighter, Raft made his first film in 1929. It wasn't until *Scarface* (1932) that his gangster persona attracted attention.

Though Raft played in over 60 films, he was perhaps more noticeable for the opportunities he turned down — *High Sierra*, *The Maltese Falcon*, *Double Indemnity*, and *Casablanca* — while accepting *She Couldn't Take It*, *Stage Door Canteen*, and *Loan Shark*.

As colorful off the screen as he was on, Raft was friendly with various Hell's Kitchen gangsters and pals with Bugsy Siegel. He lived to be 85, but at 73 was broke, suffering from emphysema and ulcers and being dunned by the IRS for $75,000 in back taxes. "When I was going good I had three servants, a publicity man, an agent, lawyers and nine million parasites," he complained. "I don't know where it all went."

Right near George, closer to the wall, is the crypt of tragic young actor **Freddie Prinze** (1954–1977). His epitaph reads, "We love you. Psalm 23." It is difficult to know what could have saved Freddie Prinze. Perhaps if he had not succeeded so quickly, had not gone from being an unknown stand-up comedian to a host of the "Tonight" show, and the star of "Chico and the Man," he would have been better able to handle success. As it was, he could do so only with cocaine, Quaaludes, and the constant reassurance of those around him. In the end that was not enough. He left a note on Shoreham Americana Hotel stationary advising "I must end it. There's no hope left. I'll be at peace. No one had anything to do with this. My decision totally. Freddie Prinze."

Across the way in Vault 4349 is **Wanda Hendrix** (1928–1981), "To know her is to love her." The petite actress, who survived being married to Audie Murphy and James L. Stack, and made a flock of B movies, died of pneumonia.

On the other side, in the Sanctuary of Reflection, is **Reginald Gardiner** (1903–1980), whose marker bears the masks of Comedy and Tragedy and the inscription, "The angels of Avalon shall be with you evermore." A British actor, Gardiner generally played the daffy Englishman in such films as *The Man Who Came to Dinner* (1941) and *Mr. Hobbs Takes a Vacation* (1962). Gardiner, who died of pneumonia, began his American career in Beatrice Lillie revues doing an imitation of a lighthouse, train, and wastebasket. In 1964 he gave a wonderful rendition of Liza Doolittle's father, Alfred, in a revival of *My Fair Lady*.

Farther back on the wall in Numbers 2301–2 is the western clothes designer inaptly named **Nudie** (1902–1984). To the left of his name is the label Nudie's Rodeo Tailors, with a cowboy roping the words. Nudie was the first to put sequins on movie cowboys.

If you walk into the end mausoleum at the back, you can find **Strother Martin** (1919–1980), who died of a heart attack. He was best known as the sardonic prison warden in *Cool Hand Luke* (1967). Six positions from the end and eight up is **Forrest Tucker** (1919–1986) of "F-Troop." Nearby is **Pamela Britton** (1923–1974), the pert blonde actress best known to television audiences for her appearances on "My Favorite Martian" and in the title role of "Blondie."

Go outside the wall and to your right to the mausoleum. Three vaults in and two up is the marker of **Michael Garrison** (1922–1966), the executive producer of the TV series "Wild, Wild West," who died after a fall in his home.

In front of the outside wall is a white marble bench dedicated to "America's beloved gospel singer" **Tony Fontane** (1925–1974). His stone, down on the grass to the left, reads, "His mission on earth fulfilled." Starting as a pop singer with the hits "Cold, Cold Heart" and "Syncopated Clock," Fontane found the Lord after a near-fatal traffic accident. A film biography, *The Tony Fontane Story*, was translated into 19 languages and shown to religious audiences around the world. Fontane died of cancer.

Catty-corner to this mausoleum wall, in Vault 3442, is pop singer **Andy Gibb** (1957–1988). Following in the footsteps of his older brothers, the Bee Gees (Barry, Robin, and Maurice Gibb), he began performing solo in his native Australia. He had two Number-1 singles, "I Just Want To Be Your Everything" (1977) and "Shadow Dancing" (1978), but his private life became more spectacular than his singing. Plagued with cocaine problems which he blamed on his break-up with actress Victoria Principal, Gibb was dismissed from the cast of *Joseph and the Amazing Technicolor Dreamcoat* in 1983. He entered the Betty Ford Clinic for treatment two years later. The 30-year-old singer died in a hospital in Oxfordshire, England, after complaining of stomach pains. The cause of death was not given.

On the back outdoor wall, Vault 3442 is that of **Harry F. Mills** (1913–1982). "Your love will remain in our hearts forever," his inscription reads. Harry was often the spokesman for the famous Mills Brothers, first a quartet and then a trio, who entertained the public for 50 years. The brothers, noted for their imitations of instruments, loosened up the traditional barbershop harmonies with their instrumental inflections. Their suave style influenced many black groups, including those that turned to rock and roll. The brothers retained a loyal following throughout their career. Among their biggest hits were "Paper Doll" and "Glow Worm."

Walk around the periphery to the wall on the side facing Vesper Drive, to the marker of **Johnny Eager–Tanner** (1924–1963) at Vault 3235. Eager–Tanner was a minor English actor. His inscription requests, "If you need me, Precious, whistle."

Down the wall farther, in Vault 3116, is **Ruth St. Denis** (1879–1968) whose epitaph reads:

> The gods have meant that I should dance,
> And in some mystic hour
> I shall move to unheard rhythms
> Of the cosmic orchestra of heaven.
> You will know the language of my wordless poems
> And will come to me
> For that is why I dance.

On the right is an Art Nouveau image of her with a large aureole and the inscription "Ruth St. Denis, Pioneer and Prophet."

"Miss Ruth," who felt herself karmically linked to the Egyptian goddess of fertility and consolation, Isis, began creating appropriate dances. Unsuccessful in New York, she established her reputation in Europe, then settled in Los Angeles. With her husband, Ted Shawn, she opened the Denishawn School of Dance, attracting such pupils as Martha Graham and Dorothy and Lillian Gish. Although she and Shawn split personally and professionally after 1931, she continued to teach and to put on spectacular recitals.

Across Vista Lane, by the curb and facing the Court of Remembrance, is **Jason Nilson Robards** (1892–1963), stage actor and father of J. R., Jr. One of his best-known roles was as Chandu the Magician on radio.

Farther down on the lawn, nearly across from the water tower, is **Ernie Kovacs** (1919–1962), whose marker bears the enigmatic words, "Nothing in moderation" and "We all loved him."

Ernie Kovacs certainly inherited the tradition of nothing in moderation from his parents. His father was a colorful Hungarian who worked on both sides of the law, and his mother a fiery, doting woman who staunchly stood up for her youngest son. In his youth in Trenton Ernie knew both the poor and rich sections, public and private schools. It was at Trenton High School that he demonstrated his theatrical talents, appearing in everything from Gilbert and Sullivan to Shaw.

Kovacs' leap to fame was not a graceful one. Continuing his studies in New York City while trying to eke out a living with bit parts, he suffered from poverty during the Depression, falling deathly ill and being hospitalized in the terminal ward during his "Welfare Island Engagement." His recuperation took over a year and a half and found Ernie back in Trenton, where he latched on with a local radio station. Starting in a 15-minute spot, Kovacs quickly expanded his time slot as listeners became aware of him and enamored of his madcap ways. Ernie would save the ads for last and run them all together, or he would create his own sponsors, such as Bash's Imported Sheep Dip, as the mood struck him. His popularity grew, and he expanded his humor to a newspaper column which dealt with everything and anything in the most iconoclastic fashion possible, including ridicule of the Pledge of Allegiance, Perry Como, and Margaret Truman.

Kovacs stayed on at the Trenton station for 10 years, ending his run in 1950 when he opted to give TV a try. First appearing as a less-than-serious host on a cooking show, he soon moved on to an early-morning show where he resumed his impetuous style, utilizing all manner of sight gags and props and continuing with his corny puns and other abuses of the spoken word. The informality of the new medium leant itself to his style, and both he and his cameramen developed many new techniques which expanded the creative use of the TV camera. During this time Ernie also hired a short, nearsighted, gorgeous singer named Edie Adams, whose chief function was to sing while Ernie thought up new routines and then fling him a prop when she was done. Eventually he married her.

Among Kovacs' greatest talents was his ability to invent comic names: his immortal lisping poet, Percy Dovetonsils, and Bessie Lederkrantz, Hecuba Baldspot, Heatcliff Coldsore, and J. Walter Puppybreath. Kovacs also leant his humor and his visage to *Mad* magazine and allowed *Mad* the use of the name Melvin Cowznofski. Of course he was already sporting his trademark moustache and the ubiquitous cigar whose size would have ridiculously dwarfed anyone with smaller, less distinctive features. Ernie moved to New York and wrote many skits, some of which he felt were "borrowed" by Steve Allen, causing a rift between the two for some time. Ironically Ernie gained national attention when he did his first half-hour filler for NBC in 1957, ironic because Ernie was silent throughout. His entire routine consisted of mime combining with yet more innovative camera techniques to create a surrealistic world which Ernie used as a foil for his humor.

The show lit up the switchboards. Among the callers were Hollywood agents and producers. Soon Ernie was on his way to Tinseltown. His career in movies proved to be less than he hoped. He got roles in *Operation Madball*, *Our Man in Havana*, and *Sail a Crooked Ship*, among others, but he never achieved any stunning success. Between movies he continued with his highly publicized TV specials, which attracted large audiences. In his spare time he applied his boundless energy to marathon late-night poker games with some of the rich and elite of Hollywood. He was no snob, however, and played similar games for lesser stakes during breaks at work with his film crew. Almost all who worked with Kovacs found him to be down to earth, generous, funny, and compulsively on the go.

On Saturday, January 13, 1962, Kovacs put in his usual long, hard day, attended a christening party, and was on his way to PJ's in Hollywood for a nightcap, when, attempting to light yet another cigar, he lost control of his car on the wet road and smashed into some telephone poles. He died almost instantly, a victim of fatigue and an unlit cigar.

To his left is his daughter **Mia Kovacs** (1959–1982), "Daddy's Girl. We all loved her too." Twenty years after her father's fatal accident, Mia died when her car ran off the road and crashed. She was thrown through the sunroof and died two hours later.

In the Gentleness section, under a tree, are two actress sisters, **Amanda Randolph** (1896–1967) and **Lillian Randolph** (1914–1980). Amanda's marker is inscribed: "An inspiration to the young actors and actresses, hers was a life of giving." She portrayed the cantankerous mother-in-law on "Amos 'n' Andy" and the maid on "The Danny Thomas Show" before dying of a stroke.

Also in this section is animator **Frederick B. "Tex" Avery** (1908–1980), one of the creators of Bugs Bunny. He is kept company by **Jack Soo** (1917–1979), who is in Plot 3980. Born Goro Suzuki in Oakland, Soo's budding entertainment career came to quick halt when he was interned during World War II because of his Japanese ancestry. After the war he changed his name and went on to star in both the stage and screen versions of *Flower Drum Song*. His most famous role was that of Sgt. Nick Yemana on "Barney Miller," where he played a world-weary detective infamous for making bad coffee.

Move down Evergreen Drive and go left on Memorial

Drive to the Enduring Faith section. Starting up the hill by the road and two positions in is **Fritz Lang** (1890–1976). Lang, the large-featured, despotic Viennese-born director, was most famous for his film *M*, the study of a child killer played with chilling, sinister perfection by Peter Lorre. Such horror was typical of Lang's movies, for he was preoccupied "with violence [and] the pathology of violence" and often centered on the underclasses for his explorations.

As a teenager Lang ran away from home to study painting. Soon tiring of this, he traveled around the world supporting himself with his artistic talents. By 1914 he had returned to Vienna, and by 1922, having been a movie director for three years, he directed his silent-film classic, *Dr. Mabuse, the Gambler*. Lang left Germany suddenly in 1932 on the very day he met with Josef Goebbels. Called to the Nazi minister's office for a reprimand, Lang had his hand only mildly slapped and was then offered a chance to help Nazi propaganda with his film expertise. Abhorring Nazism and fearing discovery of Jewish ancestry on his mother's side, Lang, a Catholic, headed for France and soon after made his way to Hollywood, where he remained until his death. He was responsible for directing *While the City Sleeps*, *You Only Live Once*, *Metropolis*, and *Fury* among many other films.

Known for his dictatorial and perfectionistic ways in the studio, Lang found these traits to be less acceptable in Hollywood than they were in Europe, but confrontations with actors and producers did little to change his attitude. Ironically his best-known contribution, the countdown to a launch, is seldom attributed to him. In *Women in the Moon*, Lang realized that audiences would only know the moment of take-off if he counted down to zero. Scientists have followed the wisdom of his ways since.

Six rows up from Lang and four in, is the marker of **Diane Linkletter** (1948–1969), bearing the inscription, "Darling, we loved you so much." Diane was a sad casualty of the 1960s. A bad LSD trip caused her to feel she was losing her mind. While discussing it with a friend in her sixth-floor apartment, Diane moved to the kitchen window and jumped out. Her terrified friend tried to stop her but could catch only at her belt loops.

Up the hill are two musicians. **C. Dudley "Pete" King** (1914–1982) is described on his marker as "A man of great integrity, his music will live forever." King was a noted conductor, composer, and arranger who made contributions to many movies including *State Fair*, *South Pacific*, and *Camelot*. He formed his own chorale and orchestra and arranged and conducted for many of the leading pop singers of his time.

Edwin Lamar "Buddy" Cole's (1916–1964) inscription notes, "Buddy's life was gifted with incredible ability to add incomparable beauty to the sounds of music. To know him was to admire and love him deeply. . . . Buddy described his life and accomplishments very simply in his hauntingly beautiful original composition 'Fulfillment.' " His monument has organ pipes on each side, and in the center a grand piano. Buddy Cole accompanied such stars as Bing Crosby and Rosemary Clooney on the piano. He died suddenly at 49 after spending the day rehearsing with Phil Harris.

Under the big tree is **Sabu Dastigar** (1924–1963) who dropped his last name at the start of his career. Sabu was actually the son of an elephant driver in Mysore, India, when he was plucked from his perch by director Robert Flaherty to play in *Elephant Boy* (1937). Arriving in Hollywood via England, he was the resident Indian for such films as *The Jungle Book* (1942), *Song of India* (1949), and *Hello, Elephant* (1952). Sabu died of a heart attack at 39.

Sabu's brother, stuntman **Sheik Dastigar** (1913–1960), is one row back. Both have markers showing a couple side by side gazing toward the mountains. The plaques bear the inscription "Till the day breaks and the shadows flee away."

Across Evergreen Drive in Sheltering Hills, about seven markers in and eight up, is **Roy Disney** (1893–1971). His inscription reads, "A greatly humble man, he left the world a better place." His wife **Edna Frances Disney** (1890–1984) is buried with him. Roy Disney was the counterweight to his brother Walt's flights of fantasy, the anchor that kept the studio firmly in place. Like all anchors, he tended toward caution, but it was his business acumen that parlayed Disney Studios into a multimillion-dollar empire. After Walt's death in 1966, Roy oversaw the creation of his last dream, Epcot Center in Florida.

Farther up the hill in Plot 266 is **Lester "Smiley" Burnette** (1911–1967), who was Gene Autry's sidekick in 81 movies and ended his career as the cheerful engineer, Charlie Pratt, on "Petticoat Junction" (1963–67). In between, Burnette, described on his monument as "A dedicated entertainer who brought joy to others," played one hundred musical instruments, collected novel cooking gadgets, and wrote *The Smiley Burnette Cookbook*.

To the right is **Helen C. Travolta** (1912–1978), "Dearly beloved wife, mother, and actress," and, of course, the mother of John. Her marker has masks of Comedy and Tragedy and a rose floral design.

HORACE HEIDT

AND HIS FAMILY

HIS CREED

"'Tis better to build boys
than mend men"

Finally, in Plot 1999 is **Jack Webb** (1920–1982). His slate marker has the dark letters of his name but nothing else on it. Although he played roles other than Joe Friday in the TV series "Dragnet," most people would be hard pressed to remember what they were.

From Sheltering Hills, go up Memorial Drive until you reach the Murmuring Trees section. The large classical marble statue there is a memorial to bandleader **Horace M. Heidt** (1901–1986) and shows a family, all dressed in togas and all with downcast eyes. The mother's head is uplifted and rests against her husband's temple. A young boy stands in between while a yet younger one sits at their feet with a ball at his side. The base bears Heidt's creed, " 'Tis better to build boys than mend men." Heidt was best known to radio audiences for his talent shows, which gave a boost to Gordon MacRae, Art Carney, Al Hirt, and the King Sisters. His later shows, featuring his band the Musical Knights, were known as "Family Night with Horace Heidt" and "The American Way." Heidt had less success with his five wives, the last of whom brought charges of domestic violence against him.

Diagonally to the right of Heidt and up the hill is comedian **Godfrey M. Cambridge** (1933–1976). Described in one obituary as "sometimes fat, sometimes thin, sometimes jolly, sometimes bitter," Cambridge weighed close to three hundred pounds and was in good spirits when he collapsed of a heart attack at age 43. He died near here on a movie set in Burbank, playing Idi Amin in the TV movie "Rescue at Entebbe."

Cambridge, a West Indian who was schooled in Nova Scotia, where his grandparents lived, encountered his first racial prejudice as a junior at Hofstra University in New York. Switching to City College, he held a number of odd jobs — from judo instructor to airplane wing cleaner — until he got his first part in the play *Take a Giant Step* (1956). His better-known films included *Watermelon Man* (1970) and *Cotton Comes to Harlem* (1971). Active in civil rights causes, Cambridge at the time of his death had successfully filed a complaint against a Connecticut real-estate broker for selling him a house that lacked such "luxuries" as heat and hot water.

At the top of this section, on the hill, is **Dar Allen Robinson** (1947–1986). His monument reads, "The World's Most Spectacular Stuntman. A true legend in our time. . . . Like him there will be no other." Robinson, who had twice survived a nine-hundred-foot free fall from the Canadian National Tower in Toronto, died in a motorcycle accident in a small Arizona desert town. He departed on the same day as Scatman Crothers, comedian Jerry Colonna, and the mother of the Dionne quintuplets.

Moving across the grass in the direction of Old North Church, in Plot 1611 you will find **Eddie Cano** (1927–1988) under a dark brown marker with a handsome bronze grand piano. Cano was a popular pianist in the Los Angeles area; his trio blended jazz with Latin rhythms.

In the same section **James A. McCarthy**'s (1904–1971) plaque points out, "No use kicking."

On the hillside opposite the Murmuring Trees section across Evergreen Drive rests **Oswald G. Nelson** (1906–1975),18 rows up from the road. Ozzie Nelson had a storybook life. At 13 he was the youngest Eagle Scout in the United States, a distinction which earned him a trip to the 1920 Boy Scout Jamboree in London. He played football and lacrosse and swam at Rutgers University, New Jersey, earning a law degree in 1930. When the Depression made jobs scarce, Nelson cashed in on his resemblance to Rudy Vallee. Buying a megaphone, he organized a band and toured the country. He married vocalist Harriet Hilliard. In 1944, after a number of guest appearances, they were given their own radio show.

"The Adventures of Ozzie and Harriet" lasted 22 years on radio and TV and gave work to the Nelson's real-life sons, Ricky and David. When the TV show ended in 1966, Ozzie felt as if he was "killing off a whole set of people loved by millions." He died of liver cancer before having to face the death of his son Rick Nelson in a plane crash. Ricky and his band were on their way to Dallas to perform in a New Year's Eve show.

Also up here is **Esther Phillips** (1935–1984). One of the great rhythm and blues singers of her time and one of the influential innovators for rock and roll, it was ironic that, for a long time, Esther Phillips was best known and appreciated in England. Among her admirers were the Beatles, who paid tribute to her in their 1965 BBC-TV special.

Phillips got her start at 13 by winning a talent contest in Los Angeles. Johnny Otis, the band leader, was in the audience and was so impressed that he offered her a job with his group. Singing both solo and with Otis, she became known as Little Esther and recorded a series of R&B hits. At 17 she decided to branch out on her own and continued her successful ways with "Ring-A-Ding-Doo." Shortly after, her career was put on hold due to serious illness. Returning in the early 1960s she recorded an international hit with "Release Me." After that she enjoyed a string of successful singles and albums and performed at many of the top jazz festivals including Newport and Monterey.

Moving into Hillside section to the right approaching the entrance, you can find cowboy sidekick **Gabby Hayes** (1885–1969) in Plot 4972. His marker says merely "George F. Hayes."

Finally, down farther to the left, is **Marjorie Main**, born Mary Tomlinson (1890–1975), best known as the hillbilly Ma Kettle in the Ma and Pa Kettle series of movies, which started with *The Egg and I* (1947).

Also In Forest Lawn Hollywood Hills

Truman L. Bradley (1905–1974), described in his epitaph as the "Golden Voice of Radio." **Robert Florey** (1900–1979), who directed the classic *The Beast with Five Fingers* (1946). **Otto Kruger** (1885–1974), reliable supporting actor who played many stage roles as well. **Joe E. Ross** (d. 1979), TV actor on "Car 54, Where Are You?" and "The Phil Silvers Show."

DIRECTIONS TO FOREST LAWN HOLLYWOOD HILLS: Take Route 101 (Hollywood Freeway) to Route 134 (Ventura Freeway) and go east to Forest Lawn Drive. The entrance is on your right at 6300 Forest Lawn Drive.

C H A P T E R   7

Home of Peace
and Calvary

*The reason so many people showed up
at his funeral was because they wanted to make sure that he was dead.*

　　　　— SAMUEL GOLDWYN (about Louis Mayer)

HOME OF PEACE

In Los Angeles there tend to be a lot of mixed marriages — at least among graveyards. Catholic and Jewish
cemeteries are frequently paired side by side or, in the case
of Home of Peace and Calvary, placed just across the road
from each other. Calvary is filled with hundreds of Victorian marble angels; one, who appears to have lost her way,
stands in lonely confusion amid carved menorahs in Home
of Peace.

The most interesting monument in Home of Peace is a
granite fireplace complete with log and two stuffed easy
chairs on either side. You will see it when you first enter
the cemetery. Continue past the fireplace to the mausoleum. It, too, is something of a surprise. It has an eastern
appearance, with windows in the shape of minarets and
arched doorways. Inside the foyer is a massive black iron
chandelier with golden glass. On each of its four sides is a
Star of David. Walk toward the chapel and turn left into the
Corridor of Memory, then go right. In the second hallway,
make a stop at the glassed-in niches. In Compartment
E1109 you will find the ashes of **Fanny Brice** born Fanny
Borach (1891–1951).

Anyone who has seen Barbra Streisand's *Funny Girl*
(1968) is familiar with the life of the plain Jewish girl from
the Lower East Side. At 13 Fanny won an amateur-night
contest by singing, "When You Know You're Not Forgotten

Rubin family memorial

by the Girl You Can't Forget." Elated, she quit school that night and entered vaudeville, winning recognition for her satire of Theda Bara and her role as Camille, with W. C. Fields as her maid. The obnoxious child, Baby Snooks, was Brice's own creation; she played her on the radio show of that name from 1938 until her death.

Brice's first marriage, in 1911 to a barber, only lasted a few days. Her next, to Nicky Arnstein, survived his imprisonment in Leavenworth, where he was placed after the mysterious disappearance of $6 million entrusted to him. Fanny divorced him after his release. Her last marriage, to showman Billy Rose, ended after eight years. Fanny Brice died of a massive cerebral hemorrhage from which she never regained consciousness.

Proceed left and then right into the Corridor of Eternal Life. Halfway back you will find the marble drawer of **Shemp Howard** (1901–1955), brother of Moe and Curly Howard. An original member of the Three Stooges, Shemp left the group only to return in 1946 as Curly's replacement. He remained with the group until his death of a heart attack while returning home from a boxing match.

Retrace your steps to the main hallway and into the other wing. All the way back is the Corridor of Immortality. Here in a large drawer (Number S-405) is producer **Louis B. Mayer** (1885–1957). Mayer, production chief of MGM, fit the usual short, feisty, cigar-in-the-mouth physical description of Hollywood tycoons — "One could have swung a scythe five and a half feet off the ground at a gathering of movie moguls without endangering any lives," as Philip French pointed out. Mayer fit the image in other ways: he was explosive, dictatorial, sentimental. Whether falling heavily to his knees to demonstrate to Andy Hardy how he should pray for his sick mother ("Dear God, please don't let my mom die, because she's the best mom in the world.") or announcing to his wife on their fortieth wedding anniversary, "I'm leaving!" Mayer was emblematic of his profession.

He indulged himself with a totally white office, white grand piano to white andirons. On the white leather walls were photographs of his favorite friends: J. Edgar Hoover, Herbert Hoover, and Cardinal Spellman. Anxious to assimilate, Mayer sponsored elaborate family Christmas parties and Easter Egg hunts. But although the former scrap-metal dealer was said to favor glitz, he produced such movies as *Dinner at Eight* (1933), *The Merry Widow* (1934), *Treasure Island* (1935), *The Barretts of Wimpole Street* (1934), and *The Good Earth* (1937). Between 1937 and 1944 he was the highest paid executive in America.

Mayer died of leukemia in 1957, after telling an associate, "Nothing matters. Nothing matters." On his deathbed he kept asking, "Is she here yet?" Each of his estranged daughters took the question to refer to herself.

Also in the mausoleum, in a room devoted to his family, is early film mogul **Carl Laemmle** (1867–1939). Tinier than his star, Mary Pickford, the German-born producer turned out 250 films in 1915, the first year that his Universal City studio was in operation. He is known for such films as *Hiawatha* (1909) and Erich von Stroheim's *Foolish Wives* (1921) and was immortalized in rhyme by Ogden Nash — "Uncle Carl Laemmle/Has a very large faemmle"—when it was discovered that 70 of his relatives were on the studio payroll. A goodly number of them are also here.

As you leave Home of Peace mausoleum, move onto the grassy area to your right, Section D. Three mausoleums back you will find one with the name **Warner**, decorated by two laurel wreaths tied with bows. Inside rest movie mogul **Harry M. Warner** (1881–1958) and director **Charles Vidor** (1900–1959), who was married to Harry's daughter, **Doris Warner**. Vidor, an Hungarian–American director not to be confused with King Vidor, directed a number of films for Columbia. Some of his best were *Gilda* (1946) with Rita Hayworth and *Love Me or Leave Me* (1955).

Although Harry Warner was president of the company he established with his three brothers, it was Jack who ran the studio. **Jack Warner** (1892–1978) rests by himself in an underground crypt marked by a fountain about fifty yards from the family mausoleums — probably because of his final quarrel with Harry. It occurred in 1957 when both brothers agreed to sell their shares in the studio. Jack held on to his instead and gained control of the company while watching the stock triple in value. Harry did not speak to him again.

But Jack Warner was used to being unpopular. Warner Brothers held their actors to the long-term contracts they signed as unknowns, refusing to re-negotiate salaries. It caused stars such as Jimmy Cagney and Bette Davis to refuse to work at the "Buchenwald of Burbank." After Warner's testimony before the House Un-American Activities Committee, in which he named names of alleged Communist sympathizers — Elia Kazan, Clifford Odets, and Irwin Shaw — he was liked even less. It seems unfair that such a man could have produced the fine films that he did: *Little Caesar* (1930), *The Maltese Falcon* (1941), *Yankee Doodle Dandy* (1942), *Casablanca* (1942), and *A Streetcar Named Desire* (1951).

To end your Home of Peace tour, make your way back to the southwestern corner (behind and to the right of the mausoleum), to the area designated Western Jewish Institute. In Plot 1, five rows of graves back, is another of the Three Stooges. **Jerome Howard** (1903–1952) lies under a monument inscribed "Beloved husband, father, and brother." Jerome was, of course, best known as Curly, the most popular of the Three Stooges. He was the lovable simpleton whose high-pitched voice, comical gestures, and injured expression brought him the laughter and sympathy of the audience. A heavy drinker, his career was cut short by a stroke which forced his retirement at the age of 42.

CALVARY CEMETERY

Calvary, just across the way, is many times larger than Home of Peace. Consecrated in 1896, it encompasses 137 acres. The fourteen Stations of the Cross, glassed-in boxes with painted plaster figures, are placed strategically. Although there are some attractive older monuments scattered along the rolling terrain, almost everyone of importance is tucked away in the main mausoleum. That building, erected in 1929, is set back on the grounds and is landscaped with formal shrubs. The main entrance is topped by three stained-glass windows and the roof bears a cross.

The best way to locate the residents is by ringing the bell inside the elevator. The attendant, Gabriel (yes, Gabriel), is very accommodating and will escort you from site to site. For do-it-yourselfers, we are providing locations as well. Everyone well known is located on the second floor.

Two actresses rest within speaking distance of each other. **Pola Negri**, born Apolonia Chalupec (1899–1987), in Block 56, Crypt E-19, is a new arrival to the mausoleum. Exotic, calculating, temperamental, Pola Negri carried her role as vamp into real life. She pursued Charlie Chaplin and Rudolph Valentino and actually married a Polish count and a Georgian prince. Yet though she could be overbearing, men at a safe distance succumbed to the charms of the green-eyed, porcelain-skinned millionairess; Adolf Hitler ran Negri's German-made movie *Mazurka* once a week for a good cry.

Negri's film career began with *Slaves of Sin* (1916) when she was 17 but ended when talkies became popular. She took a loss in the 1929 stock-market crash and spent her final years living modestly in San Antonio. Two years before she died she was diagnosed as having a brain tumor.

In Block 60, Crypt 3F, is **Ethel Barrymore Colt** (1879–1959). Although of the same generation as Pola Negri, Ethel Barrymore could not have been more different. Born to the theatrical dynasties of the Barrymores and Drews, Ethel had aspirations to be a pianist. It was not to be. When she was 13, her mother, Georgiana Drew, who was dying of tuberculosis, took an unknowing Ethel to California to keep her company. The ordeal of packing up her mother's effects and making arrangements for the coffin to be brought home effectively ended Ethel's childhood. For the next few years she made the theater rounds in New York unsuccessfully looking for work.

Barrymore finally achieved stardom in 1901, playing the lead in *Captain Jinks of the Horse Marines*. Her dark, upswept hair and regal bearing remained her trademark for the rest of her life. Other notable stage roles included *School for Scandal* (1923), *The Corn Is Green* (1940), and *The Shadow* (1915) in which Barrymore moved audiences to copious tears when she discovered after years of being paralyzed that she could walk.

In the 1940s, already a grandmother, Ethel Barrymore retired to Hollywood. She won an Academy Award for *None but the Lonely Heart* (1944), in which she played the elderly owner of a thrift shop in the London slums. She continued to play similar character roles but never kept a scrapbook or a single clipping, asking, "Why clutter up the house with a lot of dead history?" She chose to remember what she wanted to remember. Confined to bed for the last 18 months of her life because of a heart condition and arthritic rheumatism, Ethel remained serene. The evening she died she woke from a nap, asked, "Is everybody happy? I want everybody to be happy. I know I'm happy," then closed her eyes again and did not wake up.

Another group of theatrical folk are several corridors away. **Louis Francis Cristillo** (1906–1959) is in Block 354, Crypt B-1, with his wife **Anne** (1912–1959). He is better known to the world, of course, as Lou Costello who, with his partner Bud Abbott, delighted audiences with their comic routines. Abbott was the sharp; the streetwise wise guy who always had a plan. Costello was his roly-poly foil. Slow-witted, clumsy, and the object of abuse, he drew on childlike facial expressions to evoke pity.

Costello was born and raised in Paterson, New Jersey. While his father saw him moving on to medical school, young Lou's high-school career brought the boy, at least, to his senses. As a young man he made his way to Hollywood by working in a haberdashery, a slaughterhouse, and the prize ring. By the early 1930s he was back east and teamed up with Abbott at a Brooklyn burlesque. They first gained attention with an appearance on Kate Smith's radio show in 1938. Moving on to Hollywood, they had a huge hit with their second movie, *Buck Privates*. Many other well-attended movies followed, but the pair are best remembered for their skit, "Who's on First?" That hilarious routine, now enshrined at the Baseball Hall of Fame in

Cooperstown, is a classic example of clever repartee and perfect comic delivery.

At one time the plan was for both Barrymore brothers to rest at Calvary. But although John Barrymore's crypt is still there in Block 352, F-3, with the Shakespearean epitaph, "Good night, Sweet Prince," he is actually buried in the family plot in Philadelphia. **Lionel Barrymore** (1878–1954), however, is still in the drawer above.

Like the son who tries in vain to get out of the family grocery business, Barrymore attempted to escape from the theater. When he was six and pressed into service by his famous parents, Maurice and Georgie Drew Barrymore, he burst into tears instead of reciting his lines. He did little better as a teenager, appearing in *The Rivals* with his grandmother, Louisa Drew. After his wooden delivery the first night, his part was written out and Lionel was dismissed from the theater to become a painter. He broke away several more times but always returned to acting, pressured by what he called "the need to eat."

By 1904, when he had appeared in *Sag Harbor* and *Second in Command* and was already considered a star, Barrymore left again for the art ateliers of Paris. On his return to New York he signed with D. W. Griffith's Biograph Studio, acting in one-reelers with Mary Pickford, Mack Sennett, and Mabel Normand, and writing dozens himself. He stayed on in the East to distinguish himself on stage in *Peter Ibbetson* (1917), *The Copperhead* (1918), and *Macbeth* (1921).

Embarking for Hollywood in 1925 with his second wife, Irene Fenwick, Barrymore made "quickies" until 1931, when he won an Oscar for *Free Soul*. He went on to appear in *Grand Hotel* (1932), *Dinner at Eight* (1933), and *David Copperfield* (1934). In 1937, still limping from a hip injury, Lionel tripped over a cable while making *Saratoga* and snapped his hip again. This time he was left in a wheelchair. MGM, unwilling to lose him, adapted parts to his condition, starting with that of Dr. Gillespie in a series of 15 Dr. Kildare films.

Lionel Barrymore was very different from his younger brother John, who inspired wild stories with every breath he took. In later life round-faced Lionel, who did the yearly radio version of Scrooge in *The Christmas Carol*, played himself as a kind and sentimental old gent. He was extremely attached to his wife, **Irene**, constantly sending her flowers. When she died on Christmas Eve 1936 of complications from anorexia and bulimia, he had to be hospitalized himself. Barrymore never married again. He did, however, return to painting and, surprisingly, to composing music. His symphony and a tone poem in memory of his brother John were performed by the Philadelphia Orchestra under Eugene Ormandy and in Lewisohn Stadium in New York and the Hollywood Bowl. Barrymore also composed a musical setting for *Ali Baba and the Forty Thieves* (1952) and narrated it on record.

Knowing Lionel's strong family feeling — his autobiography was entitled *We Barrymores* — one can suspect he would have been happier to have John and Ethel close by. But at least Irene is here.

Taking a step into a main hallway and back into time, you can visit the very large marble drawer of **Mabel Normand** (1895–1930). The inscription reads, "Rest in Peace," a fitting hope after a turbulent life.

Mabel Normand, a petite dark-haired beauty, first modeled for illustrators Charles Dana Gibson and James Montgomery Flagg. She was brought to Hollywood from New York by Mack Sennett while she was still a teenager. After inventing the custard-pie-in-the-face action out of boredom one day, she went on to roles in *Mickey* (1917) and *Suzanna* (1922). Just before her wedding to Mack Sennett in 1915, she discovered him in a compromising position with actress Mae Busch. Busch covered her embarrassment by braining Normand with a vase.

The blow may have caused physical as well as emotional damage. Mabel became undependable and distracted and began stuffing her uncashed salary checks into a shoebox. By the time William Desmond Taylor was shot and Normand was briefly a suspect, she already had a firm cocaine habit. An incident the following year, in which her chauffeur shot a man and then was revealed to be an escaped convict, ended Normand's career. She died of tuberculosis in a sanitarium in Monrovia.

Right next to Normand is actor **John Hodiak** (1914–1955), who collapsed and died at 41 while shaving. Recently divorced from actress Anne Baxter, Hodiak was building a reputation as a gifted actor before he died. He had won critical acclaim in 1954 on Broadway for his role in *The Caine Mutiny* and was finishing a film, *On the Threshold of Space*.

Also in this building, at the other end, is California's twentieth governor, **Henry T. Gage** (1852–1924). Gage, elected in 1898, was a company man — one of many tools of the Southern Pacific Railroad. Placed in power by the wealthy Republican machine, he forced a settlement in a San Francisco labor dispute favoring management. After

"Come Follow Me"

the Hearst papers printed a cartoon showing Gage being led on a leash by Southern Pacific magnate Collis Huntington, the governor passed legislation restricting journalistic license with respect to himself.

Actor **Ramon Novarro** (1899–1968) is buried out under the grass near the front of the cemetery in a grave almost impossible to find (Section C, Plot 584). The marker gives only his name and his dates. Dark and pensively beautiful, the young Mexican hit stardom in *The Prisoner of Zenda* in 1922, following up his success quickly with *Scaramouche* (1923) and *Ben Hur* (1925). He was often compared to Rudolph Valentino, a close friend who gave Ramon a black Art Deco phallus with his name inscribed in silver to celebrate the success of *Scaramouche*.

Novarro's popularity, briefly revived by his role opposite Greta Garbo in *Mati Hari* (1931), waned after that. He maintained his spiritual quality in private life, toying with the idea of becoming a Jesuit or a Trappist monk. But a weakness for gin and for young men undermined his ambitions and eventually caused his death. On the night of October 30, 1968, Paul Ferguson, a male prostitute who had served jail time for theft, and his brother Tom paid a visit to Novarro—a visit that ended with the brutal beating death of the actor and an unsuccessful search for the $5,000 he was rumored to have kept in the house.

DIRECTIONS TO HOME OF PEACE AND CALVARY: Take Route 10 (Santa Monica Freeway) going east into Route 60 (Pomona Freeway). Exit on Downey Road going south and turn right onto Whittier Boulevard. Entrance for Home of Peace is at 4334 Whittier Boulevard. Calvary is opposite.

Rosedale and Chapel of the Pines

A cynic is a man who, when he smells the flowers, looks around for a coffin.

—H. L. MENCKEN

ROSEDALE CEMETERY

It would be easy for visitors to overlook Rosedale Cemetery, because of its lack of major personalities and its location in one of the less fashionable areas in the city. But to do so would be to miss one of the most charming spots in Los Angeles. Its monuments, interesting in themselves, stand out prominently against the palms.

After you drive in the main entrance, park catty-corner to the cemetery office. Five rows of markers in from the curb, in the first row behind a cluster of palm trees, is **Hattie McDaniel** (1895–1952), the first black woman to sing on the radio and also the first to win an Academy Award. The Oscar, for her portrayal of Scarlett O'Hara's mammy in *Gone with the Wind* (1939), was for Best Supporting Actress. In later years she played Beulah on the radio show of the same name, prompting her comment, "The only choice permitted us is either to be servants for $7 a week or to portray them for $700 per week."

When she died of cancer at 57, Hattie McDaniel had appeared in more than three hundred movies. Nearly three thousand people crowded into her funeral service at the People's Independent Church of Christ, and 125 limousines accompanied her body to Rosedale.

Continue to bear left around to the chapel. On the right side facing it, in the second row of markers from the ivy-covered wall, is **Andy Razaf**, *née* Andreamenentania Razafkeriefo (1895–1973), "Composer and Lyricist." In his role as lyricist, Razaf collaborated with Eubie Blake and Fats Waller and gave the world such classics as "Ain't Misbehaving," "Stomping at the Savoy," "That's What I Like 'Bout the South," "The Joint Is Jumpin'," and "Honeysuckle Rose." He first won notice with bawdy blues songs such as "If I Can't Sell It, I'll Keep Sittin' on It."

The grandson of a freed slave who was made United States consul to Madagascar, Razaf came to Washington from the island just in time to be born. He worked as an elevator operator in Tin Pan Alley, wrote militant poetry, and played semi-pro baseball before teaming up with Fats Waller in Harlem. Married four times, Razaf spent the last twenty years of his life in a wheelchair after a stroke.

Behind Andy Razaf under a larger stone is his mother, **Jenny Razaf Coles** (1879–1959), with one of his lyrics on her marker:

> An angel came and took her by the hand,
> And gently led her to a better land.

Across from the mausoleum, in the **Gottschalk** plot, is a tiny statue of a sleeping child. Farther down is the intriguing black slate pyramid of **Emma** and **Lewis Grigsby**. The entrance has the traditional Egyptian motifs. On the lintel are spread wings.

Around the corner is a brown stone placed on a rough-hewn gray granite block, the memorial of **Francis Murphy** (1836–1907). The stone reads: "Gospel Temperance. 'With malice toward none and charity for all, I, the undersigned, do pledge on my honor, God helping me, to abstain from all intoxicating liquors as a beverage, and I will by all honorable means encourage others to abstain.' " It is signed "Francis Murphy, Worldwide Apostle."

Francis Murphy, an Irish bon vivant who emigrated to America, fought in the Civil War before becoming an alcoholic. After his reform, he began a career as a temperance advocate. Murphy traveled through the United States, Europe, Hawaii, and Australia lecturing on abstinence and encouraging people to sign the pledge reproduced on his tombstone. In all he persuaded 16 million to become liquor-free.

Rosedale has a second pyramid nearby, this one of brown block stone. Counting five water spigots after it, in Plot N-109 is buried baseball player **Frank Chance** (1877–1924). His grave, unfortunately, is unmarked. When double plays turned by the Chicago Cubs helped to defeat the New York Giants, Franklin P. Adams of the *New York Evening Mail* lamented it in a famous rhyme which started, "These

Gottschalk memorial   *Emma and Lewis Grigsby*

are the saddest of possible words, Tinker to Evers to Chance." Frank Chance was the first baseman of this now-immortalized double-play combination. Indeed so popular did the rhyme become that it helped all three players get elected to the Hall of Fame in 1946, although based on their statistics none of the three deserved to be so honored.

If Chance's numbers do not justify his honored place at Cooperstown, he was nevertheless a respectable player and a good manager. He did double duty from 1905 to 1914 when he served as player-manager. Under his direction the Cubs won four pennants and two World Series.

Continue along the back road of the cemetery to Section 5, 28 spaces in on Row 178. There you will find the marker of **Art Tatum** (1909–1956), who died of uremia at the age of 46. Made of black marble, it shows a piano etched in the clouds. Beside it is written, "Though the strings are broken, the melody lingers on." In the upper left-hand corner is inscribed, "Someone to watch over me," with the musical notes.

Art Tatum. "No one can imitatum! No one can overratum!" That's how it was when Tatum played. Other pianists were in awe, and it is rumored that more than a few switched to other instruments after hearing the master play. Even Fats Waller announced to his audience one night after seeing Tatum walk in, "I play piano, but God is in the house tonight." Tatum's mastery of the keyboard seemed complete. His virtuosity attracted the attention and admiration even of Horowitz, Toscanini, and Godowsky.

Born with cataracts on both eyes, Tatum was permanently blind in one eye and had only limited sight in the other. Raised in Toledo, Ohio, he originally took up the violin but switched to piano in his early teens. By 17 he was wowing local audiences on his 15-minute radio show and soon garnered national syndication. In 1933 he cut his first record, "Sophisticated Lady" and "Tiger Rag." Within two years he was known internationally, and his living legend was in full gear. Oscar Peterson, the pianist now playing whose virtuosity most closely resembles Tatum's, said that he had to force himself to admit that it was only one pianist playing "Tiger Rag." Peterson developed a phobia against playing in Tatum's presence which took him years to overcome.

Tatum was, of course, in demand all over. In addition to his solo playing, he formed his own band, featuring himself and the famous blues shouter Joe Turner. Feeling hampered by a large group, however, he soon formed a trio with Tiny Grimes on guitar and Slam Stewart on bass. But it was as a soloist that he shone. Tatum's influences stemmed from players such as Waller and Earl Hines and the music of Debussy. Clearly, however, he was an original who made a deep impression on jazz artists, including nonpianists like Coleman Hawkins and Charlie Parker, for years to come.

Relatively unrecorded for years, Tatum made up for the lag when he recorded over one hundred songs for Norman Granz and Verve from late 1953 to 1955. These sessions show him in great virtuosic form; his left hand striding up and down the bass, his right filling in the melody and ornamentations of incredible intricacy. His harmonic progressions were startling in their compexity, rapidity, and originality. Yet there are those who state that no matter how impressive his records are, they are just pale intimations of the extended impromptu performances he gave in the after-hours clubs when he was most relaxed and inventive. For that's when God spoke, his disciples listened, and woe betide him who played next.

Near Art Tatum is a popular actress from the 1930s, **Anna May Wong**. The star of such pictures as *Daughter of the Dragon* and *Java Head*, she rests under a pink marble monument with an inscription in Chinese.

Return to the curb. Five rows farther along is an ornate monument to a victim of a storm at sea. One side reads, "Honor, Fidelity, Death," with an anchor entwined by a ribbon. It was "Erected by the Wireless Operators of the Pacific Coast in memory of **Lawrence A. Prudhont** (1884– Jan. 7, 1913) who died at his post." Lower down it states, "God calls away when He thinks best." On the third side is a

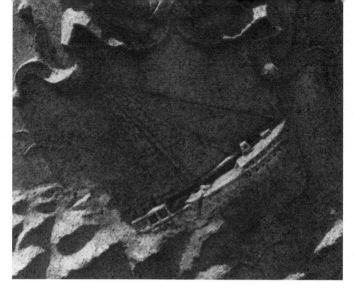

Lawrence A. Prudhont

wreath which may have contained Prudhont's image but is now empty. Below it is a bas relief of a ship sinking into the waves.

Prudhont died aboard the oil tanker USS *Rosecrans* during a storm at the mouth of the Columbia River in Oregon. The ship ran aground on Peacock Spit during a 50-mph gale; of the 37 crew members, 33 perished. Three survivors clung to the rigging until rescued, and one man swam to safety.

Slightly farther up on the opposite side of the road is a statue of a sweet child sitting on a stack of stones, engraving the name of **William F. Roller** (1890–1909). It reads, "Sleep well, my child." On the side is a poem in German.

William F. Roller (also bears the name Meyerhofer)

Chapel of the Pines

CHAPEL OF THE PINES

Around the corner from Rosedale is Chapel of the Pines, an attractive, domed building that looks more like an observatory than a mausoleum. Here is Los Angeles' oldest crematory, established in 1903. To gain admittance you must ring the bell. Once inside you will find there is very little to see. You can ask a staff member to show you any markers you would most like to visit. One popular choice, **Nigel Bruce** (1885–1958), is in a compartment the size of a mailbox. Bruce, the Englishman known to Americans as the bumbling Dr. Watson to Basil Rathbone's Sherlock Holmes, appeared in 14 Holmsian epics between 1939 and 1946.

Another well-known resident, **Ann Sheridan** (1915–1967), is down in the basement, however, still in a holding vault and not available for viewing. Known during her career as "the Oomph Girl," Sheridan was talented but short-fused. During the times she was not on strike or suspended by the studios, she filmed *The Man Who Came to Dinner* (1941) and *I Was a Male War Bride* (1949). Sheridan's three marriages only lasted a year or less — although her final union, to actor Scott McKay, was terminated by her death from cancer at age 51.

Edmund Gwenn (1875–1959), the actor who won an Oscar for his portrayal of Santa Claus in *Miracle on 34th Street* (1947), and **Harry Ruby** (1895–1974), the songwriter who gave the world "Who's Sorry Now?" and "Three Little Words," are also in vaultage and not able to be visited.

A number of other personalities passed through the Chapel of the Pines crematorium on their way to other resting places. **Jay Silverheels** (1922–1980), an actor born on the Six Nations Indian Reservation in Ontario who played Tonto in the "Lone Ranger" series between 1949 and 1957, was returned to Canada. **David Seville**, born Ross Bagdasarian (1919–1972), the creator of that lovable trio, The Chipmunks — Alvin, Simon, and Theodore — as well as the best-selling song "The Witchdoctor," was buried in Ararat Cemetery in Fresno.

Two actresses were also cremated here, but did not stay. **Marilyn Maxwell** (1921–1972) was undergoing treatment for high blood pressure and a pulmonary condition when she died at 50. Maxwell, a durable blonde who played sensual roles in forgettable films, was scattered at sea. **Rachel Roberts** (1927–1980), by contrast, was a serious actress who won three British Academy Awards, for her roles in *Saturday Night and Sunday Morning* (1960), *This Sporting Life* (1963), and *Yanks* (1980). Married to Rex Harrison for nine years, Roberts was found dead in her back yard. Her ashes were returned to Wales.

The other actors cremated at Chapel of the Pines include **Raymond Massey** (1896–1953) and **Walter Huston** (1884–1950).

Veteran actor Raymond Massey, a Canadian, played a diversity of roles but was best known for his characterizations of Abraham Lincoln. He was seen in both the stage and film versions of Robert Sherwood's *Abe Lincoln in Illinois*. In a career that spanned 50 years, Massey also played the original Henry Higgins in *Pygmalion* (1945) on stage, and the beloved Dr. Gillespie in TV's "Dr. Kildare" (1961–1966). He died after being hospitalized for three and a half weeks with pneumonia; his ashes were buried in Beaverdale Memorial Cemetery in New Canaan, Connecticut.

Although his film career lasted only 22 years, Walter Huston seems a legend in American acting. Whether playing Wyatt Earp in *Law and Order* (1932) or the Devil in *All That Money Can Buy* (1941), Huston brought a sense of integrity to each role. In 1948 he was rewarded with an Oscar for Best Supporting Actor for his performance in *The Treasure of the Sierra Madre*, which was written and directed by his son, John. Huston became ill during a luncheon celebrating his 66th birthday and succumbed to a heart attack the next morning. His ashes were given to the family.

DIRECTIONS TO ROSEDALE CEMETERY AND CHAPEL OF THE PINES: Take Route 10 (Santa Monica Freeway) and exit at Normandie Avenue. Go right on Washington Boulevard. Rosedale Cemetery entrance is at 1831 West Washington. Chapel of the Pines is located around the corner at 1605 South Catalina Street.

C H A P T E R   9

Holy Cross

and to all you others, the great,
the near-great
the featured, the extras
who pass quickly and return in
dreams saying
your one or two lines,
my love!

— FRANK O'HARA

HOLY CROSS APPEARS, at first glance, to be a cemetery filled with religious people with nothing to hide. Yet a look at some of the names on markers here — Bing Crosby, Rita Hayworth, Bela Lugosi, Sharon Tate, Mario Lanza, Gloria M. Vanderbilt, and Evelyn Nesbit — shows that although the inhabitants died as Catholics in good standing, they did not escape the vicissitudes and tragedies of American life.

The most logical place to begin a tour of Holy Cross is in the Grotto, up the hill from the main office and on your left. Grottoes, or religious caves, are the most popular setting for miracles in Europe. American cemeteries are fond of recreating them. Fronted by pools and sculpted, tufted shrubs, the Grotto at Holy Cross is made of rough-hewn rock. To one side is a cavelike opening whose roof opens to the sky. The focal point is the niche which contains an altar and, raised above ground level, the Virgin Mary, who stands with lowered eyes and hands pressed together in prayer. Facing towards her, as if in humble echo, kneels a shawled woman with clasped hands

The most prominent spot in the Grotto belongs to **Rita Hayworth**, born Margarita Carmen Cansino (1918–1987). She rests beneath a kneeling angel and under a bonsai-like tree, with a marker that reads, "To yesterday's companionship and tomorrow's reunion."

Rita Hayworth began her career as a black-haired Spanish dancer named Rita Cansino and made her first 10 movies in that persona. At 19, however, she married businessman Edward Judson, who realized her potential. He altered her hairline and her eyebrows, changed her last name to a variation of her mother's, and made her a beautiful redhead. By 1941 Hayworth had been dubbed The Great American Love Goddess by *Life* magazine, a label with which several million servicemen agreed. In what seemed the ultimate compliment, a photograph of Rita in black lace was fastened to an atomic test bomb, dropped by the B29 *Dave's Dreams* on Bikini Atoll in 1946.

Few of Rita Hayworth's movies were classics, but many of her dancing roles, including *You Were Never Lovelier* (1942) with Fred Astaire and *Cover Girl* (1944) with Gene Kelly, were great fun. Other films, such as *Gilda* (1946) and *The Lady from Shanghai* (1949) allowed her more dramatic scope.

Rita Hayworth collected interesting husbands. In 1943, after shedding Edward Judson, she married one-man production company Orson Welles but was lured away five years later by Prince Aly Khan, playboy of the Moslem world. Although their travels through Europe and her illicit pregnancy scandalized thousands, when they finally married it lasted only two years. Her next husbands included singer Dick Haymes and British director James Hill, who favored animal stories such as *Born Free* (1966) and *Black Beauty* (1971).

A	Rita Hayworth	M	Gene Lockhart
B	Sharon Tate	N	Rosalind Russell
C	Charles Boyer	O	Evelyn Nesbit
D	Bing Crosby, Bela Lugosi	P	Gene Fowler
E	Jack Haley	Q	Frank Lovejoy
F	Edward "Kid" Ory	R	Walter O'Malley
G	Jimmy Durante	S	Jose Iturbi, Ray Bolger
H	Pat O'Brien	T	Spike Jones
J	Jackie Coogan	U	Mario Lanza, Joan Davis
K	Barney Oldfield, Louella Parsons	V	Mack Sennett
L	Gloria Morgan Vanderbilt	W	Richard Arlen

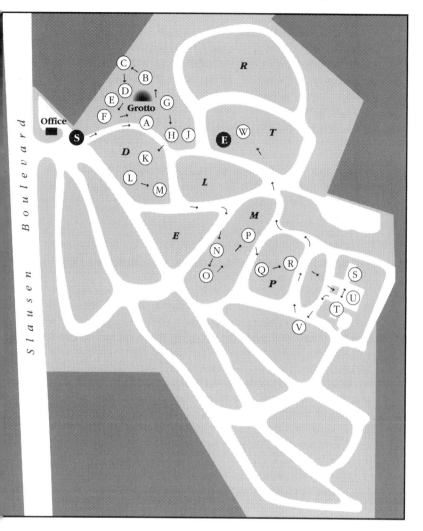

Rita Hayworth's life ended too soon, under the black cloud of Alzheimer's disease. At 53 when she attempted a stage career, she was unable to remember her lines. Her decline had been initially blamed on alcoholism. She died at 68, under the care of her daughter, Princess Yasmin Aga Kahn.

Close to where Rita Hayworth is buried is the marker of child actress **Bonita Granville** (1923–1988). At 15 she starred in the *Nancy Drew, Detective* series of movies and had ingénue roles in such confections as *Youth Runs Wild* (1944) and *Love Laughs at Andy Hardy* (1946). In later years she produced the TV series "Lassie." Granville's funeral was said to be an exact copy of her friend, Rita Hayworth's.

Walking through the Grotto area into the level garden behind, you will find a white marble marker which reads, "Beloved wife of Roman, **Sharon Tate Polanski** (1943–1969), **Paul Richard Polanski**, their baby."

Nearly 20 years have passed since the slaughter on Cielo Drive, an attack as incomprehensible now as on the sweltering night it took place. It was 12:50 A.M. when four of Charles Manson's disciples crept up the road to the estate and started their massacre. They killed Steve Parent, who had been visiting at the groundskeeper's cottage, then continued into the house and in less than an hour brutally murdered Wojtek Frykowski, Roman Polanski's countryman and friend; Frykowski's girlfriend, coffee heiress Abigail Folger; Hollywood hairdresser Jay Sebring; and the actress Sharon Tate, who was eight and a half months pregnant.

Tate was the epitome of the middle-class American girl. The daughter of a career Army officer, she was prettier than most — at six months she was Miss Tiny Tot of Dallas — but less interested in a serious acting career than in married life. Her pictures had been of the genre of *The Fearless Vampire Killers* (1967) and *Wrecking Crew* (1969). At the time of her death she was anxious simply for her husband to return home from London and for her baby to be born.

With Hollywood terrified after the murders, the police thrashed around for a logical motive. Frykowski, along with Gibby Folger, had used drugs; perhaps he was also a dealer, and the murder was drug-related. Another theory held Roman Polanski responsible, speculating that he had hired a killer because Sharon and Jay Sebring were having an affair. It was through other killings that occurred in the area that suspicion focused on the Manson "family."

Charles Manson had harbored a hatred for the Polanski–Tate house ever since he had gone there to unsuccessfully beg record producer Terry Melcher, the owner, for a second audition. He had returned to the house looking for Melcher — after the Polanskis had rented it — and had been turned away, this time by Sharon Tate and Jay Sebring. To a sick mind, that was enough cause for revenge.

Directly to the right is **Marian I. Jordan** (1898–1961), the radio actress who portrayed Mollie in "Fibber McGee and Mollie" between 1935 and 1957, and her husband, **Jim Jordan** (1896–1988), who was Fibber.

Also in this section is **Charles Boyer** (1899–1978), his actress wife **Patricia** (1910–1978), and "Our Beloved Son, **Michael Charles Boyer**" (1943–1965). Although he first went to Hollywood in 1929, Charles Boyer remained the quintessential Frenchman, retaining his accent and charm to the end of his life. He enchanted American audiences in more than 65 films, including *The Garden of Allah* (1936), *All This and Heaven Too* (1940), and *Gaslight* (1944), although the line attributed to him from *Algiers* (1938), "Come vith me to zee Casbah," was never spoken by anyone.

Charles Boyer had to painfully endure the deaths of those closest to him; his son's at 21 from a self-inflicted gunshot wound, his wife's from cancer after 44 years of marriage. Enough was enough. Two days after Patricia died, Boyer took an overdose of Seconal tablets and joined her.

The next group of markers are on the sloping lawn in front of the Grotto. In the fourth row down, slightly to the left facing the Grotto, is Harry Lillis Crosby. His marker is black, inset with white letters and an IHS cross. Next to Bing is wife **Wilma "Dixie Lee" Crosby** (1911–1952), with his parents on the other side. Bing had himself buried nine feet down so that if his second wife Kathryn wishes, she can join him here.

HARRY LILLIS "BING" CROSBY b. *May 2, 1903, Tacoma, WA; d. October 14, 1977, Madrid, Spain*. Bing Crosby liked to picture himself to the world as lazy and good-natured. He wore a battered golf hat and was seldom without a generous wad of gum. The movies he chose showed him as happy-go-lucky, entertained by his own wit. In later years he added a philosophic Catholic twinkle. The world took Bing's public image at face value, though it knew that few people reach the top without ambition.

In the beginning it was Bing's mother, Kate, who did the pushing — to go to school, to attend Mass regularly, and to stay out of mischief. (When he stole pastries from a bakery wagon and got caught, she advised juvenile authorities to keep him locked up for the night.) Kate managed to get him through Gonzaga University in Spokane with training in law before Bing detoured into a musical career. It was during his college days that he met up with a high-school student, Al Rinker, who was organizing a band.

The band eventually was reduced to a singing duo, Two Boys and a Piano. They toured the West Coast, and in 1927 they were joined by singer/songwriter Harry ("Mississippi Mud," "Wrap Your Troubles in Dreams") Barris. The three became Paul Whiteman's Rhythm Boys. Being part of Whiteman's band was prestigious, but the band also introduced Crosby to the movies when the troupe was featured in *King of Jazz* (1930). For the young singer, it was love at first frame. Though he didn't leave the Rhythm Boys immediately, Bing next made a short comedy for Mack Sennett called *I Surrender, Dear* (1931), which was based on a Barris song. Following this success, Bing, in a less-than-good-natured gesture, dropped Rinker, Barris, and his agent, Roger Marchetti, and then walked out on his contract at the Coconut Grove.

He was blacklisted by the union, but CBS was glad to pick him up for their radio network. And the movies continued. The musical shorts Bing played in grew longer as he was found to have box-office appeal along with his magnificent singing voice. A photograph from that time shows him, eyes to the right, grinning like a kid who knows he's said something cute. He went from hits such as *Pennies from Heaven* (1936) and *Sing, You Sinners* (1938) to the *Road* pictures, beginning in 1940. The first, with Bob Hope and Dorothy Lamour, was *The Road to Singapore*. Six more followed.

During this time Crosby married actress Dixie Lee (Wilma Winifred Wyatt) and fathered four sons in short order. They were his greatest contribution to the marriage. Busy with his radio and movie commitments, golf, horse racing, and financial interests (an employment agency, a music-publishing company, and a racetrack), Bing made only infrequent guest appearances at home. Only his staunch Catholicism and his mother's watchful eye on him into his sixties kept him married. When Dixie was dying of ovarian cancer in 1952, Bing sailed to Europe to make *Little Boy Lost*, arriving home only a week before she died at 40.

His second wife, Kathryn Grant, had a better understanding of life with a man's man. When he presented her with a saddle instead of an engagement ring, she guessed, as she put it, that he "only wanted a 'buddy,' not a sweet-

BELOVED BY ALL
HARRY LILLIS
BING
CROSBY
1904 ——— 1977

heart." Perhaps because of the failure of his first marriage, Bing postponed his second wedding four times. He and Kathryn were finally joined on October 24, 1957. Unlike Dixie Lee, however, Kathryn did not stay meekly at home and wait for him to join her.

Bing never outlived his popularity. *White Christmas* (1954), *Say One for Me* (1959), and *Road to Hong Kong* (1962) were his final hits, but he continued to do his annual Christmas TV show and make records to the end of his life. After a two-week engagement at London's Palladium, Bing left for Spain for a golfing vacation. On the La Moralejo course, he collapsed at the eighteenth hole. He died of a massive heart attack en route to the Red Cross Hospital in Madrid.

In the very center of the same row of markers is **Bela Lugosi** (1882–1956). His monument reads, "Beloved father," and as his will stipulated, he was buried in his Dracula cape and tuxedo. Born in Transylvania like the character he made famous, Lugosi had as many personal quirks as the Count. In real life he too exuded sex appeal and drew women helplessly into his dressing room. Five times, however, he married them, transforming himself into an American chauvinist werewolf. A wife had to be on call 24 hours a day, waiting to squeeze Lugosi's orange juice and having no interests of her own. His third marriage lasted four days. His fourth wife complained that she could not even go to the dentist without his calling to make sure that was where she had really gone.

Paradoxically his extraordinary success as Count Dracula, on stage and in films, limited Lugosi's development as a serious actor. (Walt Disney used his face as the prototype for the Devil in *Fantasia*.) He retained a heavy accent which further limited the roles he might have been offered. The frustration of unemployment and pain from a World War I injury led him to morphine, Demerol, methadone, and barbiturates. In 1955 — on the birthday of his fourth wife, Lillian, who had left him, he turned himself in to Los Angeles County authorities and began a drug-rehabilitation program. Lillian did not return to the marriage, but Lugosi remained drug-free, acting in two more films (though he played a deaf mute since he could no longer remember lines). Lugosi died in 1956 of a heart attack, clutching the movie script to *The Final Curtain*.

Three rows down is **Jack Haley** (1898–1979), who attracted notice as the Tin Man in *The Wizard of Oz*. Initially the part went to Buddy Ebsen, but he suffered a bad reaction to the aluminum dust in the make-up and had to be hospitalized. Ebsen's was not the only bad reaction to the Tin Man make-up: Jack Haley, Bert Lahr, and Ray Bolger were banned from the MGM commissary at lunchtime because it was felt their furry, rubbery, and aluminum-pasted faces were too disgusting for their fellow diners to endure.

Edward "Kid" Ory (1886–1973) rests halfway down the hill. His marker calls him the "Father of Dixieland Jazz." Born to a French-speaking Creole family in La Place, Louisiana, Ory was a young entrepreneur if there ever was one. By the time he was 13, he had formed his own band and even organized the concerts by supplying food, beer, and music, all for 15 cents. By 1910 he was in New Orleans, where his band starred for the next nine years. Among its members were future greats such as King Oliver, Sidney Bichet, and Johnny Dodds. Ory didn't do badly getting replacements. When King Oliver left, he found a 17-year-old trumpeter named Louis Armstrong to fill in. From 1925 to 1929 the roles were reversed, and Ory played in Chicago for Oliver and Armstrong. Ory's most famous composition, "Muskrat Ramble," was written during this time and recorded by Armstrong's Hot Five.

Ory retired to California but was urged out of retirement by two fans of traditional jazz. Playing with Barney Bigard and several others, the group received air time on Orson Welles' radio show, and their popularity soared. The traditional-jazz revival was on its way. Ory starred in two movies and continued to play regularly until he was 78. John S. Wilson described Ory as a " 'tailgate' trombonist, a huff-and-puff style that primarily supported the other instrumentalists." Ory was not only the most famous of the Dixieland trombonists but, according to fellow trombonist

Trummy Young, he was perhaps the only one who truly knew how to supply the proper timing and punch.

Return to the Grotto and walk behind it. In the center of the grass is **James F. "Jimmy" Durante** (1893–1980), "Beloved husband and father." The marker shows a standing cross and rosary.

Durante was unique. Seated at the piano, his felt hat pushed high on his forehead, he would play in honky-tonk style and sing in his raucous, gravelly voice one of his standards like "Inka Dinka Doo." His speech was delivered with a Brooklyn accent ("Everyone's gettin' into de act.") and emphasized mispronounced words. Most prominent of all was his nose — a large proboscis by any standard — his trademark and the butt of his humor, which he would proudly and humorously display in profile. Durante was an old-style comedian who played his persona for laughs. Even when comics gained popularity by abusing audiences, Durante maintained his gentler approach.

Starting out as a honky-tonk pianist at Coney Island, Durante gained fame in 1919 when he teamed with Lou Clayton and Eddie Jackson in vaudeville. Refining his comedy, he became a Broadway star in the 1930s and then moved on to Hollywood. For some reason none of his 29 movies captured the comic spirit of his live acts. When he turned to radio, however, he was a hit all the way, and he made the successful transition to television for seven seasons before retiring in 1956. Jimmy's famous sign-off, "Good night, Mrs. Calabash, wherever you are!" was for a grammar-school sweetheart or his first wife, Jean Olson. Take your pick. Calabash referred to a Chicago suburb they both liked.

Known to everyone as Jimmy, Durante cringed at formality. He always traveled with old friends and refused to attend any affair, no matter how prestigious, unless his friends were welcome also. He was noted for both his generosity and his optimism. "I know there are more good people than bad ones in the world. I don't mind if a gentleman scratches a match on the furniture so long as he is careful to go with the grain."

When he was 67 Durante married for a second time. A year later he and wife Marge adopted their infant daughter, Cecelia Alicia. Believing that "If y'retire, y'decay," Durante continued to perform at clubs until his health began to fail him in 1972. Honored at a show two years later, Durante, now enfeebled and wheelchair-bound, whispered his thanks and then roused himself to belt out one last rendition of "Inka Dinka Doo."

The tour continues next in the larger section, T. Use the tree by the edge of the road as a landmark. Walking back from it, you will come to a marker that commemorates the "Queen Mother of Egypt" **Nazli Fouad** (1894–1978). Next to her is her daughter **Fathaya Fouadthali** (1930–1976) with "God bless you, Mama. We love you, your family."

About nine markers down the row from the tree is Spencer Tracy's childhood pal, **Pat O'Brien** (1899–1963), who as Knute Rockne – All American won one for gipper Ronald Reagan.

For an entertaining interlude, detour four rows down and four rows to your left to the marker of **James J. Conti**. His stone, complete with a pair of dice, protests, "I'd rather be in Las Vegas." Allegedly other California gravestones have equally candid sentiments, from "I'd rather be skiing" to "I'd rather be on my boat." Although the Bumpersticker School of epitaphs may seem irreverent to some, at least markers inscribed "Foxy Grandpa" and "I Love My Poodle" tell more about the person buried beneath them than do his name and dates alone.

Farther along the treeline is **John Leslie Coogan** (1914–1984), who as Jackie Coogan achieved childhood fame in *The Kid* (1920) and *Oliver Twist* (1921). He is probably best known to contemporary audiences as Uncle Fester on "The Addams Family."

Section L contains a handful of offbeat personalities, familiar names with less-familiar lives. Right in the center under the largest tree is **Barney Oldfield** (1878–1946). "Slow down! Who do you think you are? Barney Oldfield?" Those famous words, issued to many a young driver by a concerned and perhaps frightened parent, were heard long after Oldfield had retired from auto racing. His heroic image was such that he obscured his successors for many years. There was Barney, emerging from a cloud of dust on the dirt track, cigar clenched firmly in his teeth, once again leading the pack across the finish line. His achievements may sound tame by today's standards – in 1903 he was the first man to drive a mile per minute – but given the poor condition of the tracks in Barney's day, the frequency of accidents and deaths, the crudity of the cars, their heavy weight, poor suspension, and arm-breaking steering, his success was worthy of the awe it still inspires.

Speeds increased rapidly and by 1910 Oldfield was driving his Blitzen Benz 133 mph. He was a hero not just to fans but to many children whose scooters bore the names of his cars: 999, Big Ben, Green Dragon, and Golden Submarine. After retiring in 1918, Oldfield stayed connected with the auto industry, often speaking to the public about safe driving. Entranced by the idea of driving 300 mph and breaking the world record of 253 mph, he considered a comeback in 1932 but never was able to achieve it. Having survived his races, crashes, and injuries, Oldfield died in bed of an apparent heart attack at the age of 68.

Two rows below him, and about ten markers to the left, is **Louella O. Parsons Martin** (1881–1972), "Beloved wife and mother." Whether she was beloved to the rest of Hollywood is questionable. Certainly the items she carried in her gossip columns could make or break all but the biggest stars. Even the Bard was not exempt. Commenting on the movie version of *A Midsummer Night's Dream*, Louella declared, "Shakespeare or no Shakespeare, there should be some kind of entertainment in films of this kind!" Her factual slips could also be amusing. She announced that Sigmund Freud was going to be brought to Los Angeles to advise on the film *Dark Victory*. No airplane ticket was necessary; Freud had already been dead several months.

Louella, whose third husband, Dr. Harry Martin, was head of the Twentieth Century–Fox medical department, lived in a Beverly Hills mansion herself and treated the stars as equals. (At a party where "Docky" had over-imbibed yet another time and passed out, when someone went to move him, Louella said calmly, "Oh, let him rest. He has to operate in the morning.") Knowing her power, movie-colony members would often phone her first with their news, hoping to avoid either a string of nasty innuendos or, worse, a vengeful blanketing silence. Yet Louella Parsons saw herself as no more than a kindly fan. Though her catty, garrulous style won her no Pulitzers, her column was carried in 70 newspapers, with a readership of 20 million.

On the opposite side below the big tree is composer **James Monaco** (1885–1945) with the notes to "You Made Me Love You" on his monument. He also wrote "Pocketful of Dreams" and "Row, Row, Row."

In this area are twins **Gloria Morgan Vanderbilt** (1904–1965) and **Thelma Viscontess Furness** (1904–1970). The twins, who were born in Switzerland and educated in French convents, were the toast of Manhattan as The Magical Morgans. Dominated by an ambitious mother, Gloria consented in 1922 to marry Reginald Vanderbilt, who was 48 to her 18 and who died 18 months later. Thelma wed John Converse and then English shipping executive Viscount Furness.

Both twins were in the papers again 10 years later. Gloria

was involved in the custody battle that her daughter, Gloria Vanderbilt, describes in *Little Gloria, Happy at Last*, a battle that Gertrude Whitney, young Gloria's paternal aunt, won in court. Thelma was in the public eye because of her relationship with the Prince of Wales until she left him in the safekeeping of her friend, Wallis Warfield Simpson, with the remark, "Well, Dear, look after him for me while I'm away and see that he doesn't get into any mischief." As the world later found out, Wallis kept him out of trouble by marrying him herself.

In the end, the twins were left with each other. They operated several businesses, including cosmetics and perfume lines and a dress shop. They lived together in California from 1955 to 1965 when Gloria died of cancer.

Under the largest tree to your right near the road is "Beloved husband and father" **Edgar Kennedy** (1890–1948). His bronze marker has a three-cross crucifixion scene. Kennedy's face is more familiar to many people than his name. An original Keystone Kop, he perfected the slow burn and exasperated gesture, used with good effect in Laurel and Hardy comedies.

Finally, up from the tree and left about six rows of markers, rests **Gene Lockhart** (1891–1957). Most people are familiar with the pouty, double-chinned actor as he appeared in such films as *Miracle on 34th Street* (1947) and *The Man in the Gray Flannel Suit* (1956), but fewer know that he wrote the song, "The World Is Waiting for the Sunrise." His daughter, June Lockhart, had recently started her 10-year stint on "Lassie," when he died of coronary thrombosis.

In Section M, orient yourself by the large crucifix and plantings. Right beneath them is **Rosalind Russell Brisson** (1908–1976). It is said that a Monsignor gave her his own prime spot. She actively supported many Catholic charities, though she sometimes referred to her own parish in Beverly Hills as Our Lady of the Cadillacs. In later years, battling rheumatoid arthritis, her face puffy from cortisone, Miss Russell cut back on acting. But by then she had left her mark on American entertainment.

Rosalind (named after the ferry to Nova Scotia on which her parents celebrated a wedding anniversary) initially played career women but broadened her scope as the scrappy, hair-pulling gossip in *The Women* (1939). She gave memorable performances in *His Girl Friday* (1940) and *My Sister Eileen* (1942) but created her own legend first on stage and then on screen as *Auntie Mame* (1958). The play, adapted from the book to fit her exuberant personality, might well have been titled *Auntie Roz*. At the same time she was learning to play other character roles, such as the hysterical spinster in *Picnic* (1956) and the stage mother in *Gypsy* (1962).

Russell was married to the same man, agent Frederick Brisson, for 35 years. Because of his help in her career decisions, some people called him The Wizard of Roz. Others, including Ethel Merman, who had expected to recreate her *Gypsy* stage role in the movie, referred to him as The Lizard of Roz. But Russell, whether stuffing restaurant silverware in her purse or pushing her daughter, Gypsy Rose Lee, into a stage career, did the role to perfection.

Facing the cross, move down a row and walk right three markers to **Gia Scala**, born Giovanna Scoglio (1935–1972). Although Gia Scala was a tall and beautiful green-eyed brunette, her career came to a quick end. She had appeared in *Don't Go Near the Water* (1956) and *The Guns of Navarone* (1961) and received recognition for her role as a union organizer's wife in *The Garment Jungle* (1957), but when she died at 38 of an overdose of alcohol and the medication she had been taking to control a drinking problem, she had not been offered a part for several years.

Five rows farther down and about five markers in from the right curb is **Evelyn Florence Nesbit** (1884–1967). She has a plain granite marker with a cross in the center and the simple inscription "Mother." Evelyn was a famous beauty who by 16 was one of the most sought-after models in the country. Dancing as one of the Floradora girls, sitting for drawings by Charles Dana Gibson, and posing for photographs, she gained national attention for her pose as "Innocence."

More important she caught the eye of Stanford White, the country's most famous architect and the leading light in New York's glittering turn-of-the-century social scene. While not the first, Evelyn became the best-known Girl in the Red Velvet Swing, the swing that hung from the ceiling in White's studio. There she would swing up to the ceiling and kick out the paper panels of rotating Japanese parasols. In the studio, lined with red velvet and mirrors, was a four-poster bed encircled with tiny lights of changing hue. There Evelyn was relieved of her innocence.

Eventually she swung out of White's life and into that of Harry Thaw—a wealthy, deranged idler from Pittsburgh. Thaw was given to unexplained fits of rage, insane jealousy, paranoia, sadism, and self-abasement. He would beat Evelyn with a dog whip or a cane and later, kissing her feet, beg forgiveness from "his angels, her tumtums, her tweetums, her boofuls." Thaw knew of White's previous involvement with Evelyn and, after they were married, harbored an undying hatred for the architect. He took his revenge in 1906 by shooting New York's leading citizen to death as White watched Mamzelle Champagne at Madison Square Garden. Thaw was tried twice, being acquitted the second time by reason of insanity—although he did serve time in Matteawan State Hospital for the Criminally Insane.

Evelyn did not fare well, either. Despite some support from Thaw, she suffered a drastic drop in her standard of living, moving from the plush of society and ballrooms to an apartment over a grocery store on Amsterdam Avenue. She attempted stage comebacks but was unsuccessful. Selling her story over and over, she finally confessed to being sick of the rehashings, although even as late as 1955 she was in Hollywood as a technical consultant for *The Girl in the Red Velvet Swing*. Overall she was despondent and afraid and twice attempted suicide. Of her life she stated, "Stanny White was killed, but my fate was worse. I lived." Of what she perhaps saw as an ever-hopeful return to her fabled adolescence she wrote:

> And down the long and silent street
> The dawn with silver-sandaled feet,
> Crept like a frightened girl.

To the left of the crucifix, about four rows down and 25 markers over, is Admiral **John Ford**, born Sean O'Feeney (1895–1973). His stone is inscribed, "Portland, Maine to Hollywood." When he made *Mary of Scotland* (1936), he wore the same shirt every day—the shirt he had worn while making *The Informer* (1935), which won four Academy Awards. The spell didn't work, but Ford went on to gather up Oscars for *The Grapes of Wrath* (1940) and *How Green Was My Valley* (1941). Also here is **Mary Ford** (1896–1979), "His beloved wife for 59 years."

In the upper left of the same section is newspaperman **Gene Fowler** (1890–1960), whose epitaph calls him "That young man from Denver." Although he was a prolific writer, Fowler was equally well known for such exploits as stealing a streetcar full of passengers when he was in college and living under the name, "Horace Witherspoon, Jr., Famous Polish Impersonator," when he was tired of being interrupted by calls from his studio. His books included *Father Goose*, *Mighty Barnum*, and *Good Night, Sweet Prince*, a biography of his friend, John Barrymore. Fowler died of a heart attack at 70.

If you cross the road into Section P, you will find **Frank Lovejoy** (1912–1962) 12 rows up and directly in front of the mausoleum. His epitaph reads, "Now cracks a noble heart," yet another quotation from *Hamlet*. The actor, who specialized in tough roles and co-starred in *The Best Man* (1960), died in bed of a heart attack after watching a Dodgers–Giants baseball game.

At the top of the section, in the second row of markers down from the curb, near a tree trunk spigot, is **Walter F. O'Malley** (1903–1979) and his wife, **Katherine H.** (1907–1979). Probably the most influential baseball executive of his era, O'Malley gained his greatest fame (or notoriety, depending on your geography) by moving the Brooklyn Dodgers to Los Angeles after the 1957 season. The move proved to be so lucrative that O'Malley was considered to be a visionary by his fellow owners. California was once again the site of new gold. Averaging well over two million customers a year since their move, the Dodgers have been one of the most successful franchises in baseball and perhaps the most visible.

Not that the Dodgers had been poor in Brooklyn. And there lies the rub. Was O'Malley just greedy, or was he forced to move by politicians who had stymied his efforts to build a new stadium in Brooklyn for ten years? The truth seems to lie in between. Known as a pinchpenny but offered only a site in Queens, O'Malley decided that if the team had to leave Brooklyn, California made more sense as a home than Queens, and he said goodbye. Interestingly, O'Malley was generous in personal affairs, paying all of Roy Campanella's medical bills after he had been paralyzed in a car accident, and lending words of comfort to Ralph Branca after Bobby Thomson's home run.

Starting as an engineer and later practicing as a lawyer, O'Malley became a director of the Dodgers when he was 29. With Branch Rickey he bought the team in the 1940s and became sole owner and president in 1950. Under his ownership the Dodgers won eleven pennants and four World Series.

Buried with O'Malley is Kay, his wife and childhood sweetheart. At the time of their engagement Kay was operated on for cancer of the larynx. Though cured, she was unable to speak for the remainder of her life. Walter, given the chance to back out of the wedding, refused saying, "No. She's still the same girl I fell in love with."

Continue on into the mausoleum, a long, white, modern building whose raised entrance is dominated by a large sculpted depiction of the crucifixion. The figures, Jesus and two mourners standing below, are done in an Art Deco style. The whole is backed by a glittering gold background into which is inscribed the words "We adore Thee, O

Holy Cross Mausoleum

Christ, and we bless Thee because by Thy holy cross Thou hast redeemed the world." Under them are two slender columns topped by eternal stone flames. These flank a chalice which cups a wafer that resembles the sun. On either side of the chalice are the Greek letters alpha and omega. The inscription over the door reads, "Behold the tabernacle of God with men and He will dwell with them. And they shall be His people and God Himself shall be their God. And God shall wipe away all tears from their eyes. And death shall be no more. Nor mourning. Nor crying. Nor sorrow shall be anymore. . . . Behold I make all things new."

Everything in the mausoleum is done in a light marble, giving it a bright effect. The stained-glass windows are modern but done beautifully. The faces on the figures are simplified but not inane. They include such subjects as Lazarus being raised from the dead and Christ comforting those who mourn.

Jose Iturbi (1895–1980) is in the mausoleum in a marble crypt with a cross. He is to your left in Section 16. A child prodigy in Valencia, Spain, Iturbi did not disappoint as an adult, garnering rave reviews in Europe and in the United States where he made his debut in 1929 with Stokowski and the Philadelphia Orchestra. Not content with being a pianist, Iturbi studied conducting and led the Rochester Philharmonic for eight years in the 1930s. By the 1940s he had branched out even further by pursuing a Hollywood career, appearing in many movies, usually playing himself. His popularity and record sales soared.

Iturbi fared less well with his peers and critics. Not only was he looked down upon for commercialism, his brazen attitude did little to gain him sympathy. Typically outspoken, he publicly derided women for what he considered to be their limited temperament. This did not stop him from performing duo-piano recitals with his sister, however. Undaunted by criticism and health concerns, Iturbi followed a busy concert schedule until shortly before his death.

In Section 69, two markers in and two up on your right, is **Jack La Rue**, born Gaspare Biondolillo (1902–1984). His epitaph reads, "Forever in our hearts." For over 40 years Jack La Rue was typecast as a gangster, beginning in 1934 with *Lady Killer*.

In Section 70, all the way to the top and two markers from the blue-toned stained-glass window, is **Spike Jones** (1911–1965), "Beloved husband and father." Eulogized at his funeral as a "madcap musician . . . a genius in the clothes of a musical satirist . . . [who made] people forget for a moment the nervous tension of our era," Spike Jones was surely one of a kind. Accompanied by The City Slickers, his supporting musical cast, Jones satirized just about anything musical. Supplementing more traditional instruments, Jones developed a whole range of new and, fortunately, never-to-be-replicated instruments. These included "a Smith and Wesson .22 pistol, an octave of Flit guns tuned to E flat, two octaves of tuned doorbells, an anvilphone, a crashophone [for breaking glass], a latrinophone (a toilet seat strung with catgut), and a goat trained to go *N-n-n-a-a-a* in the key of C." Add to this assorted whistles and automobile horns, and one can see that satire was never far away.

Gaining popularity in the 1930s, the group reached its peak in 1942 by mocking Adolph Hitler in the song "Der Fuehrer's Face." The record sold over one and a half million copies to an enthusiastic wartime audience. Song lyrics were not above readjustment for comic effect, as in the Slickers' versions of "You Always Hurt the One You Love" and "Chloe." The band continued their brand of comedy through the 1950s but turned to straightforward Dixieland recordings in the 1960s.

In a prime spot to the right of the altar and facing it is **Joan Davis** (1912–1961), an actress best remembered for her television stint in "I Married Joan" (1952–1955).

Right next to Joan Davis is Mario Lanza and his wife, **Betty Lanza** (1922–1960).

MARIO LANZA (ALFREDO ARNOLD COCOZZA) *b. January 31, 1921, Philadelphia; d. October 7, 1959, Rome.* Mario Lanza had a large voice, housed in an even larger body. From childhood, Alfredo Arnold Cocozza was a warm-hearted boy, but also a boy who was used to having his own way. When his mother bought him a violin to further his musical education, he tossed it out the window. (Undaunted and wiser, she next bought a piano.) Among his friends it was the rule that Freddy had first crack at any willing girls. It was a privilege he insisted on throughout his life.

After high school Freddy, who loved opera, told his mother he wanted to sing professionally. She brought him to a voice teacher, who agreed that he had talent and suggested he begin learning foreign languages and taking voice lessons. Then in a coup that was retold in his first movie, Freddy was moving a piano when he was offered a chance to be "overheard" by conductor Serge Koussevitzky. Freddy sang for him and was given a scholarship to the Berkshire Music Festival at Tanglewood. Around that time he adapted a variant of his mother's maiden name, Maria Lanza, as his own.

Recognition was not immediate. During World War II Lanza sang in the military chorus Winged Victory and was selected for the film of the same name in 1944. Over the next few years he tried to promote himself by giving concerts. After a successful appearance at the Hollywood Bowl, Lanza attracted the attention of Louis B. Mayer. MGM offered him a seven-year contract but could not find a suitable vehicle for their wide-shouldered classical singer. They finally devised *That Midnight Kiss* (1949), about a truck driver who moves a piano and is discovered for the opera. It was followed by *The Toast of New Orleans* (1950), about a fisherman who is discovered by the opera.

By then a strange pattern was developing. Mario would be encouraged to fatten up so as to be in full voice when the music for the film was prerecorded, then was expected to deflate like a balloon for the filming itself several weeks later. A diet of grapefruit and little else melted away the pounds, but also left the singer nervous and paranoid. It may have been the start of his drinking problem. Ironically the public cared far less than his movie bosses how much Mario weighed. They mobbed him wherever he went, breaking into his hotel rooms to plunder souvenirs and attempting to literally tear off his flesh. Though the press excoriated him for his temperamental behavior, his weight fluctuations, and his habit of urinating without benefit of bathroom, it had little impact on his popularity. *The Great Caruso* (1951) grossed $19 million for MGM in less than a year

In 1953 Lanza prerecorded the music to *The Student Prince* but was in no shape to make the movie, and MGM was not in the mood to coddle their star. After several bitter battles, the studio shot the film with another actor, Edmund Purdom, lip-synching Lanza's songs. Lanza next turned to concert appearances. But instead of opening at The Sands, Las Vegas, as scheduled, Mario, inebriated, stayed in bed. When Jimmy Durante announced to the audience, "Mario Lanza will be unable to sing for you tonight. He is a very sick boy and under an oxygen tent," he was laughed off the stage.

Mario, Betty, and their entourage of four small children and nurses picked up and moved to Rome. There he successfully filmed *The Seven Hills of Rome* (1958) and gave tours in London and Germany. The only cloud in Roman skies was Lanza's association with gangster Lucky Luciano. Luciano, exiled by the American government, convinced the tenor to sing at a charity benefit in Naples. When Mario skipped rehearsals, he was visited by two men who informed him that if he did not do the benefit he would never appear in public again. Mario, opting for less radical treatment but still refusing to sing, checked into the hospital for a new weight-reduction program.

There he was told by doctors that his heart was bad. Betty was told that he had pneumonia. Later, when his chauffeur entered Lanza's hospital room, he found an empty IV jar attached to a tube, pumping air into the patient's body. By then the singer was comatose. No one could say whether he had died of an embolism, a heart attack, the reduction therapy, or an "accidental" injection. But the Student Prince was dead at 38. Betty, her own system ravaged by alcohol and amphetamines, followed him the next year. They were laid to rest together at Holy Cross, after Mario was brought here from a gravesite at Calvary.

Like Rudolph Valentino, Jean Harlow, and Marilyn Monroe, who also died under a cloud of mystery, Mario Lanza has remained in the American imagination. His fan clubs, from California to England, are still going strong.

On the opposite side of the chapel and toward the back in Section 35 is **Ray Bolger** (1904–1987). Forever typecast as a scarecrow, Bolger had the distinction of outliving everyone else in *The Wizard of Oz* cast, including the Wizard, Frank Morgan, and the Wicked Witch of the West, Margaret Hamilton. So thin and flexible-jointed was he that his legs truly appeared to be made of straw.

Bolger preferred the designation "comedian" rather than "dancer," but it was for his dancing that he initially won acclaim, first in the number "Slaughter on Tenth Avenue" choreographed by George Balanchine and performed in *On Your Toes* (1936), and then for his soft-shoe routine in "Once in Love with Amy" from *Where's Charley?* (1948). It was that song he was called on to perform in practically every TV appearance. After *The Wizard of Oz*, Bolger appeared in several other films including *April in Paris*

(1952) and *Babes in Toyland* (1960). He died of cancer in a nursing home.

To the right of the mausoleum when facing it, in Section N, and down 10 rows is **Mack Sennett** (1890–1960), designated "Beloved King of Comedy."

Sennett's epitaph is no exaggeration, although it might be more accurate to call him the Father of Slapstick. More than any other director in the new industry he had an instinct for sight gags — a trail of bumbling Keystone Kops, a face with a custard pie just thrown in it, the look of a couple when the lake they're rowing on starts to drain. In his first year in Hollywood, he cranked out 140 films, a pace that quickly turned his hair white.

But those were the best years for the Old Man, as he was nicknamed. Silent movies were his medium; once talkies took control, Sennett's grip on the industry loosened. By then his star, Mabel Normand, was in the throes of scandal and drugs. His comedian, Fatty Arbuckle, had lost his career in disgrace. The 20-room mansion in which he had given such outrageous parties — at 11:00 P.M. a gong would sound warning the straitlaced to leave — was only a memory. In his last decade Sennett lived modestly at the Garden Court apartments in Los Angeles, sometimes giving advice to another resident, young Marilyn Monroe. Before dying after kidney surgery, he mused, "I thought the audience stayed forever and kept on laughing."

In Section T, right in the shadow of the Madonna with child, is **Conrad N. Hilton, Jr.** (1926–1969). His marker reads, "In memory of our loving father." Nicky Hilton, the son of the chairman of the Hilton Hotels Corporation, died at 42 of cardiac arrest. He stepped into the spotlight briefly in 1950 when he married 18-year-old Elizabeth Taylor. The marriage ended a year later.

Facing the Madonna, walk right to Tier 56, Grave 130. Right under it is **Richard Arlen**, born Cornelius van Mattimore (1900–1976). Richard Arlen's career crested at the start with his roles in the Oscar-winning *Wings* (1928) and in *The Virginian* (1929). The quality of his pictures declined, but he took some revenge when he appeared before the House Un-American Activities Committee in 1947 and told them, "There are certain groups of parlor pinks or influences that we would be better off without in Hollywood," then went on to identify the evildoers as "mainly screenwriters."

DIRECTIONS TO HOLY CROSS CEMETERY: Take Route 405 (San Diego Freeway) to the Slauson Avenue exit going east. The entrance to Holy Cross is on the left at 5835 West Slauson Avenue.

C H A P T E R   10

Mt. Sinai and Hillside

Here in nature's arms I nestle,
Free at last from Georgie Jessel.
—EDDIE CANTOR (composing his own epitaph)

MT. SINAI MEMORIAL–PARK

Visiting Mt. Sinai Memorial–Park is an interesting way to learn Jewish history. The cemetery gives guided tours on request, but it is compact enough to walk around on your own and not miss anything. Of particular interest is the Memorial Monument, a stark, frightening sculpture done by Bernard Zakheim to commemorate Holocaust victims. It can be reached by taking the third left after coming into the park. The Heritage, a mosaic 145 feet long based on a painting by Neil Boyle, details Jewish participation in American history—the Revolutionary War, the Gold Rush, and Immigration—as well as scenes from Hester Street and the Lower East Side.

Mt. Sinai, whose Hebrew name, *Bet Ha Hayim*, means "House of the Living," was dedicated in 1953. It is at 5950 Forest Lawn Drive and is adjacent to Forest Lawn Holly-wood Hills, on the outskirts of Burbank. Like everything else in Burbank, home of movie studios and false facades, Mt. Sinai has felt the influence to a degree. Some time ago visitors watched, fascinated, as plaster-and-chickenwire boulders were set in place here.

To begin your tour, keep to your right until you come to the Heritage mosaic. In the Heritage Gardens, on your right as you face the mural, is comedian **Phil Silvers** (1911–1985). He is in Vault 1004, which has a leaf-and-acorn design. Although he played in film comedies before and after the TV series which made him a household name, Phil

Silvers will forever remain Sergeant Ernie Bilko. "The Phil Silvers Show," originally titled "You'll Never Get Rich," centered around Bilko's shady money-making schemes. Silvers met death easily. According to a daughter, he answered some fan mail, lay down to take an afternoon nap, and never woke up.

In the Garden of Shemot, in the center of the cemetery, opposite a Zodiac mosaic recreated from the floor of a sixth-century synagogue in the Jezreal Valley in Israel, is **Zev Lahav**, a.k.a. Laurence Merrick (1926–1977). His epitaph reads, "Always in our hearts." Merrick was best known for his documentary film, *Manson*, which was filmed during the celebrated murder trial of Charles Manson and his confederates. It was nominated for an Academy Award. Merrick did not escape violent death himself. He was shot in the back at his film school by a disgruntled actor to whom he would not give a part. His assailant escaped initially but was captured later.

Continuing to your left you will find **Lee J. Cobb**, born Leo Jacoby (1911–1976). His inscription, "Ay, every inch a king," is from Shakespeare's *King Lear*, a part Cobb played to perfection at Lincoln Center in 1969. Earlier in his career he had immortalized another role on stage, that of Willy Loman in *Death of a Salesman* (1949). In between these two roles, Cobb made movies and played Judge Garth in the TV series "The Virginian" from 1962 to 1966. Legend has it that Frank Sinatra paid for Cobb's final hospitalization and burial here.

Further left, in an individual garden across from the second small wall mural, is **Bruce Geller** (1930–1978) with the inscriptions, "A man greatly loved" and "His words were music." Bruce Geller was the creator, writer, and producer of the original TV series "Mission Impossible." The show's method of giving its agents taped assignments which would self-destruct immediately ("Your mission, if you decide to accept it, is to blow up the Kremlin.") has passed into American folklore. Geller died at 47 when the twin-engine plane he was riding in, piloted by ABC vice-president Stephen Gentry, crashed near Santa Barbara.

Finally, along the wall in Crypt 6418, is **Billy Halop** (1920–1976), "Beloved son and brother." Halop's greatest achievement came as a teenager when he played the Dead End Kid Billy, in first the play and then the movie *Dead End* (1937). (The title came from the sign at the end of the slum street on which Billy and the others grew up.) The phenomenally successful Dead End Kids were then placed in several other films, such as *Little Tough Guy* (1938) and *Angels with Dirty Faces* (1938). Halop stayed in Hollywood, accepting bit parts. His last appearance was in "All in the Family."

Move next to the Courts of Tanach, just across the road. As you come in, on your left is **Herschel Bernardi** (1923–1986) in Crypt 52250. His crypt has the masks of Comedy and Tragedy and a menorah on each side, as well as the message, "Heshy, you were the greatest moment in my life," from his wife, Teri. Bald and beaming, Bernardi was a standard character actor in B movies. His films often had names like *Crime, Inc.* (1945) and *Stakeout on Dope Street* (1958), but he was familiar to early TV audiences for his role in "Peter Gunn" (1958–1961).

Moving onto the grass, in Plot 1856 rests **Barry J. Crane** (1927–1985), a famous contract bridge player who was murdered. Crane, who had won more titles than anyone else in the history of the game, was found beaten to death in the garage of his luxurious townhouse. When he died at 57 his career total of master points was 35,000.

Finally, also in the grassy area, is a longtime observer of the Hollywood scene, **Sidney Skolsky** (1905–1983). His pounded-brass marker bears the title of his book, *Don't Get Me Wrong, I Loved Hollywood*. Skolsky started as a gossip columnist for several New York papers, including the *Daily News* and the *New York Post*. In later years he wrote a column, "Tintypes," working out of an office above Schwab's drugstore in Hollywood—the drugstore where Lana Turner was *not* discovered in 1936, but where Harold Arlen wrote "Over the Rainbow" in 1939. Skolsky, who loved being involved, freely gave out advice to stars such as Al Jolson.

HILLSIDE MEMORIAL PARK

Al Jolson, of course, was what made Hillside Memorial Park. According to legend, the Mammy Singer had plunked down his money to be buried in a more status-laden cemetery when Hillside approached him with an offer he didn't refuse. Jolie's widow paid $9,000 for the plot and another $75,000 for the monument itself. However it came about that Al wound up here, it was a wise decision. His monument, seen from the freeway, has become one of LA's landmarks.

Designed by architect Paul Williams, the six-columned marble structure is topped by a dome. The ceiling of the dome bears a mosaic depicting Moses amidst clouds holding the Ten Commandments. Jolson's tomb stands underneath. To one side of this structure is a dark, three-quarter-sized statue showing Jolson in his classic pose: on one knee and singing with outstretched arms.

Al Jolson memorial

Allegedly Jolson told his last wife, Erle Galbraith Jolson, that he wanted to be buried near a waterfall. If so, his wish was granted in grandeur, for from in front of the tomb water cascades 120 feet down the hillside. The falls are stepped and give a uniform blue color to the water.

AL JOLSON (ASA JOELSON) *b. May 26, 1886, Seredzius, Lithuania; d. October 23, 1950, San Francisco.* "When Jolson enters, it is as if an electric current had been run along the wires under the seats. . . . He speaks, rolls his eyes, compresses his lips, and it is all over. You are a life member of the Al Jolson Association. He trembles his under lip and your heart breaks with a loud snap. He sings and you totter out to send a night letter to your mother." So wrote Robert Benchley in 1925 in *Life* magazine.

In person, Al Jolson was magic, though before a movie camera his acting was on a par with a high-school student attempting mime, and placed in front of a radio microphone, he stiffened up like a corpse. Al needed his audience with nothing in between. Even then, his nervousness was legendary. When he appeared before a packed house, buckets were stashed in the wings so he could throw up on his way on or off. But Jolson was playing for high, primal stakes: the attention of a mother who had deserted him by dying when he was a child and the adulation of a rabbinical father—which was never forthcoming. Nevertheless each performance gave the boy, Asa Joelson, a deceptive second chance.

During the early years of his life, Al's father was a stranger. Moshe Reuben Joelson left his family in 1890 and came to America to try to establish himself. When he was appointed to a large temple in Washington, DC, in 1894, he sent for them. It was less than a year later that Asa came home from Hebrew school and heard piercing screams from his mother's bedroom. Naomi Cantor Joelson had been an unusually accomplished young woman, the daughter of a wealthy Lithuanian family. But that afternoon she looked through Asa, her favorite child, as if she didn't know who he was. The terrified boy watched the doctor pull the sheet over his mother's face.

Asa, who Americanized his name to Al the way his brother Hirsch had changed his to Harry, began to run the streets. At one point he ended up at St. Mary's in Baltimore — the reformatory Babe Ruth made famous — after he refused to give his correct name and address. By the time he was 12, his only goal was to appear in vaudeville. He did so without much success for the next eight years.

Jolson's break came when he began applying burnt cork to his face and chalking his lips to match the whites of his eyes. Thus disguised, he could relax, crack jokes, and belt out a song. Although he didn't always perform in blackface — a device considered exotic and inhibition-releasing rather than racist — he employed the same full-voiced, dramatic delivery whatever his make-up. The number of songs popularized by and identified with Jolson is awe-inspiring: "Swanee," "My Mammy," "Rock-a-Bye Your Baby with a Dixie Melody," "Sonny Boy," "California, Here I Come," "You Ain't Heard Nothing Yet," "April Showers," "The One I Love Belongs to Somebody Else," "Keep Smiling at Trouble," "There's a Rainbow 'Round My Shoulder," and "Avalon," to name only some.

In 1909 Jolson, who had been doing vaudeville spots with increasing success, joined Lew Dockstader's Minstrels for eight months. In retrospect it seems strange, a successful tree retreating to the forest, but the move brought Jolson to the attention of Lee and Jake Shubert. The Shuberts bought his contract and began featuring him in their New York extravaganzas: *La Belle Paree*, *Vera Violetta*, *The Whirl of Society*, and *Bombo*. From 1911 to 1937 Jolson wowed them on the New York stage and in related tours. But by 1931, with *The Wonder Bar*, Jolie's star was shining less brightly.

By then he was involved in the infant sound-movie industry. *The Jazz Singer* (1927), the first talkie, was by virtue of its sheer existence an immediate hit. *The Singing Fool* (1928) was even more successful. He followed it with others, *Big Boy* (1930) and *Hallelujah, I'm a Bum* (1933). But the Jolson magic did not project well through celluloid.

Al Jolson

Only on stage could he make each enraptured viewer feel he was talking and singing to him alone. Jolie projected the vulnerability and appeal of the motherless boy; men as well as women found him irresistible.

Off stage Jolson was considered less lovable. His first three wives suffered greatly from his neglect. He preferred to park them at home while he golfed, played poker, went to the races, and toured in his shows. Sometimes remorseful, he would send for a wife and, after several days of husbandly attention, dispatch her home with a snarl. His marriage to Ruby Keeler lasted from 1928 to 1939 before she sued him for divorce. There was also the ongoing question of Jolson's bisexuality—he brought his close friends along even on his honeymoons—but he was basically a man's man, interested in aggressive pursuits rather than domestication.

Rabbi Moshe Joelson never responded to his son's success in the way Asa hoped. Early on he pretended to be naively disappointed that his son was not the show's manager but "only a star." Years later he cut off Al's description of his new show because it was time for some *real* entertainment—"Amos 'n' Andy."

Jolson, home from entertaining the troops in Korea, seemed happier in his fourth marriage. But, typically, he was with his cronies playing gin rummy when he suffered his fatal heart attack. Feeling for his pulse, the 64-year-old singer murmured sadly, "Oh, I'm going," and died.

Hillside Mausoleum rises just behind Jolson. On a sunny afternoon—and they all seem to be here—it has an oddly joyous feeling. The simply styled windows allow the rooms to be washed in light. And with a center atrium, part of the mausoleum is outdoors. Go first through the main door and left into the garden. Halfway down on your left you will see the crypt of **David Janssen**, born David Harold Meyer (1931–1980), which bears the declaration, "My love is with you always." Between 1963 and 1967 Janssen *was* "The Fugitive," Dr. Richard Kimble, hotly pursued by the detective who believed he had murdered his wife. In each episode Janssen almost caught the true killer and was almost caught by the law himself. Janssen, who made his movie debut at 15 in a Sonja Henie film, died unexpectedly of a heart attack at 49.

Three drawers up from Janssen is **George A. Jessel** (1898–1981), designated here as "Toastmaster General." Married four times, one of them to Norma Talmadge, Jessel began singing at 9 in a nickelodeon. He achieved stardom in the stage version of *The Jazz Singer* (1925) and, had he not been on the outs with the Warner brothers, might have taken the film role away from Jolson as well. Jessel, who went on to produce musicals for Twentieth Century–Fox, was a man of outspoken views. Dressed in a military uniform, he once appeared on the "Today" show to designate the *New York Times* and *Washington Post* as "Pravda."

Although he received his Toastmaster nickname from the many bond dinners, inaugurations, and USO tours in which he was involved, Jessel's real specialty was funerals. Beginning with Al Jolson and Fanny Brice, anybody who was anybody was eulogized by Jessel. The comedian threatened to write and tape his own tribute, saying that he wanted his inscription to read, "I tell you here from the shade it is all worthwhile." The inscription is still to come.

On the same wall is comedian **Dick Shawn** (1929–1988), born Richard Schulefand. The most popular films he made included *It's a Mad, Mad, Mad, Mad World* (1963) and *What Did You Do in the War, Daddy?* (1966).

Return to the front door where you began and take the hall to the right. Make your first left down the Corridor of Contentment and go straight through the Hall of Graciousness. At the end, in a huge black sarcophagus, are **Mary Livingstone Benny** (1906–1983) and Jack Benny. He is described as "Beloved Husband, Father, And Grandfather, A Gentle Man."

JACK BENNY (BENJAMIN KUBELSKY) *b. February 14, 1894, Chicago; d. December 26, 1974, Holmby Hills, CA.*

Holdup Man
Your money or your life.

Jack
(Long pause . . . one of his longest.)

Holdup Man
Quit stalling! I said your money or your life.

Jack
I'M THINKING IT OVER!

Benny Kubelsky, the son of an immigrant Russian Jew and his brokered American wife, grew up in Waukegan, Illinois, where he was renowned for his talent on the violin. In fact he outgrew the town's best teacher and by the age of 8 was taking lessons from a high-priced professor of music in Chicago. At great sacrifice his parents paid $15 per lesson for their budding prodigy. Unfortunately young Benny's practice habits did not justify the expense. His work in school was similarly poor, and by 13 he had quit school and ended his formal lessons.

The violin continued to play an important role in his life, however. He was first a violinist in a vaudeville theater, then played on stage in tandem with a pianist, and finally in the early 1920s opened as a solo act with comedy bits thrown in between musical selections. As his career gradually narrowed and defined itself, the violin became a prop and then a crutch. He no longer played, but he couldn't perform without it. In placing his first name last he went from Ben Bennie to Ben K. Benny, and by 1919 to Jack Benny.

In Jack's vaudeville career he made lifelong friends of such fellow performers as George Burns and Bob Hope, and shorter-lived acquaintances with others like Violet and Daisy Hilton, a talented Siamese-twin act. By 1926 Jack was making over $1,000 per week and was courting Sadye Marks, a young salesgirl for the May Company in Los Angeles. In order to make time, he visited her counter almost daily, buying pair upon pair of stockings while she led him on and teased, "How sheer? What size? With or without garters?" On January 14, 1927, they were married.

As Sadye joined Jack on stage, her persona also changed: her hair was dyed blond, her nose was bobbed, and her name was changed to Mary. Soon Jack was doing movies, but without great success. His real break came with an appearance on Ed Sullivan's radio show in 1932. Upon hearing him, an advertising executive was amused enough to refer Canada Dry as a sponsor, and in 1933, his first year on radio, Jack was voted Most Popular Comedian on the

Air. By the early 1940s the legendary cast, including Mary (now Mary Livingstone), Don Wilson, Rochester, Phil Harris, and Dennis Day, was in place, and the show was a Sunday-night staple for millions of Americans.

Besides the stars, the "Jack Benny Show" offered a cast of memorable characters such as Gertrude Gearshift (Sara Berner) and Mable Flapsaddle (Bea Benaderet); the railroad PA announcer; Professor LeBlanc, Jack's violin teacher (Mel Blanc); Mr. Kitzle (Artie Auerbach); the racetrack tout (Sheldon Leonard); and the obnoxious character who always answered "Uhyesssssss" and then proceeded to annoy Jack in every way possible (Frank Nelson). Along with these dubious lights were standard gags such as Jack's stinginess, the opening of Jack's subterranean money vault, and his old Maxwell automobile.

Jack inspired universal loyalty and admiration. He was generous with his money and paid his staff well. Having an unusual sympathy for the feelings of others, he did not indulge in cruel humor. Jack doted on Mary and their adopted daughter, Joan, and let Mary have her way, sometimes extravagantly, with the house and decorating. Unassuming and unpretentious, he stayed off stage when he wasn't working. But he loved being entertained and was famous for literally falling on the ground in hysterics, anyplace, anytime, when someone tickled his funnybone.

In time the show's characters and gags became hilariously predictable. Listeners knew what was coming next and laughed all the harder when it came. The same was true of Jack's mannerisms. He is still a standard imitation for many mimics; his hand resting lightly on his cheek, "Well, ya see. . . ." or his outraged, "Well!" He parlayed the obvious into classic comedy and became a man beloved by the public and his friends while doing it. And all in just 39 years.

To the left of the Bennys, opposite the stairs and in the second row up, is another funnyman, **Eddie Cantor**, born Edward Israel Iskowitz (1892–1964), with his wife **Ida** (1892–1962). Unlike some of his contemporaries such as W. C. Fields and George Burns, Eddie Cantor's face and humor are not imprinted on the American consciousness. Some people may remember his googly-googly eyes, but the films which helped make him successful—*Kid Boots* (1927), *Whoopee* (1930), and *Ali Baba Goes to Town* (1937)—are no longer shown. In the 1930s Cantor switched to radio comedy. A board game, "Tell It to the Judge," was published based on one of his shows, and the radio audience came to feel they knew his wife and five daughters. Ida, who was celebrated by Eddie's theme song, "Ida, Sweet As Apple Cider," was often the butt of his humor as well.

In later years Cantor was involved in charitable ventures. He is credited with coining the name "March of Dimes." Eddie and Ida died within two years of each other, of heart ailments.

Continue up the stairs. To your right, in the second section, is **Ira Grossel**, a.k.a. Jeff Chandler (1918–1961). When he arrived in Hollywood in 1947, Chandler's prematurely gray hair helped attract notice, but for a long time he played only Indian roles. Most of his later films were adventures such as *Ten Seconds to Hell* (1959) and *Merrill's Marauders* (1961). He was still active when what began as surgery for a slipped disc escalated into abdominal bleeding; blood poisoning eventually took the life of the 42-year-old actor. Chandler's pallbearers included his baseball friends, Bill Rigney and Hoby Landrith, and another leading man of the day, Tony Curtis.

A number of minor characters have also made Hillside their last home. **Allan Sherman** (1924–1973), who delighted millions with his recording, "Hello Mudduh, Hello Fadduh/Here I Am at Camp Granada," is one of them. Sherman, who won a Grammy Award for his performance of his song in 1963, collapsed and died of respiratory failure while entertaining friends. The 48-year-old entertainer had been battling asthma, emphysema, and obesity.

Orchestra leader **Percy Faith** (1908–1976) and producer-songwriter **Arthur Freed**, born Arthur Grossman (1894–1973), are in the same row in a small outside garden. Percy Faith, who arranged and conducted more than 45 easy-listening albums, won an Academy Award nomination for "Love Me or Leave Me" (1955). Arthur Freed wrote a number of popular songs including "Pagan Love Song," "All I Do Is Dream of You," "Temptation," "Singin' in the Rain," and "You Are My Lucky Star." He also produced musicals for MGM, two of which—*An American in Paris* (1951) and *Gigi* (1958)—won him Oscars.

Meyer Harris "Mickey" Cohen (1913–1976), lovable racketeer, is no doubt charmed to find himself among the entertainers in Hillside. Mickey's aspirations for living well began at age 9 when he was involved in a bootlegging operation. As a teenager he became a prizefighter and gained entrée into the glamorous world of gambling. Mickey ran various nightclubs and a men's clothing store but spent the years between 1952 and 1955 and between 1961 and 1972 in prison for income-tax evasion. He survived being shot in a restaurant, having his house bombed, and a beating with a metal pipe in prison to die of natural causes.

Outside, in the Mt. Olive section in Block 5, is an actor who met a tragic end. After making his film debut in *The Blackboard Jungle* in 1955, **Vic Morrow** (1932–1982) played in a variety of movies, from *God's Little Acre* to *The Bad News Bears*. He died while filming a sequence for the movie *Twilight Zone* at 2:30 A.M. at Indian Dunes Park, 40 miles northwest of Los Angeles, on a set simulating a Vietnamese village under attack. Debris from explosives hit the helicopter carrying a camera crew. In a terrible imitation of life, it crashed on Morrow and the two Vietnamese children he was carrying, killing all three. The pilot and camera crew were also injured.

DIRECTIONS TO MT. SINAI MEMORIAL–PARK: Take Route 101 (Hollywood Freeway) to Route 134 (Ventura Freeway) and go east to Forest Lawn Drive. The entrance is past Forest Lawn Hollywood Hills on your right at 5950 Forest Lawn Drive.

DIRECTIONS TO HILLSIDE MEMORIAL PARK: Take Route 405 (San Diego Freeway) and exit at Sepulveda-Centinela. Go south on Sepulveda Boulevard, then turn left and proceed to 6001 Centinela Avenue.

Entrance to Mt. Sinai

CHAPTER 11

Inglewood Park and Valhalla

I saw the ghosts of children at their games
Racing beyond their childhood in the shade,
And while the green world turned its death-foxed
page
And a red wagon wheeled,
I watched them disappear
Into the suburbs of their grievous age.

—STANLEY KUNITZ

INGLEWOOD PARK

With its towering palm trees, Inglewood Park Cemetery, founded in 1905, has a tropical look even for California. The Spanish Mission buildings have orange-tiled roofs and wide arches, and the names — Capistrano Gardens, Sunset Mission Mausoleum, and Mausoleum of the Golden West — evoke memories of forgotten romance. The names of those interred here — Betty Grable, Paul Bern, Edgar Bergen, and Ferde Grofé — add to the mystique.

The customs here are exotic as well. As you begin to drive around the cemetery you see what appear to be the remains of a community picnic: beer cans, food wrappers, liquor bottles. A closer look shows they are not strewn on the ground, however, but sit neatly by the monuments, gifts to the deceased of favorite things. According to a groundskeeper, these gifts sometimes include roast pork and headless chickens — leading to speculations about other kinds of gifts for the dead.

Another regional custom, one that is found in many California cemeteries, is that of having a special section for

babies and young children. At Inglewood the area is closest
to the office. In its center stands a statue of two cherubic
children reading a book. The statue bears the inscription:

I have just to shut my eyes,
To go sailing through the skies.
To go sailing far away
To the pleasant land of play.

Gifts are also left here, including a replica of a birthday
cake and small toys for a 6-year-old at one grave. One of the
most touching children's memorials in Inglewood is that of
Norman Spencer Chaplin, the son of Charlie Chaplin,
who was born severely deformed. His marker reads simply,
"The Little Mouse, July 7–July 10, 1919."

Leaving this section, named the Garden of Verses, and
moving to the right, you will come to the Mausoleum of the
Golden West. Going into it is like entering a garden. Light
bursts through the colored-glass roofs and through the
huge stained-glass windows at the end of each hall. Most of
the brass holders on the crypts contain flowers. At the end
of the Sanctuary of Dawn is a window showing the mission
at San Luis Rey with a beautiful assortment of flowers and
shrubs leading up to it. Halfway down on the right, in Crypt
A78 is **Betty Grable** (1916–1973).

Contrary to myth, her "million-dollar" legs were only
insured by Lloyds of London for $500,000. Yet they were
certainly her most valuable asset. In 1946–1947 Betty Grable was the highest-paid woman in America, well-recom-
pensed for such movies as *Mother Wore Tights* (1947) and
When My Baby Smiles at Me (1948). Her greatest fame
came as a World War II pin-up in a photo that showed her
from behind in a white bathing suit, blonde curls piled high
on her head, smiling invitingly over her right shoulder.
Betty Grable, a heavy smoker, died of lung cancer at 56.
Former husbands Jackie Coogan and Harry James attended
her funeral.

Going in the opposite direction, in the Sanctuary of
Faith, look for Crypt E324 and the memorial of composer

A   Garden of Verses
B   Betty Grable, Ferde Grofé, Paul Bern
C   Lillian Leitzel
D   Edgar Bergen
E   Lyman Wesley Bostock
F   William "Buckwheat" Thomas
G   Willie Mae "Big Mama" Thornton
H   James J. Jeffries

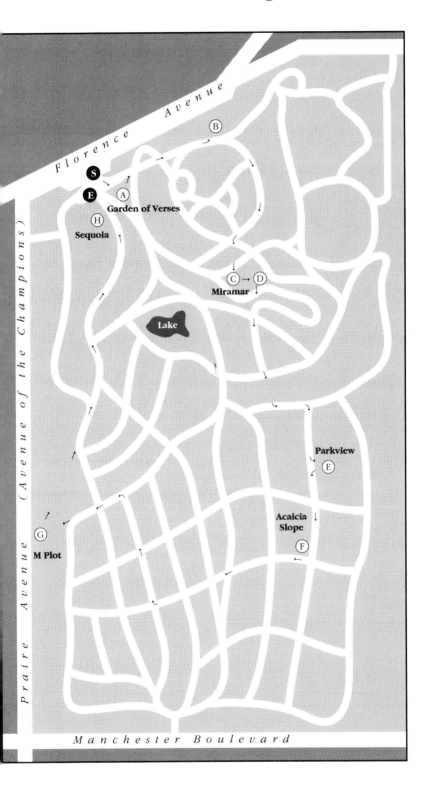

Ferde Grofé (1892–1972). Running away from his Los Angeles home at 14, Grofé earned his musical experience by playing piano in bawdy houses. He expanded his talents to arranging and orchestrating popular songs and earned a place with Paul Whiteman's band in 1919, where the two men did much to develop the style known as symphonic jazz. Most notably, Grofé arranged Gershwin's "Rhapsody in Blue" for its premiere, as Gershwin had neither the time nor expertise for the task at that point. Grofé's own scores gained him popularity in his day, and his "Grand Canyon Suite" is still frequently heard. It was the first piece of American music to be recorded by Toscanini, and the theme for the section of the suite entitled "On the Trail" may be best remembered by some as the lead-in for Johnny on the Philip Morris commercials.

On the opposite side of the mausoleum and halfway down the corridor, on the very top of the first glassed-in niches (F96), are the remains of **Paul Bern** (1890–1932). Paul Bern's story is an unhappy one. A slight, sensitive man who was known around MGM as a good listener, Bern was a scriptwriter turned producer when he married starlet Jean Harlow. Bern evidently hoped that her on-screen magic as a sex goddess would help cure him of his greatest handicap: child-sized sexual equipment which rendered him impotent. Instead she ridiculed him, and they fought. They continued to quarrel until he shot himself in the head two months after their wedding.

Coming out of the mausoleum, turn right and follow the road around to the Miramar section. You will be able to see at a distance the statue of **Lillian Leitzel** and **Alfredo Codona**. It shows him as a winged figure slipping upward out of his embrace; although classic in style, their faces are accurate portraits of the two acrobats. Beneath the sculpture is a bas relief of two trapeze rings, one with a broken rope, and the words, "In everlasting memory of my beloved Leitzel Codona, Copenhagen, Denmark, February 15, 1931. Erected by her beloved husband, Alfredo Codona."

The Dainty Miss Leitzel, as she was known on circus posters, was a third-generation performer, specializing on the trapeze. With her second husband, Mexican Alfredo Codona, she had attempted to form her own circus. When that failed, they went back to individual appearances. At a performance in Copenhagen, Lietzel fell 45 feet with no safety net. Codona rushed to her side from Berlin, where he had been performing with an acrobatic troupe. Leitzel died an hour later.

His monument lies on the ground below hers with the

dates October 7, 1893–July 30, 1937. Their statue, created by the Seitz Memorial Company, has no sculptor's name.

Walking to the left of the Codonas in the Miramar section, you can find the **Bergren** family marker, an upright stone flanked by two large arborvitae. Despite the spelling variation, the in-ground plaque marks the last resting place of **Edgar Bergen** (1903–1978).

Everybody loves a dummy. Charlie McCarthy, manned by Edgar Bergen, was one of the best loved ever. Lacking undue modesty, Charlie once told an interviewer, "Bergen is nothing without me." Mortimer Snerd might have said the same thing and been believed, so convincing were the personalities Bergen crafted for his dolls. The Swedish comedian created the top-hatted, monocled McCarthy in 1925. They played the vaudeville circuit together until Bergen developed his own radio show in 1936.

Besides fathering actress Candice Bergen, the ventriloquist acted in a number of movies without Charlie McCarthy, including *I Remember Mama* (1948) and *The Hanged Man* (1964). Bergen, 75, had announced his retirement 10 days before he died in his sleep after a performance in Las Vegas. He was buried here alone. Charlie McCarthy, slated to go to the Smithsonian Institution, quipped, "Well, I won't be the only dummy in Washington."

Four rows of markers back and to the right of Bergen is the monument of **Billy Mac Bunnell** (1911–1986), inscribed "US Veteran, World War II." It has the unusual epitaph, "This cat lived, and he was also loved." Nearby in this section is another interesting inscription: "Why care by what meanders we found the center of the labyrinth? Men have perished trying to find the place which we together found."

Head back to the main road and up to Acacia Slope. Near the far right-hand corner, two rows of markers from the end and two rows in is **William B. Thomas** (1931–1980), better known as Buckwheat from the *Our Gang* comedies. Thomas, who joined the company at age 3 and helped them make mischief for the next 10 years, was found dead of a heart attack at 49. Police entered the window of his home when neighbors became concerned after not seeing him.

Up at the top of the cemetery, in the Cherry Blossom section, is a monument that dominates the area. It is gazebo shaped with a wrought-iron canopy, Greek columns, two bronze flames, and, standing in a pool of water, two marble sarcophagi. The names on them appear to be **Vari** and **Mayton**, with the words "Love, Understand, Be Kind."

The family to whom the plot belongs, the **McKinleys**, were the original owners of this land.

In Section M, all the way back against the barbed-wire fence, opposite the intersection of Regent and Prairie Streets, is **Willie Mae "Big Mama" Thornton** (1926–1984). She is buried with **Kenny V. Barton** (1965–1984). Thornton was known best as a blues shouter whose songs "Hound Dog" and "Ball and Chain" were brought to greater fame in their white covers by Elvis Presley and Janis Joplin. When Thornton was a young woman, her over two hundred pounds earned her the nickname "Big Mama." Her style was reminiscent of the older blues singers such as Ma Rainey and Bessie Smith, but she also served as a link between blues and rock and roll. As if not content with her aggressive singing, Thornton also played the drums and a pungent country-style harmonica.

In Sequoia, the section closest to the entrance, there is a wrought-iron archway with a hedge, two benches, and beautiful plantings. The flat sarcophagus is inscribed, "This is the illumined resting place of the holy soul **Thornton Chase** (1847–1912) who is shining in the horizon of eternal life ever like a star." Also in this division, catty-corner to the office and three rows back from the road, is the large solid-block monument of **James J. Jeffries** (1875–1953). The bronze plaque identifies him as the "World Heavyweight Boxing Champion from 1899–1906." Jeffries, son of a street-corner preacher, twice defeated Gentleman Jim Corbett. In 1910 he came out of retirement as the Great White

Hope against Jack Johnson in Reno but was knocked out of the ring for good. His Spring Street saloon in LA was closed down by Prohibition. With two defeats under his belt Jeffries retired to a ranch in Burbank.

Almost in the center of the Parkview section, under a brown marble marker, is **Lyman Wesley Bostock, Jr**. (1950–1978), "Beloved husband, son." On the left is a baseball player hitting a ball, and on the right is the symbol for the California Angels — an A with a halo on top. Bostock, a young star outfielder, was one of the highest paid players of his day. He died of a gunshot wound acquired when a man tried to kill the woman with whom he was riding in a car.

VALHALLA MEMORIAL PARK

Valhalla Memorial Park, located at 10621 Victory Boulevard in Burbank, near Burbank Airport, reflects the trend of modern cemeteries to feature a few large works of statuary dedicated to specific groups and insist that individual markers be flush with the ground. Valhalla, founded in 1923, inaugurated that style sooner than other cemeteries. If you drive in the entrance from Victory Boulevard and make the first left, you will see on your right the Veterans' Monument. It shows a large bronze combat helmet held aloft by an upright rifle and designates the area for veterans and their families. On the monument are verses adapted from a Sir Walter Scott poem:

> Soldiers rest, the warfare o'er.
> Dream of fighting fields no more.
> Sleep the sleep that knows not breaking,
> Morn of toil nor night of waking.

Just beyond the first curve is the outside Mausoleum of Hope. In Row C, Crypt 34, is actress **Bea Benaderet** (1894–1968). Benaderet is most familiar as the voice of Betty Rubble in "The Flintstones" (1960–1964), though older audiences will remember her from radio as the next-door neighbor on the "Burns and Allen Show." At the time of her death from lung cancer, Benaderet was playing the mother, Kate Bradley, on the TV series "Petticoat Junction."

Continue up the road, turn left, and stop at the Heritage Fountain. If it doesn't upset you to find something so obviously European transplanted to Southern California, you will be impressed by its heroic proportions and baroque artifacts. The large circular fountain is made from dark stone and is layered like a wedding cake. It is decorated by many ornate features and is topped by a young maiden in a classical pose. The stone has been softened by

Heritage Fountain

the weather and by the mist generated by the fountain's many arching sprays of water.

Make your first right after the fountain and stop at the second wall enclosing the Garden of Hope. Behind it lurks funnyman **Oliver Hardy** (1892–1957). He is interred in the ground, but a plaque against the wall reads, "A genius of comedy. His talent brought joy and laughter to all the world." It was placed there in 1977 by the Sons of the Desert and is bordered with bronze roses. Born in Atlanta, Hardy gained theatrical experience as he went through college and then law school. He made his first picture in 1921 and in 1926 was teamed up with Stan Laurel in the Hal Roach studios.

Surprisingly agile for his three hundred pounds, his frame was topped by a bowler which was too small for his head. The hat was a frequent if inadvertent target for the blundering Laurel, whose inept but well-intentioned efforts and overliteral attention to commands set the stage for Ollie's famous slow burn and withering scorn. Ollie was the conniver, the one in charge, whose plans to gain money or impress women always seemed to backfire. At the end of a Laurel-and-Hardy movie if Ollie was getting any attention from women, it was usually in the form of a tongue-lashing by his wife or girlfriend. Of their over two hundred films the comic pair is best remembered for their seasonal classic, *Babes in Toyland* (1934).

Hardy died of complications resulting from a paralytic stroke he had suffered almost a year before his death. Laurel, himself recovering from a stroke, was forbidden to attend the funeral by his doctor but mourned Hardy's departure as he would have a brother's.

Retrace your steps to the fountain and to Section D, the large area to your right just past it. Look for curb designation 6411 and go up eight rows of markers. Here rests another famous voice, that of Jiminy Cricket in *Pinnochio* (1939). The marker for **Cliff Edwards** (1895–1971) comments, "In loving memory of 'Ukelele Ike.' "

Right next to him is **Mitty Morris** (1874–1953), "Mother Morris, Founder of Faith Home Missions."

Also in Section D, in Plot 6657, is the man known as **Gorgeous George**, born George Raymond Wagner (1915–1963), whose marker bears the epitaph, "Love to Our Daddy." Here is a wrestler who could give Andre the Giant lessons and teach the Hulk a bit about showmanship. George, whose favorite color was orchid, would be preceded into the wrestling ring by a valet who perfumed the ring, whereupon he would mince in to "Pomp and Circumstance." Bleached blond curls flashing, he would remove

his fur-trimmed robe and step into the ring. That he usually lost made little difference. Afterward he would climb into his orchid-colored Cadillac and return to the turkey farm he owned near Beaumont, California.

Despite his birds, the wrestler died broke, succumbing to a heart attack on Christmas Day. Loyal fans buried him here in an orchid-covered coffin.

A fitting climax to this visit would be to continue straight back to the Portal of the Folded Wings — an interesting metaphor for death. This structure is an ornate mass of carvings with an unusual blue, yellow, and rust domed and tiled roof. It was built to honor the pioneers of American aviation and dedicated on the fiftieth anniversary of powered flight, December 17, 1953. Used as a landmark for flyers landing at nearby Burbank Airport, it has plaques to notables such as Amelia Earhart and Richard E. Byrd. The most famous figure actually interred here is **Charles Edward Taylor** (1869–1956), who designed and built the engine of the Wright brothers' plane in 1902. He later pioneered in engines for cross-country flights.

Also buried in Valhalla is actress **Gail Russell** (1924–1961). Russell, a dark-haired beauty, was plucked out of high school and hyped as "the Hedy Lamarr of Santa Monica." Although she had never done any acting and was morbidly shy, Russell passed a Paramount screen test and was given small roles. In 1944 she starred in a ghost story, *The Uninvited*, then co-starred with Diana Lynn in *Our Hearts Were Young and Gay*. To calm her terror of performing, she began to drink. Her films became fewer, her drunken-driving charges more frequent, until she turned reclusive and stayed home to paint. Russell was found dead at 36, surrounded by empty vodka bottles.

DIRECTIONS TO INGLEWOOD PARK: Take Route 405 (San Diego Freeway) and exit east on Manchester Boulevard. Turn right on Prairie Avenue at the cemetery to reach the main entrance at 720 East Florence Avenue.

DIRECTIONS TO VALHALLA MEMORIAL PARK: Take Route 101 (Hollywood Freeway) and exit east on Victory Boulevard. Entrance is on the left at 10621 Victory Boulevard.

Portal of the Folded Wings

CHAPTER 12

Mission Hills

May Memory restore again and again
The smallest color of the smallest
day:Time is the school in which
we learn,Time is the fire in
which we burn.

— DELMORE SCHWARTZ

SAN FERNANDO MISSION

For decades California missions were placed along the coastline like beacons, the only hope of civilized life. Although there is enormous charm in their rough white stucco walls and orange-tiled roofs, they were not intended to be decorative. In the 1700s, when the mission priests were trying to tame a desert and support hundreds of newly converted Indians who had left their homes, life was more precarious than pleasurable. Each mission had cells housing wooden pallets for beds and bright, crudely woven blankets which served as bedding. The mission grounds contained a chapel and an agricultural center as well.

Each mission also had its own burial ground. The San Fernando Mission, founded in 1797, is no exception. Its cemetery is tiny and beautiful, giving no hint that over 2,500 souls have been laid to rest here. The cemetery was intended first for "Christianized Indians," but it also holds Spanish and other nationalities, as well as five priests. The graves are a combination of homemade wooden crosses and pieces of unmarked slate.

There are just two larger markers. One, of white marble, is that of the **Menendez** family, dedicated to **Maria Espirito Capigaras** (1836–1906), with the inscription, *En paz descanse recuerdo de su hijo.* (Rest in peace, from your son.) The other named marker, behind the hedge next to the church, is that of **Luisa Straube** (1876–1907), and bears the epitaph, "In peaceful rest." **José Antonio**, one of the first

Interior courtyard

natives christened at the mission, April 7, 1798, is the earliest recorded interment.

The other dead here were buried multiply, wrapped in mats and placed directly into the ground. In frontier days, when survival was the primary concern, there was no time for coffins and floral tributes. The most charming marker in the cemetery, though attached to no name, shows two clay bluebirds on a roughly carved stump. Most of the paint is worn off.

Although the modern Mission Hills Cemetery is adjacent to the old mission churchyard, you cannot get there from here. Retrace your steps out of the mission and turn right. Turn right again onto Stranwood Avenue then into the new cemetery. The large section diagonal to the office, containing the Statue of the Sacred Heart of Jesus, is Section C. Walk to your left until you see the number 64 on the curb, and go in five rows. The marker with the flowers and rose-colored inset is that of **William Frawley** (1887–1966), best known to Americans as Fred Mertz on "I Love Lucy" and later as Fred MacMurray's co-star on "My Three Sons." Before television, Frawley had a long film career as a supporting actor, usually as a cigar-chomping taxi driver or a comic gangster.

Continuing left to the curb designation 409, walk back toward the statue. Near it, in Row 416, you will find scientist **Lee DeForest** (1873–1961). The flat marker shows an angel kneeling at a cross with lilies scattered around her. Often called "the father of the radio," the triode DeForest invented in 1906 made wireless telephony practical and

Oldest marker in the burial grounds

helped found the radio industry. DeForest also designed the first high-powered naval radio stations.

From DeForest's marker walk diagonally back toward the curb to Plot 247, three rows of markers in. The cemetery's best-known inhabitant, **Ritchie Valens**, born Richard Valenzuela (1941–1959), lies under a flat marker inscribed with five notes from "Come On — Let's Go." To the left is a cross with a rosary around it. Beside his name is inscribed "Beloved Son."

The biographical movie, *La Bamba*, begins with a striking image: adolescent boys in a playground, positioned like dancers on a stage, are shooting baskets. Their arms move in the slow motion of a dream; the orange ball arcs endlessly across the blue sky. Then a plane circles overhead. It is joined by another. The planes smash against each other, burst into flames, and fall to earth. Richard Valenzuela awakes from his nightmare. Yet the image of the sunny days of childhood cut forever short is chilling.

Valenzuela was a Mexican teenager living in the San Fernando Valley when his mother, Connie, arranged for him to give a concert at a local hall. He was discovered there by Bob Keene of Del–Fi Records, who auditioned him, shortened his name to Ritchie Valens, and brought out his first hit single, "Come On — Let's Go," in September 1958. It was followed by his biggest hit, "Donna," which he wrote after a misunderstanding with his Anglo girlfriend, Donna Ludwig. By then Ritchie had left high school to make personal appearances. He was not pleased when he had to fly to Philadelphia in order to appear on "American

Bandstand," but his fear of flying lessened after that trip. Ritchie's premonition of death in a plane crash persisted, however.

With the success of "La Bamba" in January 1959, Ritchie made a Winter Dance Tour of 13 cities. He was billed with renowned rock-and-roll singers Buddy Holly, J. P. Richardson (The Big Bopper), and Dion and the Belmonts. Tired of traveling on an unheated bus that kept breaking down, Holly chartered a four-seat plane to fly from Clear Lake, Iowa, to Moorhead, Minnesota. The Big Bopper talked one of Holly's band members into giving up his seat on the plane, and Valens, who had a cold, tossed a coin with Holly's guitarist, Tommy Allsup, and won his seat.

Minutes after taking off from the Mason City, Iowa, airport in light snow, the plane crashed into a farmer's field, plowing the distance of two city blocks before, smashing into a fence. Everyone on board, including 17-year-old Ritchie Valens, died. As if it had happened in the silence of a dream, the sound went unheard. The wreckage was discovered the next day.

Continue up the road to Section D and to the curb marked 241. If you go in 14 rows of markers and 6 rows to your right, you will come across old-timer **William Bendix** (1906–1964). The border decoration resembles that on *National Geographic* covers, and the inscription reads, "Forever in our hearts." Bendix is best known, of course, for his role as a harassed aircraft worker and family man in "The Life of Riley." As a bat boy for the Giants and Yankees, he fetched hot-dogs for Babe Ruth, then had the chance to portray his hero in *The Babe Ruth Story* (1948).

Bendix appeared in more than 50 movies, often as a broken-nosed tough. His last role, before he died at 58 of pneumonia and malnutrition arising from a stomach ailment, was on the TV show "Burke's Law." Standing here, you find it easy to imagine Bendix materializing in the persona of Chester A. Riley, looking around and complaining, "What a revoltin' development dis is!"

EDEN MEMORIAL PARK

Perhaps it is because Groucho Marx's ashes were once stolen from here and deposited on the doorstep of Mt. Sinai Cemetery in Burbank, or because even now some people do not think too kindly of Lenny Bruce. Whatever the reason, Eden Memorial Park does not want the locations of its well-known residents given out—a wish that will be respected. Nevertheless, because of its occupants, this cemetery cannot be ignored. If you visit, admire the metal gates which are topped with outlines of the symbols for the tribes of Israel. As you wander around you may stumble upon one or more of the cast.

The most appropriate resident of any cemetery is in Eden Park: **John Brown** (1899–1957), best known as the lugubrious-voiced Digger O'Dell, the "friendly undertaker," on both radio and TV versions of "The Life of Riley." While attempting to break into show business, the British-born actor in fact worked for an undertaker in New York City.

In the mausoleum, in a modest vault with just his name and a star of David, rest the remains of one of America's funniest men:

JULIUS HENRY "GROUCHO" MARX *b. October 2, 1890, Manhattan; d. August 19, 1977, Los Angeles.* Those who haven't been swayed by the five-and-dime Groucho disguises and have looked closely, know that for years Groucho wore greasepaint and not a mustache. That extravagant smear, the highlighted eyebrows, the glasses and cigar, and the stooped, striding walk all became trademarks, creating one of the most recognizable figures of the twentieth century. One of the most revered also, for George Bernard Shaw thought Marx to be the era's greatest actor, and an admiring T. S. Eliot carried on a correspondence of long standing with Groucho, who spoke at the poet's funeral.

Groucho followed Chico and Harpo into the tenement world of East 93rd Street in Manhattan. His father, Sam, must have made the pants too long, for he was a less-than-successful tailor. Because her brother, Al Shean of Gallagher and Shean fame, was a vaudeville star, Groucho's mother, Minnie, felt that there must be talent in her sons. She pushed the boys, but on their own they achieved little. At 16 Groucho joined a traveling act only to be abandoned in Denver. He was forced to work in a grocery store in Cripple Creek, Colorado, for two months before he could raise the fare home.

Collectively the boys did little better. Minnie was their agent, and armed with their mother's chutzpah and little else, Groucho, Harpo, and Gummo joined forces with the luscious-figured but erratic-voiced Janie O'Reilly as the Four Nightingales. These rare birds seldom trilled their way into the hearts of their audiences. Although they gradually added slapstick and cornball humor to their act in a routine called "Fun in Hi Skule," 1914 found them still touring the smallest towns in the country with little success. It took an insult to correct their approach. Playing in

Nacogdoches, Texas, the group found their audience leaving, preferring the antics of a runaway mule. The locals soon filtered back in, but by then Groucho was in a rage. Determined to match them insult for insult, he devastated them with brilliant wit. "Nacogdoches is full of roaches," he roared. But the rubes loved it and the art of insult, however slight, was born to the act.

Soon Janie was gone, and Chico brought his amusing and up-tempo pianistic talents to the group. The boys' nicknames grew out of their character traits, Groucho's coming from his clouded disposition. Continuing to refine their act, the boys met with increased success and by 1924 were a hit on Broadway in *I'll Say She Is*. 1929 found them in Hollywood, featured first in *The Cocoanuts* and then in *Animal Crackers*, which displayed Groucho's eventual TV theme song, "Captain Spaulding," and some memorable lines. "One morning I shot an elephant in my pajamas. How he got in my pajamas I don't know. . . . But that's entirely irrelephant."

By 1935 the brothers, minus Gummo, were working with Irving Thalberg, who bore a reputation for being late or leaving guests in his office for "a minute" only to return an hour or two later. The fourth time this happened to the brothers, they ordered potatoes from the commissary, stripped naked, lit a fire, and roasted the potatoes in the office fireplace. Upon his return Thalberg was shocked but amused and never again late for the Marx Brothers. But of course Thalberg was a fan, though not an uncritical one. Feeling that their previous movies lacked a story line, he urged them to make the plot more cohesive. In a tight story the anarchy of their humor would be all the more pointed. One result was their most famous collaboration and arguably the Marx Brothers' best movie, *A Night at the Opera*.

Deflation of pomposity and the rules of status quo through insult and chaos were at the core of their humor. Many of the movies featured Groucho as an unsavory suitor and fleecer of a rich widow (usually played by Margaret Dumont). Giving flattery and taking it away, often in the same sentence, Groucho's flagrant if dubious groundwork set the stage for Chico's and Harpo's madcap activities. In the end confusion and the Marx Brothers reigned.

By the 1940s the boys were getting tired of doing movies. They retired with *The Big Store* in 1941 but were unfortunately lured back for two more films several years later. In the meantime Groucho branched out into radio and emceed a new quiz show, "You Bet Your Life." With Groucho's ad libs the show became a huge hit and won the Peabody Award. The move to TV didn't disrupt the show at all. With the gimmicks ("Say the magic word, and the duck comes down, and you win fifty dollars.") and Groucho continuing as before, the loyal fans heard some of Groucho's most memorable lines. When one contestant with 13 children was asked why she had so many, she could only reply, "I love my husband," to which Groucho rejoined, "I like my cigar too, but I take it out once in a while."

His three marriages failed, but he was a loving father to his children. A closet sentimentalist, Groucho was chary of giving affection and was even shy under all the bluster. His insults seemed more compulsive than mean. He was generous with large purchases and parsimonious with small. Buying an expensive car, he might later walk some distance to avoid a parking fee.

Groucho's old age was sadly less successful than his prime. In his eighties he became involved with Erin Fleming, his secretary and companion. A battle developed over whether Ms. Fleming's influence was salutary and whether she or a family member should act as Groucho's conservator. The family eventually won the bitter affair. Groucho may have been beyond it all at that point, but always having to have the last word, he had made sure that his epitaph was ready: "I hope they buried me near a straight man."

The outside marker of Lenny Bruce is likewise very plain. Beside his name, dates, and a Jewish star, it has the words, "Beloved Father — Devoted Son" and the epitaph, "Peace at Last."

LENNY BRUCE (Leonard Schneider) *b. October 13, 1925, Bellmore, NY; d. August 3, 1966, Los Angeles.* Lenny Bruce wasn't always "Dirty Lenny." He was Lenny Penny first, a little Jewish kid growing up in what was then rural Long Island. His father, a quiet and remote man, raised, loved, and spoiled his son and was never forgiven. His mother, Sally, pursued a career in entertainment and played in and out of Lenny's life. A sometimes pal, a sometimes sister, a sometimes mother, she was forgiven. Lenny was neither beaten nor mired in poverty as he later portrayed. But he was lonely.

At 17 he enlisted in the Navy. Two and a half years later and desperate to get out, he finagled a dishonorable discharge by playing the latent-cum-blatant homosexual. Known as a kook in the Navy, he attempted stand-up comedy. Affecting debonair dress, he succeeded only in looking like a pimp, just another third-rate comic hanging around Hanson's drugstore in Manhattan with the other would-be stars. It was there, however, that he came into contact with Joe Ancis, whose manic, offbeat humor became the model for Lenny's. Ancis, known as The Funniest Man In New York City, was never a professional comic, but his humor encompassed any subject or fantasy. Lenny was hooked and began to practice that sincerest form of flattery. It took years for Lenny's own voice to emerge, and it was always rooted in Ancis'.

Lenny began to work the burlesque circuit as an emcee and a comic. There he met a voluptuous stripper named Honey, who became his wife. He also began to immerse himself in the jazz and drug scenes. In fact drugs became a common point in the marriage between these two insecure people. Theirs was a stormy relationship marked by arguments, infidelities, threats, and occasional fights. Passions and jealousies ran high, and when Honey resumed drugs after the birth of their daughter, Kitty, she was busted, with Lenny as the almost certain informer, and served two years in jail. She later gained revenge by calling Lenny at late hours asking him to guess who was making love to her at that time. Their love-hate relationship continued up to the time of Lenny's death.

As a comic Lenny first gained attention with an appearance on Arthur Godfrey's TV show. With time he lost his inhibitions, and even his clothing, gaining notoriety when he appeared naked while emceeing a burlesque show. His reputation snowballed, and he became one of the leading "sickniks," appearing on Steve Allen's show and featured in *Time*. His humor matured and ranged and raged over a myriad of subjects from current events to his personal life. He freewheeled and improvised and spat it out in coarse language. Yet even that language was subject to Lenny's ridicule, for he would take an offensive word or phrase and repeat incessantly until, losing all meaning, it became mere senseless noise and the absurdity of meaning and connotation became obvious. His audiences were enthralled, invigorated, insulted, and outraged. Nothing was sacred, nothing taboo.

Lenny's fame drew attention to his narcotics habit. By the late 1950s he was spending over $1,000 a week on drugs: methadrine, dilaudid, heroin, cocaine, and marijuana to name a few. He was hooked on the spike, and his arms were a mass of scar tissue and hematomas. Bruce stayed out of serious trouble by conning doctors with his charm, fame, and lies into giving him prescriptions for the "legal" drugs. But everything began to feed upon itself: his "filthy" mouth and mind led to his drugs, and the drugs to his mouth. He was offensive to society, and he started to be busted for obscenity.

As the circle spun faster Lenny fed into it with his obsessive behavior. Rather than settle for a slap on the wrist as punishment for his offenses, he demanded complete vindication, even in the drug cases. He went through one attorney after another, looking for the most famous one, the one who would save him. He read voluminously in the law, badgered his attorneys in court, and attempted to represent himself.

Such actions were manic, childish, and ultimately self-destructive. He was a little boy raging at authority, simultaneously thumbing his nose and seeking punishment. His performances deteriorated into long-winded accounts of his dissolving personal life. His body became bloated and, increasingly paranoid, he lived in his home in the Hollywood Hills with a string of women: comedian groupies. His mother and Honey were frequent visitors.

It has been said that Lenny secretly subscribed to the conservative standards that he so cynically satirized. But whether he was a disillusioned romantic, an acute, slashing observer, a tantrum-throwing child, or all three, Lenny more than scratched life's surface; he punctured it. He was found dead in his bathroom, naked, his pants by his ankles and a needle in his arm.

DIRECTIONS TO SAN FERNANDO MISSION: Take Route 405 (San Diego Freeway) and exit east on the San Fernando Mission Boulevard. The entrance to the cemetery is on the left at 1160 Stranwood Avenue. To reach the old mission, continue farther and make the first left.

DIRECTIONS TO EDEN MEMORIAL PARK: Take Route 405 (San Diego Freeway) to the Rinaldi exit east. The cemetery entrance is around the corner at 11500 Sepulveda Boulevard.

A Gate of Eden

J.W. HUGGINS
DEAD
Aug. 1898.

CHAPTER 13

San Diego Cemeteries

What did it matter where you lay when you were dead? In a dirty sump or in a marble tower on top of a high hill. You were dead, you were sleeping the big sleep, you were not bothered by things like that. Oil and water the same as wind and air to you. You just slept the big sleep, not caring about the nastiness of how you died or where you fell.

— RAYMOND CHANDLER

MOUNT HOPE

Mount Hope Cemetery, burial ground of the pioneers, was founded in 1869. Since then it has expanded to 169 acres and absorbed several smaller cemeteries whose stones lay piled in a gully at the back. Perhaps because Mount Hope was geographically so far from the Eastern–Victorian influence, there are few carved monuments. Most markers in the older section are granite blocks and steles. The private mausoleums are functional but plain. One stone says only "**J. W. Huggins**, Dead."

The historic section of Mount Hope is deep into the cemetery. To reach it, take Horton Avenue across the San Diego–Arizona Railroad tracks and go left onto Hope Avenue. Near the corner of North Oakwood and Hope is the white marble stele to **Alonzo Erastus Horton** (1813–1909) who was born in Connecticut and came to California in 1851 during the Gold Rush. He made his first fortune not from gold, however, but from the ice he sold to miners during the summer. While visiting San Diego in 1867, he picked up 960 acres of what would become the heart of the city for $265, then proceeded to create the town. He paid his construction laborers in land. (He also demanded that they vote Republican). Like Horace and Daeida Wilcox, the founders of Hollywood, Horton offered free land to churches.

A. E. Horton did not go easily into the cemetery he founded in 1869. Attributing some of the credit for his long life to Warner's Hot Springs, considered the "fountain of youth," he finally lay down here at 96 years.

Nearby, the stele of Colonel **C. T. Noell** (d. 1887) has the epitaph, "An honest man is the noblest work of God."

Another, more visually interesting, monument in this section of the cemetery is small and shows a dead bird made of marble. It is dedicated to **George Vergez**, who died June 20, 1892, at 5 years and 9 months. Above the name the inscription reads, "Our darling Georgie is at rest."

Also here is a huge stone cross to the **Babcock** family. **Elisha S. Babcock** is best remembered as the builder of the Hotel del Coronado (1888), which was developed to pique interest in the residential lots the owners hoped to sell in the area around it. The gambit worked. Tourists came to

Babcock family

Kate L. Sessions

gawk at the menagerie of caged monkeys and the huge turtles which roamed the lawn carrying children on their backs, as well as more adult delights. And thousands more came to buy land in an area which Babcock and his partner, H. L. Story, advertised as close to Paradise: "There is not any malaria, hay fever, loss of appetite, or languor in the air; nor any thunder, lightning, mad dogs, cyclones, heated terms, or cold snaps."

The first person in **Kate L. Sessions**'s family to be buried in Mount Hope was interred in 1895. It is probable that the pioneer horticulturist herself planted the twisted juniper under which family members lie. Her marker, located close to the road between Hope Avenue and the tracks, reads, "Kate L. Sessions, 1857–1940." Sessions was responsible for much of the horicultural beautification of San Diego.

The **Brannan** plot is right across Hope Road and up slightly on the hill. It reads, "'**Sam' Brannan** (1819–1889), California Pioneer of '46. Dreamer — Leader — Empire-Builder." It seems accidental that Sam Brannan ended up buried in San Diego. A Mormon who came to Yerba Buena (San Francisco) in 1846 with hopes of becoming the city's first millionaire, he made his fortune but was excommunicated in the process. Brannan was a printer by trade and started the territory's second newspaper, the *California Star*, but he made his real money by promoting tales of gold at Sutter's Fort — where coincidentally he had the only supply store.

Brannan's passion for money got him into deep water

more than once. He was accused of pocketing the tithes he had been collecting from faithful Mormon settlers to send back to Salt Lake, and as a city councilman he was charged with misappropriating public funds — but he had other passions as well. Darkly handsome and a great lover of champagne, he entertained royally, built houses for his mistresses, and was finally divorced by his wife for "notorious intemperance." Perhaps to assuage his own guilt, he became active in starting a vigilante committee in San Francisco, which hung a man in 1851 for stealing a safe.

A decade after Brannan heralded the Gold Rush, he discovered hot springs in the Napa Valley and proclaimed his spa discovery the Saratoga of the West. Legend has it that Calistoga got its name from an inebriated Sam trying to pronounce his resort "the Saratoga of California" and coming out with "the Calistoga of Sarafornia." Drunk or sober, Brannan continued to lead an exuberant, high-profile life but became careless with his funds and by the end of his life had lost his fortune. He died, plotting a comeback, in a boarding house just north of San Diego in Escondido.

Also in the older section are **Alta Hulett**, the first woman attorney in America; **Aubrey Davidson**, organizer of the Panama–California Exposition of 1915, whose tan stucco Spanish-style buildings serve as the city's cultural center; and **Nathan Harrison**, whose epitaph describes him as "Born a slave and died a pioneer."

Raymond Chandler is in one of the new sections nearer the entrance (Lot 1577, Division 8, Section 3). Find the corner of Tweed and North Canyon Avenues, walk down from the Tweed side for seven rows, then count eight markers in from the other road. Chandler rests under a black marble marker which has above his name the inscription, "In Loving Memory," and below it, "Author."

RAYMOND THORNTON CHANDLER *b. July 23, 1888, Chicago; d. March 25, 1959, La Jolla.* Raymond Chandler was as fascinating in his own way as his mysteries are in theirs. His detective novels, especially *The Big Sleep* and *The Long Goodbye*, are classics and have been filmed again and again. His characters and Southern California settings resonate with a special, bright color. But where his detective, Philip Marlowe, is wisecracking and heroic, Chandler himself felt victimized by life's disappointments. Like an irritable child who demands to be left alone, then fidgets to attract attention, Chandler could never decide what he wanted from other people.

By the time Raymond was 7, his father, a railroad engineer, had disappeared from his life. Chandler and his Irish

mother, Florence, returned to London, where his grandmother and aunt lived. Their welcome was half-hearted.
Although Raymond received a good classical education at
Dulwich College, near London, his wealthy uncle would
not pay to send him to a university afterward. Instead, the
19-year-old passed a civil-service examination which led to
a job keeping records of supplies. It is to his credit that he
quit six months later to write. Chandler's poetry was ama-
teurish, with a lot of "dew a-twinkling on the grass," but he
did well writing articles and reviews. The income was insuf-
ficient to live on, however, and in 1912 he sought his
fortune in America.

Chandler joined the Canadians for World War I, then
moved back to California to a job arranged by friends.
Eventually he became vice-president of the Dabney Oil
Syndicate. In 1924 he married Cissy Hurlburt, a beautiful,
soft-haired model 18 years his senior. By 1930 Chandler
was out of control, tossing off women and martinis as
frantically as a Dashiell Hammett detective. When a friend
canceled their Saturday tennis game to stay home with his
sick wife, Chandler went upstairs and tried to drag her out
of bed. Embarrassed at their horrified reaction, he went
downstairs and pointed a gun at his head.

Chandler's alcoholism and adultery did not go
unrewarded. In 1932, at 44, he was fired from his job, but
the company's original owners, knowing his burning need
to write, awarded him a monthly stipend. Freed to do so,
Chandler turned his life around. He stopped drinking, re-
newed his relationship with Cissy, and began to look for a
proper literary genre. Despite himself, he was attracted to
the pulps. Like a man who has married a whore with plans
to reform her, he spent the rest of his life trying to upgrade
the detective novel into literature.

Chandler's first published story, "Blackmailers Don't
Shoot," appeared in *Black Mask* magazine in 1933. He
spent the next five years writing short fiction which was
published in *Dime Detective* magazine as well as *Black
Mask*. His debut as a novelist came with *The Big Sleep*
(1939). *Farewell, My Lovely* followed the next year. The
milieu was Los Angeles; the action included masquerades,
shootings, double-crossings, and enough alcohol to float
Beverly Hills into the Pacific. Philip Marlowe was squarely
in the mode of the wisecracking private investigator who
smokes like a fiend, lives by his own moral code, and takes
enough physical punishment to destroy a street gang. By
writing his novels in the first person, Chandler allowed
Marlowe to deliver such bon mots as, "It was a blonde. A

blonde to make a bishop kick a hole in a stained glass window."

Humphrey Bogart, Robert Montgomery, and Dick Powell all took a turn bringing Marlowe to life on screen. Chandler worked on the screenplays of his own novels and collaborated on the script of *Double Indemnity* with Billy Wilder. An original screenplay, *The Blue Dahlia*, won an Edgar and an Academy Award nomination. Chandler insisted that he had to be drunk to complete it. The studio obliged, plied him with liquor and had doctors standing by to give him vitamin shots.

Raymond Chandler grew more acerbic with age. His sarcasm now spilled over into personal relationships; the help he hired generally lasted less than a week. When Cissy died in 1954 at 84, Chandler rewrote history to characterize her as the one light of his life, but he was genuinely bereft. He staged a suicide attempt two months later and continued drinking heavily. His alcoholism led to the pneumonia that became his last illness. Although he was lionized in London at the end of his life, only a handful of people saw Chandler buried at Mount Hope. But as Philip Marlowe pointed out, "What did it matter where you lay once you were dead? . . . You just slept the big sleep, not caring about the nastiness of how you died or where you fell."

The tall white marker that dominates this section of the cemetery belongs to the Fraternal Order of Eagles. The tablet on it was dedicated by a local aerie in 1925.

CYPRESS VIEW MAUSOLEUM

Cypress View Mausoleum adjoins Mount Hope, but you have to leave the latter and go around to Imperial Avenue via 36th Street to get to it. Founded 60 years ago, the mausoleum has artistic aspirations akin to those of Forest Lawn, but for our purposes only one celebrity. She lies in the Great Hall, on the left as you come into it, in a large bronze urn under glass. Inside are the remains of **Amelita Galli–Curci** (1882–1963); her married name is Samuels. Galli–Curci was the great coloratura soprano of opera's so-called Golden Age. Her recording of "Caro nome" from Verdi's *Rigoletto* was called by Harold Schonberg "probably the greatest performance ever put on a disk." Another critic described her as "an Italian girl with the face of Lucrezia Borgia and the heart of Dante's Beatrice, whose voice was like juggling golden apples."

All this from an unaffected, diminutive singer who started her musical studies as a pianist in Milan. It was only at the urging of the composer Pietro Mascagni, that she began vocal studies at the age of 16. Galli–Curci quickly gained fame in Italy and South America, but her American debut in 1916 with the Chicago Opera was unheralded. Perhaps this was to her advantage, for she captured and dazzled the unsuspecting audience and critics with the purity and beauty of her voice. In 1921 she made her Metropolitan Opera debut and continued there until 1930, when she retired from the stage for a career of concert tours.

Galli–Curci's career was cut short when a goiter impaired her voice in 1936. Surgery was required, and she attempted a brief but unsuccessful comeback. She accepted her fate philosophically and with humor, likening a mature coloratura to "a stout middle-aged actress playing Juliet. And why?" Her views on opera in general were just as

Cypress View entrance

forthright. She declared that opera was dying and filled with platitudes. Having little use for the "high culture" approach to her art, she felt that American opera was afraid of being corny when that was just what was needed. Galli–Curci spent her retirement years with her husband and piano accompanist, Homer Samuels, in southern California, where she fulfilled the "need to converse with and caress the trees."

Cypress View is proud of its five hundred works of art, most of which run to classical marble statuary, from nymphs to collections of puppies. There are also many religious stained-glass windows illustrating scenes from the life of Christ. The most satisfying windows are those with simple nature or nautical themes such as the one entitled "Crossing the Bar." But again it is a matter of taste. If you love Forest Lawn, you will be happy here.

GREENWOOD CEMETERY AND CATHEDRAL

Farther up Imperial Avenue is Greenwood Cemetery. Take a moment on your way to the mausoleum to look at the monuments. The Cathedral Mausoleum is at the back of the cemetery and toward the left from the main entrance. Dedicated in 1918, it has some beautiful windows. The one at the end of the short hall opposite the entrance shows a vivid garden with a blue mountain in the background and Southern California foliage.

The remains of another singer of renown are here. Madame **Ernestine Schumann–Heink** (1861–1936) is interred in the Corridor of Sunshine, not far from the entrance. Born in Prague, then part of Austria, the great contralto spoke only her mother's native Italian until she was 9. Her mother taught her to sing Italian arias by ear, and her training was furthered when she attended a convent school in Prague. There she was identified as a true contralto because of her ability to sing in the tenor clef. First encouraged by a French diva, she was nevertheless harshly rejected by the director of the Vienna Court Opera, who spared little in decrying her lack of looks, figure, and personality. Fortunately the royal opera at Dresden disagreed, and her career was launched.

After 20 years of singing in Europe, Schumann–Heink made her American debut in Chicago in 1898 and later returned with great success—enough to inspire her to become an American citizen in 1905. She was considered the preeminent Wagnarian contralto of her day and broadened her scope in America by starring in several movies for MGM. Married three times and the mother of eight, she was torn with divided loyalties during World War I, as she had sons fighting on both sides and lost one son on each. Nevertheless her efforts to support the American soldiers were tireless and earned her tremendous love and respect from the veterans. She was an honorary officer of the American Legion and had a VFW post named after her.

At one time very wealthy from her singing and her investments, Schumann–Heink's fortunes slipped badly due to her generosity and the Depression. Her voice declined as well and reduced her to singing simple German lieder, such as Brahms' "Lullaby" and "Silent Night." Her audience remained loyal, loving, and admiring. She had become the "beloved American mother" who addressed the country on Mother's Day only one year before her death urging American mothers to avoid bridge and to quit smoking.

Nine family members were gathered by her deathbed and heard her last words. "God bless him," she said, referring to the sender of a telegram which read: "Just a San Francisco urchin who heard you sing at Lotta's Fountain years ago sends his love and wants you to get well."

DIRECTIONS TO SAN DIEGO CEMETERIES: Take Interstate 805 to Market and 36th Streets. The main entrance of Mount Hope Cemetery is at 3751 Market Street. To reach Cypress View Mausoleum, turn left on Market Street out of Mount Hope Cemetery to 36th Street. Go left, then left again on Imperial Avenue to where the mausoleum is located. Greenwood Cemetery is farther up Imperial Avenue, close to Interstate 805.

SAN FRANCISCO BAY AREA

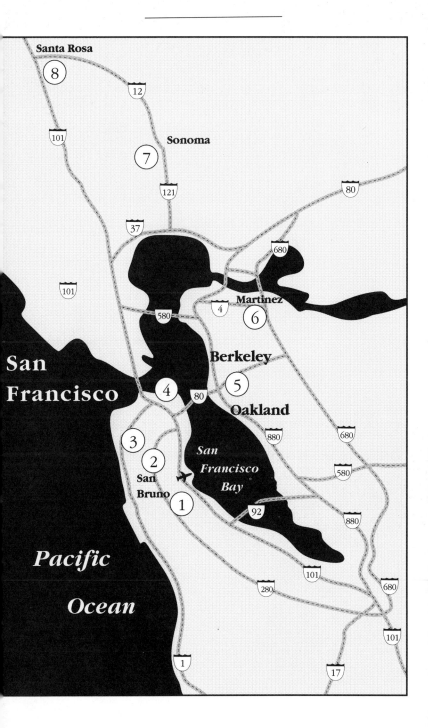

Military Cemeteries

The dead do not need to rise.
They are part of the earth now and
the earth can never be conquered
for the earth endures forever,
it will outlive all systems of tyranny.
Those who have entered it honorably . . .
have already achieved immortality.

— ERNEST HEMINGWAY

THE PRESIDIO

If you stand at the podium at the entrance of this historic military cemetery and look out over the rows and rows of markers, you will have the eerie sensation of addressing the dead, a sensation heightened by Lincoln's Gettysburg Address, carved on a large white marble wall behind you. But though the markers ranged before you may seem identical at first glance, there is considerable diversity here. When the Presidio was made a national cemetery in 1884, there were already about 240 people interred here. Before that it was an Indian burial ground.

Take the first road after the entrance all the way to your right. You will come to a section with a small sandstone statue of a young boy in uniform. It commemorates **Thomas Thompson** (d. March 25, 1899), killed in the Spanish–American War when he was 20. An inscription reads:

Sleep on, brave Tommy, and take thy rest.
God took thee home when he thought best.

Farther up in this area, on an island by itself, is a monument about five feet tall with a carving of an eagle. The shield in front of the eagle reads, "To the Unknown Soldier Dead," and the noble bird's expression seems anguished. One of the 408 buried under this Unknown Soldier's monument may be Captain **Abraham Johnston**, aide-de-camp to General Stephen Watts Kearny and known to historians as "Old Stove Bolts," who was killed in 1846 in the Battle of San Pasquale. When Johnson was exhumed for shipment home, his plain pine box was confused with those containing iron stove parts. A merchant who had ordered army surplus got considerably more than he bargained for. Worse than that, several hundred iron bolts received a military burial.

A number of generals are buried here as well. **Frederick Funston** (1865–1917) was about to be discharged after little action during the Spanish–American War when he was posted to the Philippines to put down an insurrection. After daringly capturing the insurgent leader, Emilio Aguinaldo, Funston was made a brigadier general. Also here is a comrade who did not fare as well. **William Rufus Shafter** (1835–1906) led an expedition in the Spanish–American War. His unit suffered many casualties, and Shafter was criticized for being unprepared and poorly equipped.

Thomas Thompson

Return to the cemetery entrance. In the first section is a statue showing a soldier in Civil War dress and holding a flag. It was dedicated to the "Regular Army and Navy Union of the United States of America by the Pacific Coast Garrisons, Memorial Day, 1897." The bas reliefs show cannons, swords, shields, eagles, a ship resembling the *Monitor*, and the Congressional Medal of Honor.

Although many of the markers in this section have simply a name on a shield with "USA" carved beneath and no dates or other particulars, a few give more information. The monument of **John Harrigan** (1851–1900) explains that he "died at Presidio, San Francisco, of disease contracted in the service of his country." **Charles Stulz**, "killed in action at Calumpit, PI, April 24, 1899, age 24 years and 4 months," rests under a monument with a circular bas relief of a fat dove with a leaf in its mouth.

In the Officer's Circle, halfway up, look for a monument that has been described as a "granite bathtub," in the center of its row. Complete with clawed feet like a lion's paws, the tub is the memorial of **William H. L. Barnes** (1834–1902). In the same row, nine markers in from the east side, is the plain marble marker of "Pauline C. Fryer, Union Spy." It does not give her full name — **Pauline Cushman Dickinson Fitchner Fryer** — or any other hint of the fascinating personality beneath it.

Born in 1833, Pauline received a scanty education and was recruited, at 18, for a variety show in New Orleans. Her career as an actress was disrupted by the Civil War in several ways. Her husband, musician Charles Dickinson, enlisted in the Northern army and died of dysentery in 1862. On stage in *The Seven Sisters*, she followed directions to drink a toast to the Southern cause and was expelled from the theater. But the perils of Pauline had only begun. She took a loyalty oath to the federal government and was the first woman commissioned by the army as a Union spy. Instructed not to carry any information, she was captured by the Confederates with military maps in hand and sentenced to be hung in 10 days. Pauline was saved, not by a hero, but because the Southern army forgot to take her along when they retreated from Shelbyville, Tennessee.

Cushman was acclaimed for her bravery and commended by Abraham Lincoln. Wearing her federal uniform, she lectured for many years; but nothing quite recaptured the glories of the war. She was widowed a second time, and then separated from her third husband, Jerry Fryer, in 1879. Her children died young. Amid hints of alcohol and narcotics, Pauline tried to supplement her income with

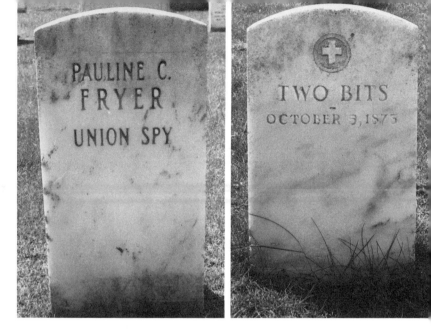

sewing. In 1893 she committed suicide and was given a semimilitary funeral.

In the left-hand section as you come out of the Officer's Circle, in the second full row on your left and 14 markers in, is a gravestone inscribed "Two Bits, October 5, 1875, Indian Guide." He was brought here from the cemetery at Fort Klamath, Oregon, when it was abandoned.

Before leaving, walk to the top and back of the cemetery for the most spectacular view of all. Looking down, you can see the bay, the Golden Gate Bridge, and the mountains beyond it. The rows and rows of old white markers in the foreground take on the poignance of time from this perspective.

PRESIDIO PET CEMETERY

Down in an area of the Presidio closer to the Golden Gate Bridge is an unexpected delight. In what other kind of cemetery would you find markers that read, "Our Knucklehead, Parakeet to Paradise"; "Faye, a loving dog of the Mange family"; or simply, "A G.I. Pet. He did his time."?

This is a tiny cemetery for the animals of military personnel living on the base. Although there are some granite and engraved headstones, most of the markers are homemade. In the front of the cemetery, instructions for burial are given: "Keep graves in line, using only space necessary and use decent headboards with name and type of pet. This is a military pet cemetery. Private expenses are high, and please stop stealing very little equipment available and my flowers. Thank you."

If you walk around, you may find a favorite epitaph or pet name. Here are some of the most appealing:

Mr. Bird, a canary

Bilbo Baggins, white mouse.

Skipper, Best damn dog we ever had. Bird dog, world traveler, 1965.

Here lie our beloved rats, Chocolate and Candy.

Trouble, 1956–1965. He was no trouble.

There are more serious monuments as well, evocative of other times and places. One carved stone reads:

Butch, beloved Chinese lion-dog, born Nanking, China 10 March 1947
Died 3 December 1963. General and Mrs. I. B. Keiser.

On the back of another marker is a bronze plate that reads:

Sooty. 1971–1986. Who would have thought the loss of one such very small Siamese cat would have created such a very large void?

After visiting this cemetery, that sense of loss is easy to understand. As you walk around the pet cemetery, you will be struck by the genuine emotion expressed here — everything repressed in the formal cemeteries is given free rein in this square of earth.

Family Pets at the Presidio

SAN BRUNO/GOLDEN GATE NATIONAL CEMETERY

In San Bruno, a naval cemetery, no matter what one's rank was in life, in death everybody is equal. The markers, from that of Admiral Nimitz to the lowliest steward, are of identical size and shape. Dominating the cemetery at the front is a hill with a white marble edifice and a flagpole. The flag is flown at half mast a half-hour before the first service of the day and kept there for a half-hour after the last service has ended.

The cemetery's most famous resident, Chester Nimitz, is at the junction of Circle and Plaza Drive, around the bend on Plaza where the first row starts, in C–1–1. The only difference between the marker inscribed to "Chester W. Nimitz, Fleet Admiral U.S. Navy (1885–1966)" and that of the other inhabitants is that it has five stars instead of the usual cross.

CHESTER WILLIAM NIMITZ *b. February 24, 1885, Fredericksburg, TX; d. February 20, 1966, Berkeley, CA.* Born over two hundred miles inland from the Gulf of Mexico, Chester Nimitz grew up poor in small-town Texas, his only sailing being rides in a prairie schooner and his only exposure to the sea being through his grandfather's stories of life in the merchant marine. Often he heard these stories in his grandfather's Nimitz Hotel, whose facade resembled a steamboat. Nimitz didn't even know of the existence of the Naval Academy. Attracted by the glamor of Army officers stationed near his home, Chester made West Point his first choice when he came to college age. Needing a free education, he accepted an appointment to Annapolis only because all the openings for West Point had been filled. In 1901 he journeyed to Annapolis and for the first time saw the ocean.

In 1905 Nimitz graduated seventh in a class of 114 cadets and was assigned to his first ship. He was fortunate to have graduated at a time of revival and recognition for the US Navy, stemming largely from its victories in the Spanish–American War. Although not a participant in the Great White Fleet's cruise around the world, Nimitz did have command of his own destroyer by the unheard-of age of 22. His excellent record saved him after he was court-martialed and reprimanded for running his ship aground. When promoted he skipped from ensign to lieutenant and was assigned to submarine duty.

Here Nimitz displayed his abilities as a quick study. He became a leading expert on diesel engines and recommended their installation in submarines. While on shore leave in Massachusetts, Nimitz met and then in 1913 mar-

ried Catherine Freeman. In starting a family both Chester and Catherine proved to be quick studies again, for the first of their four children was born 10 months later. While Nimitz continued to serve on both surface vessels and submarines, the family followed the familiar routine of shifting residences so common to the service. He rose rapidly through the ranks, being promoted to rear admiral by 1938. Along the way he was responsible for integrating aircraft carriers into the fleet and for developing the circular formation for fleet activities.

In 1941 Nimitz was offered the job of commander in chief, US Fleet, the second highest position in the Navy. Knowing he was junior to at least 50 other admirals, he turned the job down, fearing the resentment such a promotion might engender. By the end of the year, however, the Japanese had attacked Pearl Harbor, and the recently appointed Admiral Kimmel had to step down in undeserved disgrace. With the war on, Nimitz did not turn down his next offer, commander in chief of the Pacific Fleet.

Nimitz's position was not altogether an enviable one. He had to report to Admiral Ernest J. King, a man noted for his unsmiling severity, while at the same time he had to control the Pacific Fleet and its strong-minded leaders, such as "Bull" Halsey, "Terrible" Turner, and "Howling Mad" Smith. As if that weren't enough, Nimitz also had to contend with the enormous ego of his army counterpart, General Douglas MacArthur. That Nimitz was successful is a strong testimony to his organizational skills and his judgment of character. An even-tempered man who rarely swore, Nimitz was strict but also able to overlook minor indiscretions. He did not search out the limelight as did Halsey and MacArthur but rather preferred to maintain some semblance of a quiet, private life.

Nimitz's administrative philosophy was to assign out all work except that which only he could perform. Under his leadership the US Navy gradually regained control of the Pacific from the Japanese, starting with the Battle of the Coral Sea, moving on to the victory at Midway, and culminating with the Central Pacific offensive. As the war progressed, Nimitz was able to see the growing importance of air power and gave increased responsibility to his air commanders. In so doing he defied the traditionalists who wanted all control to rest with the surface fleet.

With victory secured, Nimitz was appointed to his life's goal: chief of naval operations, the highest job in the Navy. He served for two years, went on to work for the United Nations, and then finished his career with the Navy. Perhaps it was time, for he saw the military being overrun with civilians and increasingly manned with weapons which promised more civilian deaths. In his retirement in Berkeley he liked to walk through Tilden Park, where he planted yellow lupine as he went, pushing the seed into the ground with his cane. The trail has since been named The Nimitz Way.

The Admiral underwent back surgery at the age of 80 and never fully recovered his health. He slipped into a coma some months later and succumbed to pneumonia on a late February afternoon. He was laid to rest on his 81st birthday.

Prior to his death Admiral Nimitz made arrangements with fellow Pacific Fleet Admirals Raymond Spruance, Kelly Turner, and Charles Lockwood that they would all be buried with their wives near himself and Catherine. Perhaps the closest to Nimitz personally was Admiral **Raymond Spruance** (1886–1969), a Baltimore native who graduated a year behind Nimitz at the Academy. Spruance gained command of the Navy's forces at the Battle of Midway when Rear Admiral Fletcher's ship was disabled. His planes sank four Japanese carriers, thus providing the first major victory for US forces in the Pacific and striking a crippling blow from which the Japanese never recovered. Known for his coolness under pressure, there were those who felt him to be too cautious. Nevertheless he later served as Nimitz's right-hand man and then commanded the Navy's forces during the battles of Iwo Jima and Okinawa. In November of 1945 he was promoted to commander in chief of the Pacific Fleet to fill the vacancy left by Nimitz's ascension to CNO. After his retirement he served as ambassador to the Philippines from 1952 to 1955.

Richmond Kelly "Terrible" Turner (1885–1961) was born in Portland, Oregon, and graduated from the Naval Academy in 1908. He earned his wings at Pensacola in 1927. During World War II he was charged with organizing supplies, transports, and the initial movements of the amphibious forces. He was known for his intelligence, energy, and temper and was highly regarded for his tactical skills which played such an important role in winning back many of the Pacific Islands in 1944 and 1945.

Charles Lockwood (1890–1967) was commander of submarines in the Pacific Fleet during World War II. He was largely responsible for honing in on and correcting the problems that plagued US torpedos during the first two years of the war. As a tactician his deployment of submarines during the Battle of the Philippine Sea (better known as the Marianas Turkey Shoot because of the large number of Japanese planes shot down) helped greatly to foil the strategy of Admiral Ozawa. After the war he served as inspector general for Admiral Nimitz.

In the row behind Admiral Nimitz and to the right one marker in C–15A is a stone inscribed "Leo J. Ryan, Jr., U.S. Navy (1925–November 18, 1978)" with "N.C." under it. Congressman **Leo Ryan** was a character in the San Francisco tradition of flamboyance. A Nebraskan by birth, he began his career as a history and English teacher, then moved from the San Francisco City Council, to the California State Legislature, to the United States Congress. In the style of pioneer reporter Nellie Bly, Ryan often disguised his true identity to learn the inside story. Whether being carted off to Folsom Prison for a week in leg irons or living with a black family and teaching in Watts during the race riots of 1965, he thrived on dangerous situations.

Yet he did not approach his last congressional junket, to Guyana, with his usual zest. He was going as himself this time, both to investigate the strange world of Jim Jones and to secure the release of People's Temple members unable to break free from the religious colony. After several delays, Ryan and selected newsmen were allowed to tour the compound at Jonestown and stay overnight. They planned to leave the next morning taking 17 defectors, but the portents were bad. While still at Jonestown, Ryan nearly had his throat cut by a Temple member trying to prove himself.

The convoy finally left for a nearby airfield but was ominously followed by a truck from the compound. Before the group could board the plane, Leo Ryan and three reporters were gunned down fatally by Temple "angels." Nine other people were injured in the attack. Hearing the news, Jim

Jones finally had the excuse for the mass suicide he had played at several times. Over the next few hours he induced 912 of his spiritual children to join him in death. This second assault was not discovered until the bodies from the congressional trip had been returned to California.

In his will, Leo Ryan stated that he wanted the "Navy Hymn" played at his funeral and pointed out that he had always liked H. L. Mencken's epitaph: "When I depart this vale of tears, if you have some thought to please my ghost, forgive some sinners and wink your eye at some homely girl."

Percy Kilbride (1888–1964), a private in Company B, 317th Infantry, 80th Division, World War I, is deep in Section 2–B. You can locate him by finding the section in the 3700s; his marker is closest to the chain-link fence by the freeway. Kilbride is best known as Pa Kettle in the seven Ma and Pa Kettle movies he made with Marjorie Main between 1947 and 1956. In them he played a hard-boiled farmer whose pants were held up by a length of rope. Kilbride's placement right beside the freeway seems ironic. He was hit by a car crossing a street and died of his injuries two months later.

Because feelings have run so high in San Francisco concerning **Dan White**, the cemetery does not want his location given out. His marker, identical to the thousands of others here, has on it the inscription: "Daniel J. White (1926–October 21, 1985), Sgt. U.S. Army, Vietnam." Unlike some religious burial grounds, military cemeteries do not discriminate against murderers or suicides. If you have been honorably discharged from the service, as Dan White was with three medals, there will be a space for you here.

As one of 16 children, Dan White grew up competitive and strait-laced. After serving in Vietnam as a paratrooper, he joined the San Francisco police force in 1969 and switched to the fire department in 1973. Actions considered "impulsive" by the police department earned him meritorious awards for bravery as a fireman. In 1977 he ran for the San Francisco Board of Supervisors on a platform that attacked "splinter groups of radicals, social deviates, incorrigibles." White won, but the following year he resigned, saying that he could not afford to live on the $9,600 stipend he received.

It was when he tried to rescind his resignation a short time later that the trouble occurred. Fellow Supervisor Harvey Milk, who was gay, was adamantly opposed to White's return, as was a vocal faction from White's own district. On the day that Mayor George Moscone was going

Golden Gate Cemetery

to announce White's replacement, the Vietnam veteran, carrying a .38-caliber revolver, entered city hall through the basement and shot Milk and Moscone to death.

White's defense was based on a plea of diminished capacity, in part invoking the "Twinkie defense"—that Dan White was a junk-food addict whose senses had become addled by too much sugar. He served five years in Soledad State Prison, a sentence many considered too light, on a conviction of voluntary manslaughter. His early release from jail may have upset White as much as it did his detractors. Less than two years later, he entered his garage, hooked up a rubber hose to his car's exhaust pipe, and ended his life with carbon monoxide.

DIRECTIONS TO THE PRESIDIO: The Presidio is located in San Francisco at the entrance to the Golden Gate Bridge and can be reached by driving north on Route 101. Inside the Presidio, turn left on Lincoln Boulevard to reach the cemetery's main entrance.

DIRECTIONS TO SAN BRUNO/GOLDEN GATE NATIONAL CEMETERY: Drive south from San Francisco on Route 101 to San Bruno. The cemetery is close to the freeway with the main entrance on Sneath Lane.

Mission Dolores

*There are only two or three human
stories, and they go on repeating
themselves as fiercely as if they
had never happened before.*

— WILLA CATHER

MISSION SAN FRANCISCO DE ASSISI, located at Dolores and
16th Streets, is not the grand basilica on the corner with
the pale beige spires and carvings. It is the simple white-
stucco mission with a tiled roof next door. Sixth in the
chain of 21 missions along the El Camino Real, it was
formally dedicated in October 1776. The current building,
begun in 1782, is the oldest in San Francisco and survived
the 1906 Earthquake.

To get to the burial ground, you must enter through the
mission's bookstore and go into the chapel on your right.
The chapel houses an appealing collection of carved, polychromed statues of saints and early priests; the roof and
beams are painted gray, cream, and rust in a zigzag design.
There are several graves here as well. In the back of the
church under a small cement plate is **William Alexander
Leidesdorff** (1810–1848). Leidesdorff, a seaman of Danish
and West Indian parentage, arrived in Spanish California in
1839 and became a naturalized Mexican citizen in order to
obtain a land grant. Before his premature death at 38, he
was the treasurer of San Francisco, handling municipal
assets of $4,476 in 1847.

In the front of the chapel is the grave of Lieutenant **Don
José Joaquin Moraga** (d. July 13, 1785), interred in the
church April 8, 1791. Along with Juan Bautista Anza and
Junípero Serra, Moraga was one of the founders of Mission
Dolores.

The cemetery, to your left and outside, is filled with
roses and is a pleasant place to wander. Most of the names

in it are Irish; half of the women are named Bridget. Although he is buried at Carmel and not here, there is a large statue of Junípero Serra, "Founder and first president of the California missions, 1713–1784."

We will be making a circular tour, so take your first left onto the path that runs parallel to the chapel. As you start down the path, the first monument of note you will see is the one enclosed by a metal crib. It is "Sacred to the memory of the late deceased James Sullivan who died by the hands of the V. C. May 31, 1856, age 45 years." Also inscribed on it is, "Remember not, O Lord, our offenses nor those of our parents. Neither take thou vengeance of our sins." The "V. C." on the marker does not refer to the Viet Cong. It stands for Vigilante Committee, a group of citizens who banded together to combat lawlessness in the lawless San Francisco of the 1850s. Like similar groups, it got quickly out of hand. This victim, **James "Yankee" Sullivan**, was executed either for inventing a new device to stuff a ballot box or for stealing a horse.

Continuing down the path, you will next see the tall stele of Del Capitan **Luis Antonio Argüello** (1784–1830), first governor of Alta California. Halfway up the stele there is a floral decoration and cross with another cross on the top.

Catty-corner to the Argüello stone is a marker with a weeping willow and two steles. It is the family monument of **Athalie Baudichon**, who, with his children **Charles** and **Blanche**, was a victim of the explosion of the steamboat *Jenny Lind*, April 11, 1853. The inscription is in French, one of very few in the garden.

In the second full garden to your right is **Don Francisco de Haro** (d. 1849), first *algonde* (mayor) of San Francisco, 1835.

At the end close to the street are several markers with Victorian sentiments. The stone to **Bridget Flynn** (d. 1863) shows a woman kneeling at a cross amid small trees and grass in bas relief and reads:

> The mortal coil is broken,
> But her soul is in the skies.
> And in the Spring Eternal
> The body now shall lie.

Mary Farrell, who died in 1880 at 5 years of age, has a small angelic bas relief and the inscription:

> Weep not for me, my parents
> When you stand around my grave.
> Think where I've gone.
> Prepare to follow me.

Starting back up the other side of the garden, you will see the tomb of **James P. Casey** which reads, "Sacred to the memory of James P. Casey who departed this life May 22, 1856 age 27 years. May God forgive my persecutors." Casey's marble plaque appears to have been added to a brownstone monument belonging to a fire-engine company. It has fire hats in each corner and downturned torches crisscrossed on the end. Casey was also a victim of the VC, but in his case his crime is known. Before coming west and serving as a member of the San Francisco Board of Supervisors, Casey had served one and a half years in Sing Sing prison in New York for larceny. When a newspaper editor, James King of William, dredged up the old scandal, an annoyed Casey shot him in the chest. King actually died from the unsterile sponge used to plug the bullet hole, but Casey was taken out of jail by the Vigilante Committee, given a "trial," and hanged.

Across from him is another fireman's monument, this one commemorating "Thomas Murray who lost his life in the discharge of duty as a fireman on the night of January 28, 1855, age 26 years." On top of the monument is a fireman's belt, ladder, and torches, and on the bottom a wonderful tangle of hoses, fire horns, and tassels.

Thomas Murray

Also in this section is the Grotto, a Lourdes shrine with a statue of Mary in a high niche and a kneeling figure to the left. The worshipper's face is so badly marked that she looks like a smallpox victim. The shrine is dedicated to "The Forgotten Dead," people whose simple wooden crosses had deteriorated and who, when the cemetery was consolidated to its present size, were replaced under the Grotto.

Walking back, look toward your left for a marble monument whose bas relief shows a man and a woman weeping beside a stand with an urn. "Sacred to the memory of Charles Cora, a native of Italy, who died May 22, 1856, age 40 years." **Charles Cora** died on the same date and at the same hands as James P. Casey, but his crime was different. One evening at the theater, US Marshal William H. Richardson and his wife were accidently seated next to Cora and his mistress, Arabella. When Cora spoke to them, Mrs. Richardson took umbrage. Several nights later, Richardson invited Cora to step outside the Blue Wing Saloon and, according to some witnesses, threatened him with a knife. Cora shot him to death.

Cora's first trial ended with a hung jury, but while he was incarcerated awaiting a second trial, the VC came for James P. Casey. As an afterthought, they returned for Cora and hung him too.

Buried on top of Cora is **Arabella**, who died in 1862 at age 35. Belle, as she was nicknamed, was a minister's daughter from New Orleans who owned a chain of expensive whorehouses. It is fitting that, having strayed from her roots, in death she eschewed the missionary position.

The nearby statue of an Indian woman is labeled "**Tekakwitha**, Lily of the Mohawks." It is mounted on a marble stele which says, "In memory of our faithful Indians." Since the cemetery's inception, 5,515 Indians have been buried here in unmarked graves.

In the center garden is an elaborate stone about five feet tall whose bas relief shows a woman looking at a marker with a cross in a cemetery. At the top are stylized clouds with an angel face. The monument is called "The Last Tribute of Love" and is in memory of **Annia Coffey**, "a native of Ireland who departed this life November 20, 1866, age 34 years":

> I go from thee,
> God only knows how I have shuddered thus to tread
> The lone and shadowed way.
> Faith tells me that I soon may know the joys the blessed find.
> And yet I falter while I cast
> A lingering look behind.

Annia Coffey

In the back of the garden, on the opposite side from where you entered, is an interesting in-ground slab with the names of the family members each inset on a separate metal cross. Also here is a bas relief which is not a religious scene but a broken mast. Its inscription reads: "Sacred to the memory of **William Brodrick**, born in London, England, died November 9, 1860, age 30 years."

DIRECTIONS TO MISSION DOLORES: From the center of San Francisco, take Market Street north to 16th Street. Make a right and go two blocks to Dolores Street where the mission is located.

Murphy grave

Cypress Lawn

"Rosebud."

Citizen Kane — ORSON WELLES

CEMETERIES HAVE TRADITIONALLY been placed outside city limits — a fact that did not occur to early San Franciscans until they realized their dead forebears were taking up valuable real estate. In 1902 city fathers passed a law forbidding further burials within city limits and in 1914 issued eviction notices to Laurel Hill Cemetery at Lone Mountain and several others. Only those interred at Mission Dolores and the National Cemetery in the Presidio were exempt. The exhumation order was successfully fought by preservationists until 1940, when removal of the bodies from Laurel Hill began. Many of them were brought here.

The founders of Cypress Lawn were quick to see the handwriting on the wall and started the cemetery in nearby Colma in 1892. Although other burial grounds were being established in Colma at the same time, Cypress Lawn was the place of choice for the wealthy and esteemed. With its sloping lawns, duck pond, and castlelike entrance gates, the cemetery resembled a country estate, and early San Franciscans treated it as a park. Trolley cars would post signs telling when the red gum trees were in bloom. As you come into the cemetery area of Colma from San Francisco, the older section will be on your left off Hillside Boulevard. Go past the mausoleum and park on the main road where the monuments begin.

The first collection of markers are not those of famous people but are wonderful examples of Victorian cemetery art, erected in an era when stone manifestations of grief were de rigueur. On your right is the **Pope** mausoleum with a classic window showing an angel, her eyes shut and one hand raised; three infant angels hover around her head. Inside the mausoleum is a triple fountain of marble figures. The charming, larger-than-life-sized angel just down the road, complete even to the lace on her robe and the tasseled pillow on which her foot rests, belongs to **John Barton** (1813–1900). Nearby on a granite mattress is **George Henry Sanderson** (1824–1893) whose stone bears the epitaph, "God's finger touched him and he slept."

At the first corner on your right is a lovely Art Nouveau figure of a woman, arms raised above her head, head cast to one side with a willful expression. It belongs to **Thomas Valentine** (d. 1896) and **Jenny A. Valentine** (d. 1916). Between the names is the Hebrew word *Mizpah* (The Lord watch between me and thee while we are absent one from another.) Across the road is the tall stele of **Jefferson G. James** (1829–1910), which bears his cameo resembling a penny.

Turning right at the corner, you will find a surprising treasure inside the Hobart mausoleum — a marble sculpture of a young teenager, hair resting simply on her shoulders, holding the sides of her dress as if she is about to curtsey. Inside the mausoleum are some famous San Francisco surnames, including **Baldwin** and **Crocker**.

On the corner, in the plain mausoleum to your left, is **Rudolph Spreckels** (1872–1958). The youngest son of Sugar King Claus Spreckels, Rudolph was also the family rebel. When the asthmatic Rudolph was 17, his father offered him an education at Yale, a trip around the world, or a place in the sugar business. Young Rudolph chose the last, later breaking with his father and amassing enough of a fortune himself to retire at 26. Spreckels later turned on his class by financing a San Francisco graft investigation and declaring himself a pacifist during World War I. He steadfastly squelched attempts to make him an ambassador to Germany or a US senator. After losing his fortune during the Depression, he lived modestly in San Mateo, dying in a three-room apartment.

The impressive bronze statue next to Spreckels is that of

A	Rudolph Spreckels, Charles De Young	H	Arthur Brown
B	Hearst Family	J	Lillie Hitchcock Coit
C	James Clair Flood	K	Lefty O'Doul, George Inwood
D	E. J. "Lucky" Baldwin	L	Crocker Family
E	Thomas Oliver Larkin	M	Louis P. Drexler
F	Arthur Rogers	N	William Sharon
G	Claus Spreckels	O	Lincoln Steffens
		P	Gertrude Atherton

Cypress Lawn

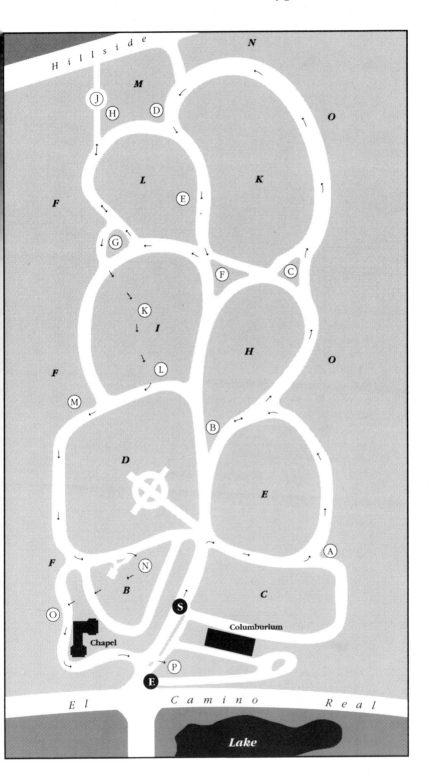

Charles De Young (1845–1880). Charles and his brother, Michael, came from France and borrowed $20 from their landlord to launch the *Chronicle* in 1865. From a modest theater playbill, it ballooned into a nineteenth-century *National Enquirer*. Not everyone enjoyed this new form of entertainment, however. Charles was slapped with libel suits, beaten with a cane, and bludgeoned with a pistol. When Baptist minister Isaac Kalloch ran for mayor against the *Chronicle*'s candidate, De Young dredged up an adulterous affair which the clergyman had at 19. Kalloch counterattacked from the pulpit, accusing Mother De Young of running a whorehouse and calling the brothers "hyenas of society."

De Young waited outside Kalloch's church, then shot the preacher twice when he came out. He was captured when the carriage in which he was fleeing overturned. Kalloch survived his wounds and was elected mayor out of sympathy. De Young, out on bail, continued his journalistic attacks until the minister's son broke into the newspaper office and killed him six months later. In an interesting verdict, the younger Kalloch was acquitted on self-defense. As one of the jurors explained, "I would have done the same thing myself."

Going up the road between Sections G and E, look out on your right for another wonderful angel, standing on a pile of flower-covered rocks. One of her arms is broken off, the other is holding a horn. It is the memorial of **J. K. C. Hobbs** (1846–1902). In the ground is a standing marble pillow with the names of two of the family's children. If you look toward the center of Section E, you will see a large white pyramid to **Carroll Cook** (1855–1915) and his wife **Lena** (1857–1899). A metal plate on the pyramid points out "Other wives and mothers have done well but she excelled them all."

At the corner of Sections E and H is the massive Greek-columned mausoleum to the **Hearst** family. A plain iron door divides the glass into triangles. The family name was removed from the outside of the mausoleum during the 1970s after the kidnapping of Patti Hearst, although it appears inside. **George Hearst** (1820–1891) was the first family member interred here. Although he made a fortune locating silver and copper mines in the West, were it not for his wife and son he would be no more famous than fellow Comstock Lode barons James Flood or James G. Fair. Unpretentious and nearly illiterate, Hearst bought the seat in the US Senate in 1887 which he had held, filling a vacancy, the year before.

CHAS de YOUNG

When he died in Washington, DC, of what the *San Francisco Examiner* described as "a complication of diseases, resulting primarily from a serious derangement of the bowels," George Hearst was warmly eulogized. President and Mrs. Benjamin Harrison attended his funeral along with many others, then the body was shipped west for burial. In San Francisco the *Examiner* sent a floral tribute that was a reproduction of its front page; despite the rain, 15,000 San Franciscans stood and watched the funeral procession make its way to Cypress Lawn.

Phoebe Apperson (1842–1919) was tiny, pretty, and refined when, at 19, she eloped with the grizzled roughneck. Whether it was his fortune or the chance for greater adventure that drew her is unclear; perhaps she saw something else in George Hearst—his kindness and his affection for humanity—which her parents did not. But she did not lower her own standards to meet his. Once established in San Francisco, she became involved in cultural projects, traveled back and forth to Europe with young Willie, and eventually adopted the University of California at Berkeley as her own. Donating buildings and endowing scholarships to deserving students made up for a certain disappointment in her own son's colorful lifestyle. Phoebe Apperson Hearst died after suffering from the influenza which claimed so many lives at the end of World War I. She did not live to see her son's fantasy, San Simeon.

WILLIAM RANDOLPH HEARST *b. April 29, 1863, San Francisco; d. August 14, 1951, Los Angeles.* Unlike the scornful treatment accorded Charles Foster Kane after his death in *Citizen Kane*, William Randolph Hearst received full honors. An editorial cartoon showed the Statue of Liberty wearing a black armband and collapsed in a sorrowful swoon. Earl Warren, Douglas MacArthur, and Bernard Baruch were honorary pallbearers. Wearing a dark suit and a tie with the family crest (instead of the wrinkled green suits and screaming hand-painted ties he favored), Hearst lay in state while several thousand San Franciscans filed by. The only one close to the deceased who was not invited to the funeral was his mistress of 32 years, Marion Davies.

That would have infuriated him. For 88 years Hearst had things exactly as he pleased. As a young child Willie was precocious but given to pranks such as locking himself in his room, lighting red flares to shine under the door, and yelling, "Fire!" It was a method he used to keep those closest to him off balance and thus maintain control. His high-spirited attacks on Harvard University while a student there kept him the focus of attention, though they culminated in his expulsion in his junior year for sending personalized chamber pots to each of his professors.

Willie spent the following year in New York City working as a reporter on Joseph Pulitzer's *World*, then persuaded his father to give him the *San Francisco Examiner*. His father was reluctant. The *Examiner* was a moribund 8-page sheet which George Hearst had bought as a political organ to promote himself for the Senate and which had done its job. Nevertheless he turned the sickly sheet over to his son. William Randolph Hearst published his maiden edition on February 4, 1887.

Hearst's personal audacity was now reflected in his newspaper. News was judged by the standard of what *might* have happened. The paper promised all the "tragedies and romance of life in every edition" and did its best to provide just that, with screaming headlines about murders, scandals, and municipal incompetence. When gore was scarce, the paper created human-interest stories, in one case floating couples over the city to be married in hot-air balloons. Like his father, Hearst championed the cause of the common man—but whether from a love of humanity or an appetite for controversy, who could say?

In any case, Hearst could not rest until he defeated his mentor, Pulitzer. He bought a modest New York paper, the *Journal*, in 1895, then lowered its price to a penny and plundered the staff of Pulitzer's *World* for himself. To imagine the *Journal*'s impact by 1898, one would have to picture the contents of the *New York Post* with the political clout of the *New York Times*—and triple it. The *Journal* successfully fought Consolidated Gas to achieve a rollback of its usurious rates and campaigned for a living wage and a 10-hour day for workers.

As history is now aware, Hearst declared war on Spain a full three months before Congress and slanted enough stories against the "Spanish butchers" to achieve it in April 1898. His power was frightening. Lincoln Steffens pointed out from the opposite coast that, "Mr. Hearst has waged as many good fights as any reformer I know. There isn't room even for a list of the good things Mr. Hearst has done or tried to do. There isn't room either for a list of the bad, the small things he has done; the scandals he has published, the individuals he has made to suffer beyond their deserts."

As the century rolled over, Hearst turned his energies to politics and marriage. The day before his 40th birthday, he married his companion of five years, 21-year-old Millicent Willson. Millicent, the daughter of a vaudeville performer and a chorine herself, quickly developed a sense of what the name Hearst should mean. Despite his later pleas for a divorce, she hung onto it tenaciously, producing five sons who were raised jointly between Millicent in New York and grandmother Phoebe in California.

The year he was married, Hearst was elected to Congress from New York and served to mixed reviews. He ran unsuccessfully for mayor of New York City in 1905 and 1909, and for governor in 1906. His real goal, however, was the presidency—a logical choice for someone who could buy almost anything else. With the zeal of Citizen Kane building an opera house for his wife Susan and forcing her to sing despite ridicule, Hearst pursued the presidential nomination in 1904, 1908, and 1912. The only reason the Democrats did not openly laugh was because he already owned nine papers and commanded millions of votes.

In 1917 Hearst's life turned another corner. He plucked young Marion Davies out of Ziegfeld's Follies and sent her to acting school. Already drawn himself to the possibilities of film, he determined to make her his star. He never did, but Marion's sparkling personality filled his life with unsuspected pleasures and filled their California homes with friends and excitement. Never good at small talk, Hearst was too used to giving orders to understand the give-and-take of friendship. His intense devotion to Marion brought him friends as a by-product and a companionship he never could have anticipated. Unable to give her the one thing she craved—marriage—he lavished everything else on her. In turn she repaid him emotionally, and even financially in 1937 during a downswing in his empire.

Part of Hearst's financial troubles then were brought on by his extravagant purchases and homes. San Simeon was only one of Hearst's estates in California, but he lavished $30 million on what he modestly called "the ranch." Perhaps in tribute to his mother and their early trips, he scoured Europe for priceless works of art and brought them back. And San Simeon was in a constant state of alteration at the whim of Marion or himself. Yet it was not a cozy place. In the last years of his life Hearst retreated from his castle/theater/museum/spa. He died of a brain hemorrhage in the pink stucco mansion in Los Angeles which he had built for Marion.

As you come up to the crossroads you will see a very pretty angel on the **Frederik C. C. Anderson** (1865–1906) monument.

Across the way on its own island sits the **Flood** mausoleum, flanked by two tall palm trees. The structure is plain in design but impressive in size. Before he became one of the wealthiest men in California, **James Clair Flood** (1826–1889) was known as the best bartender on the coast. With his partner in San Francisco's Auction Lunch, William O'Brien, Flood bought up claims which the miners who

James Clair Flood

came there for lunch believed were exhausted and eventually bought into the Comstock Lode. Each of the partners escaped with $20 million after stock purchases. Flood went on to found the Nevada Bank in 1876, but he was never able to serve whiskey, as he had boasted he would, over the counters of the rival Bank of California.

Across from Flood are an interesting collection of mausoleums. That of **William Prentice Morgan** (1838–1902) has a wonderful ironwork gate with an angelic figure of aged bronze showing her hair flying and eyes shut. Next to it is **Charles G. Lathrop**'s mausoleum, with a beautifully intricate curved door, a lily design over glass. The marble angel to the memory of **Lucy Seymour** (1843–1884), has the verse,

> Angels ever bright and fair.
> Take oh! take her to your care.

Also in this area is the mausoleum of **Elias Jackson "Lucky" Baldwin** (1828–1909). It has a charming stained-glass window showing an angel with permed hair. According to legend, Baldwin, already a wealthy man, directed his lawyer to sell some mining stock but forgot to give him the key to his lock box, where the certificates were stored. By the time he returned from an extended cruise, the mine had come in, and he was worth two million dollars more than when he left.

Opinion is divided as to whether Baldwin was a bon vivant, living a strange and wonderful life, or simply a lecherous tightwad. He faced numerous lawsuits over unpaid debts and attracted paternity hearings like lint to his black-velvet suits — when he was 60, his defense in one case was that the mother, half his age, was too old and ugly for him to have gotten involved with. His lasting gift to California was the Santa Anita racetrack.

William Matson (1840–1917) has a large four-columned monument with an M worked into the ironwork of the windows. When Matson arrived in San Francisco, the effects of the Gold Rush were still being felt. Housing under a canvas shelter with four redwood posts cost $800 a month. Everyone was up in the gold fields, with no one left to do laundry. When people began shipping their good clothes to China and Hawaii to be cleaned, the fledgling Matson Lines started doing a booming business. (It took three months for the laundry to come back clean.)

To his left is the very impressive monument of **Thomas Oliver Larkin** (1802–1858), inscribed "First and only U.S. Consul to California, 1844–1846, Monterey." The monument shows an angel kneeling, looking down at Larkin's sculpted cameo with a huge palm in her hand. Larkin was a shrewd Yankee who had settled in Mexican California when he was made "Consul." During the subsequent American takeover, he worked hard to ease the transition.

The **Niebaum** mausoleum next to Larkin is interesting for its delicate filigree design work, emphasizing the arched doorway and doors bearing his name.

The monument on the small island, that of **Arthur Rogers** (1848–1902), is completely under the Egyptian spell. Outside are two sphinxes. Four mummylike heads decorate its ironwork door, and there is also the symbol of spread wings with a circle and asps.

Two angels complete this part of the tour. The kneeling angel across the way from the Rogers memorial is inscribed "In memory of my beloved sister **Jenny Roosevelt Pool**, Eternal Rest." The **Dolbeer** mausoleum has a beautiful oversized door with an angel, her hands flat against it, looking sorrowfully to one side.

If you walk into the interior of Section I, you will find a fairly tall marker to "**George**, Husband of Susan and Lydia E. **Inwood**, Fell asleep in Jesus May 4, 1901, age 88 years." The inscription that follows is startling:

> My experience in life's trials and faith. Take ye heed everyone of his neighbor and trust ye not in any brother. Jer. 9:15. By doing this I have been defrauded out of thousands of dollars by the wicked that borrowed and payeth not again. Psalms. 37:21. The bands of the wicked have robbed me but I have not forgotten thy law. Psalms 119:61. They have done it for greedy filthy lucre's sake. I Tim. 33, Titus 1:7–11. The

Jenny Roosevelt Pool

congregation of the hypocrite shall be desolate. Job 15:34. The Lord will abhor the man handling the word of God deceitfully. II Cor. 4:2. The wicked shall be brought to the grave and remain in the tomb. Job 21:32. For the love of money is the root of all evil. I Tim. 6:10. Woe unto him that increaseth that which is not his. Heb. 2:6.

Also in this section, but with a totally different epitaph, is **Lefty O'Doul** (1897–1969), under an upright brown marble marker with white bat and ball on it. His inscriptions include: "The man in the green suit," and "He was here at a good time, and had a good time while he was here," and "Record 254 hits 1929 season, National League Batting Champion, Philadelphia Phillies .398 1929, Brooklyn Dodgers .368 1932." Engraved on the ball is .349, his lifetime batting average. As his epitaph attests, O'Doul was a good-natured soul. He started his career as a pitcher but soon recognized that his popularity with the batters did not stem from his personality. Returning to the minors, he took up what must have seemed to be the easy art of hitting and turned himself into an outfielder. And in fact he did make hitting seem easy. One year after his return to the majors at age 31 he won the batting championship. He finished his career with the Giants in 1933.

In the minors O'Doul was tremendously popular with children. Loading his pockets with baseballs, he would throw them to the young fans when he reached left field. In an effort to cut down on this daily expense, the owner of the San Francisco Seals, O'Doul's minor-league team, initiated Kid's Day, which featured O'Doul, with four sacks of balls, standing on the grandstand roof above 10,000 screaming children. He pitched the balls down until the sacks were empty and he could no longer lift his arm.

After his retirement as a player, O'Doul returned to the Seals as a manager, where he helped to develop Joe DiMaggio. Later he served as a batting coach and worked with Willie McCovey before he rose to stardom in the majors. O'Doul traveled often to Japan, where he noticed and encouraged the Japanese enthusiasm for baseball and upon his return did much to inform the American public of baseball's popularity in that country. In San Francisco O'Doul was a well-loved celebrity who operated a restaurant bearing his name.

Finally in Section I is the intriguing monument of **Edward H. Hammer** (1825–1885) and **Mary A. Hammer** (1843–1876). It shows his cameo, eyes oddly raised with one going halfway into his head, as if trying to see the bust of the young woman above him. Their name is spelled out in twigs.

The immense mausoleum of **Claus Spreckels** (1828–1908), father of Rudolph, sits on its own island. Inside in the center is a marble statue of four children holding up an urn. Spreckels began as an immigrant grocer in San Francisco. To counteract high sugar prices he built a sugar-beet refinery to process the local crop. When Hawaii was annexed in 1876, he went out there to make a deal. Legend has it that he won Maui in a poker game with the King of Hawaii. In any case, it was the start of his reign as Sugar King. When Claus died of pneumonia, even his rebellious son Rudolph was at his side. Two other sons succeeded in having Rudolph disinherited, however.

The large white sarcophagus of **Arthur Page Brown** (1859–1896) is so overgrown with evergreens and trees on each side that only part of his name and the word "ARCHITECT" under it emerge. Brown, who spent three years under the tutelage of Stanford White's firm, McKim, Mead, and White, helped shape the face of San Francisco. He originally established his own firm in New York, but presently looked for a new city to conquer. The opportunity came in 1888 when Mrs. Charles Crocker, widow of the president of the Southern Pacific Railway, invited Brown to design a fitting mausoleum for her husband in Mountain View Cemetery in Oakland.

A number of Brown's subsequent buildings were lost in the Earthquake of 1906, but Trinity Episcopal Church, modeled on Durham Cathedral in England, survived, as did the Swedenborgian Church of the New Jerusalem. Perhaps Brown's most ambitious project was the Ferry Building at the harbor, a gray Colusa sandstone structure with a 240-foot Spanish tower and Roman Revival pavilion. Brown, who was better at designing structures than actually supervising their construction, was involved in the last stages of the ferry terminal when the carriage in which he was riding plunged off a 15-foot bridge. The new carriage horse, a former steeplechaser, had bolted wildly and crushed Brown when they landed.

For three and a half months Brown, mangled and unable to whisper a coherent sentence, lay dying in his Burlingame home. Unable to move at all without excruciating pain, the architect finally succumbed. William Crocker and James D. Phelan helped carry him to his final rest.

In the small round circle at the back between Sections M and F is the **Hitchcock** mausoleum. The family's most famous member, **Lillie Hitchcock Coit** (1843–1929), is no doubt disappointed by the structure's lack of fire-fighting decoration. Lillie, who at 15 was the mascot of the Knickerbocker Engine Company 5, had a lifelong love affair with

Guarding the Newhalls

conflagration. As a debutante and young matron, she would rush away from dances, weddings, and funerals to watch the latest fire. When she left part of her fortune to San Francisco, the grateful city erected Coit Tower in her memory. The fact that the top looks like a fire-hose nozzle is not accidental.

Also in the back is the Children's Section, a place too sad to spend much time in. One marker shows a cat playing with a ball of yarn. There are many lambs, hearts, and cherubs back here.

Along the road between Sections F and I is the white marble monument of **Albert Gallatin**, showing a bas relief of a maiden looking down at her oil lamp. It no doubt relates to the biblical parable of the wise and foolish virgins, those who had their lamps trimmed and ready for the master's coming, and those who didn't. On either side of the maiden is a long stone bench.

Farther down in Section I are two enormously appealing lions, heads on their paws. One has a cranky expression, as if he is doing what he's supposed to but not enjoying it. The other, open mouthed, looks more fierce and less resigned. They are guarding the monument of **H. M. Newhall** (1825–1882).

At the corner where Sections F, D, and I meet is a seated woman, so large as to be startling. In her hands she holds two-foot-long keys. The statue is the monument of **Louis P. Drexler** (1836–1899) and **Elise A. Drexler** (1866–1951).

If you veer to your left temporarily in front of Section I, you will reach the large mausoleum of the **Crocker** family, although Charles Crocker, the patriarch, is buried in Mountain View. The bronze door shows an angel with an enigmatic expression. Her eyes are closed; her left hand rests against her face, her right hand holds a flower. In the shadow of Crocker is a flat gray mound the size of a twin-bed mattress. Beneath it rest **Grace** and **H. Noble** (1844–1929), founders of Cypress Lawn Memorial Park.

Returning to the road along Section F, at the next intersection, you will find the wonderful monument of **Lloyd Tevis** (1824–1899) and his family. The monument has a commanding bronze figure of an angel, hands placed in restraint. On either side are two male angels in shallow bas relief. The circular wording reads, "I will lay me down in peace and take my rest."

Lincoln Steffens (1866–1936) is on your right in a small vault, set halfway into the ground. His plain structure, with just the name Steffens on it, does not give a fair picture of the man beneath. A journalist and native son of San Francisco like William Randolph Hearst, Steffens came from a pioneer family sufficiently prosperous for him to grow up in the Victorian mansion in Sacramento which later became the Governor's Mansion, and to explore the area on horseback, as described in *The Autobiography of Lincoln Steffens* (1931). His memoir also records his disappointment with his education at the University of California and his journalistic career.

Steffens, a slender figure with rimless glasses, a Van Dyke beard, and bangs, returned from Europe in 1892 to become a reporter on the *New York Evening Post*. He covered the Wall Street Panic of 1893 and city politics, gradually developing the philosophy that municipal graft and corruption were not isolated acts of wicked politicians but developed from the system itself, whether in New York, Chicago, or Paris. As the muckraking era got into full swing, Steffens left newspaper journalism to write magazine pieces. These were collected in *The Shame of the Cities* (1904).

Although he traveled everywhere news was breaking, Steffens' real gift was as a consummate interviewer, able to make people confide in him the truth as they understood it. Nonjudgmental, he made friends with the great political bosses of his day even as he was critical of the systems they promoted. An optimist who chose to find that the glass was half full, he saw Russia and America forging societies in which "the generous, industrious producers and the brave, imaginative leaders of the race shall be fit to survive."

Toward the end of his life, Steffens settled in the artistic community of Carmel with his second wife and new son, who had prompted an article, "Becoming a Father at Sixty Is a Liberal Education." He died of a heart attack at 70.

Lloyd Tevis

After seeing Steffens, retrace your steps to the road between Sections B and D. As you walk along it, you will notice on your right two flat tables held up by columns. One is the memorial of **Frederick William Sharon** (1857–1915), the other to **William Sharon** (1821–1885) and Lady **Florence Emily Fermor–Hesketh** (d. 1924), daughter of William Sharon.

William Sharon won no awards for popularity. A small, dapper figure and sharp operator, Sharon cashed in on the revival of the Comstock Lode — principally by lending Bank of California money to mine managers and mill owners, then foreclosing on them. Later he turned on his principal supporter, William C. Ralston, who deeded his mansion and the Palace Hotel to Sharon. Under a dark cloud of disgrace, Ralston soon after went out too far during his daily swim and drowned.

In 1874 Sharon bought a seat in the United States Senate, but he missed the sessions five out of six years and, as his obituary put it, "made no figure at Washington." Back at home, the 62-year-old was rousted out of his afternoon nap and arrested for adultery, pursuant to a lawsuit brought by one Sarah Althea Hill, who alleged that they had been secretly married. A trial followed, first finding the marriage valid, then overruling the finding. The day before he died of angina pectoris, Sharon issued a deathbed nonconfession in which he vowed he had never even bought Miss Hill dinner.

Sharon's daughter, Lady Fermor–Hesketh, who had married and taken up residence in England, was brought here after dying suddenly in the home of the Duke of Grafton. During her lifetime she lost a fortune in the San

Francisco Earthquake in 1906 and a son who disappeared mysteriously in Dublin in 1910.

Right next to the Sharons is Columbarium I, a large building with an interesting domed tiled roof. It is multi-leveled inside, with arch-shaped openings. These are filled either with carved stones or an openwork design so you can see the urns behind. Worked into the ancient tile floor are the words, "Disturb not the ashes of the dead."

Behind the Sharons in Section B is the mausoleum of **Walker Coleman Graves** (1849–1920). Its most interesting feature is a bench that has a carved head at each of its four corners. The two female heads appear fairly benign; the men, with pointed tongues sticking out, are bacchanalian.

Across from the Sharons, in Section D, is a road shaped like a cross within a circle. Not surprisingly, this area belongs to the Episcopalians. In its center are several ornate crosses. One is to **William Ingram Kip** (1811–1893), first bishop of California, another to **William Ford Nichols** (1848–1924), the second bishop of California. Right off the circle is a man with a drooping moustache, **William E. Meadows**, who died in 1896 at 49. The lament below him reads:

> We miss you from our home dear,
> We miss the sunshine of thy face.
> But thy memory will be cherished
> Till we see thy heavenly face.

On your way out, stop in the newest mausoleum and visit Gertrude Atherton. Getting to her memorial will require some effort. To gain entrance, press I and II together, then press V and turn the lever to open. Atherton is in Section H, Niche 3, up on Tier 5.

Despite her stuffy name, **Gertrude Franklin Atherton** (1857–1948) was anything but a dowager. Raised by her grandfather after her parents were divorced, she described her father as an alcoholic who taught her "to stand on the table when he was giving a dinner party and kick the plates into the laps of the guests." At 19 she ran off with George Atherton, her mother's suitor, who, she commented later, "talked a good deal but he never said anything." He died when Gertrude was 30, and she took her young daughter—although she considered maternity "a highly specialized form of martyrdom"—to Europe.

From there she launched her literary career in earnest, with such titles as *The Doomswoman*, and *American Wives and English Husbands*. Writing one thousand words a day, Atherton was considered by critics to be a prolific but uneven writer. At the turn of the century she returned to California and wrote several iconoclastic histories of the state, such as *The Splendid Idle Forties* (the 1840s) and *California: An Intimate History*. Atherton had the distinction of having one of her books, *Black Oxen* (a novel about a controversial method of physical rejuvenation), banned in Rochester, New York, in 1923. Perhaps the work was, to some extent, autobiographical. She lived to be 90 before she succumbed to age-related ailments.

Cross the road to the new section for a briefer tour. You may want to detour first to the older mausoleum on this side, called the Catacombs. It has beautiful stained-glass ceilings in purple iris designs, which let in a lot of light, and some beautiful Carrara-marble interiors.

Next drive past the large in-ground sundial to your left. Right above it is the striking white marble monument to **Hiram Warren Johnson** (1886–1945). It resembles a skyscraper with an eagle on the top; a flag and palm fronds are built into the lower design. On the back is the children's prayer, "Now I lay me down to sleep. I pray the Lord my soul to keep." Other quotes on the monument include: "Without a sign, his sword the brave man draws, And asks no omen but his country's cause," from Homer; and "This single face in life and death and all eternity. The people. Lord. The people are good enough for me," from Kipling.

Beside Johnson is **Minnie McNeal Johnson** (1869–1955), designated as "Wife and mother. 'The Boss.' By his side she fought the good fight."

A son, **Hiram Warren Johnson, Jr.** (1886–1959), is also here, as is Major **Archibald McNeal Johnson** (1890–1933). "To live in hearts we leave behind is not to die."

Hiram Johnson, governor of California from 1910 to 1916 and United States senator from California between 1917 and 1945, had presidential aspirations, but he was singularly unlucky in the way he approached them. In 1912 he ran on the Bull Moose ticket as Teddy Roosevelt's partner, and lost. In 1920 he turned down an offer to run as vice-president to Warren Harding; two years later, Calvin Coolidge, who had accepted, became president when Harding died. During his tenure in California, Johnson worked for workmen's compensation and the protection in the workplace for immigrants, unskilled laborers, and women. In Congress he was known as an uncompromising isolationist, voting against entry into the League of Nations, and the World Court, and against ratification of the United Nations' charter.

Continue driving into the cemetery, bearing right, to get to the Pioneers Monument. On your way you will pass the **Whittell** Egyptian vault with its extraordinarily expressive sphinxes outside. On the bronze door are Egyptian faces.

Pioneers Monument

The monument to the early pioneers commemorates, in part, those who were moved out of Laurel Hill Cemetery in downtown San Francisco. The bronze statues show a pioneer family: the mother is holding a small child on her lap and pointing into the distance. The father is poised in back of them with a shovel. In granite on the wall behind is a striking set of images. One is of a sailing ship emerging from the stone, another shows the back of a covered wagon heading into the distance. These are superimposed over a stylized sun. The base reads, "Their visions and their dreams came true."

To the right of the sculpture is a huge stele. On the back wall it reads, "Laurel Hill Memorial. To commemorate the California pioneers," and then gives the story of Laurel Hill:

> From the ends of the earth, desire and a love of the wide blue sky of freedom led men to California. The gold of her foothills they converted into streets and cities. Through their labor, broad valleys became fields of waving wheat and in sunlit clearings they planted vineyards. They harnessed mighty rivers; they felled the trees of the lofty forest and with their timbers built churches and homes, schools and factories, bridges and ships. Here along the western frontier they failed and triumphed; labored and died. And were laid to rest beneath the foothill pines or within sight of the mountains they once crossed, or within the sound of the sea they once sailed. In their best, bravest city—San Francisco—there was a hill called Lone Mountain. To the west of it lay sand dunes and the sea; to the east of it the young city they had built beside the great bay. On the slope of Lone Mountain in May 1854, the pioneers dedicated the 57 acres of ground that came to be

known as Laurel Hill Cemetery. It was to be, they believed and hoped, their last home of all. One by one these builders of the California commonwealth and their wives and sons and daughters found their way to this last home to sleep beneath its laurel and oaks and whispering cypress trees. The years rolled by and the city grew. And as it grew Laurel Hill became an island surrounded and imperiled by the currents of living interests and ambitions. In 1902 by order of the San Francisco Board of Supervisors Laurel Hill was closed to further burials. Formal attempts to force abandonment of the cemetery came in 1913 and again in 1924. Both attempts failed. In April 1937 the San Francisco Board of Supervisors for the third time passed an ordinance demanding evacuation of Laurel Hill so its land could be converted to housing and street development. In May 1937 the board was presented referendum petitions bearing the signatures of 21,000 protesting San Franciscans. It refused to repeal the ordinance and at the election that following November the citizens of San Francisco upheld the ordinance and ratified the action of the Board of Supervisors by a vote of 82,983 to 65,920. The Laurel Hill Cemetery Association's 35 year struggle to save the last home of the pioneers was ended. Removal from Laurel Hill began February 26, 1940. Some remains were placed by descendants in other cemeteries. Most of them were brought here to Cypress Lawn, and now 35,000 of San Francisco's pioneer dead lie in the underground vault a few paces north of this tablet.

In love, honor, respect and gratitude, the Laurel Hill Cemetery Association erected this memorial to them. It was dedicated in their names and in the memory of their valor, love of country and devotion to God. As you stand here, open your heart to the pioneers. They gave you great cities, a fair, free land of mountains, a broad sea and the bluest of skies. Open your heart to them and trust the best that was in them all and they will also give you wisdom and humor and above all courage. For they are your fathers.(1953)

The remains of Laurel Hill Cemetery can be seen back in San Francisco at the St. Francis Yacht Club, where the marble and granite of the early markers were broken up to be used as breakwater fill. Workers were paid 80 cents a ton to cart the monuments away. At the end of the jetty some of the stones have been used to form an elaborate sound organ. If you put your ear next to one of the pipes, you'll hear the sound of the ocean roaring. The plaque reads:

The Wave Organ is dedicated to Frank Oppenheimer (1912–1985), founder and director of the Exploratorium. The stone used in the construction of this work was once part of a cemetery in Laurel Heights. The jetty forming the marina yacht harbor was partially built with the material taken from that cemetery, which was demolished in the 1950s.

Back in the newer sections of the cemetery are two people without markers. One is a Hell's Angels gang mem-

The Wave Organ

ber who was buried with his motorcycle. To prevent disinterment of the Harley–Davidson, the cemetery does not give out the location. The other site is not kept secret, but it is lacking a headstone. **Tom Mooney** (1882–1942), considered the West Coast counterpart of Sacco and Vanzetti, spent 22 years in San Quentin on what was widely agreed to be a trumped-up charge. A maverick iron molder, Mooney attempted to lead a wildcat strike among streetcar workers in 1916 and attracted the wrath of the powerful United Railroad Union. When 10 people were killed by an explosive during a Preparedness Day parade (signaling a readiness to enter World War I), Mooney was indicted.

The trial was a farce. One of the witnesses who testified that he had seen Mooney at the bombing scene was later tried for perjury when it was found he had written a friend to "come to California and make some money by testifying against Mooney." Mooney attracted such diverse supporters as Woodrow Wilson and Mayor Jimmy Walker of New York, but it took until 1939 for a California governor, Culbert L. Olson, to pardon him.

Obstreperous as ever when he was released from jail, Mooney attempted to get a legal separation from his wife, Rena, who had faithfully supported his cause over the years. (Mooney claimed they had been incompatible for the last 16.) Rena fought it, and he dropped the action. By then he was suffering a terminal case of stomach ulcers; in the last year and a half of his life he was never out of bed.

DIRECTIONS TO CYPRESS LAWN: Take Route 280 south from San Francisco and exit onto Route 82 to the Colma exit. The older section of Cypress Lawn cemetery is on your left, the newer is on your right along El Camino Real.

Colma Cemeteries

Oh, write of me not "Died in bitter pains"
But "Emigrated to another star!"
— HELEN HUNT JACKSON

COLMA IS A CITY of nearly half a million people, but only 700 of them are upright. Actually the latest figures in this City of the Dead give the living population as 731. Located south of San Francisco, Colma was chosen as the area's burial ground in the late 1800s when it was completely rural. Special railroad lines with stops at each of the larger cemeteries were soon established, and funeral trains began bringing both bodies and Sunday visitors. Wakes were often held at historic Molloy's Tavern at 1655 Mission Road, where you can still get Irish coffee and examine framed Colma memorabilia.

To the cemetery buff, Colma is a marvelous smorgasbord. Cypress Lawn, which is covered in the preceding chapter, demands full concentration, but you can drift quickly through the other Colma cemeteries, picking up a striking monument here, a colorful eccentric there, and in the noshing develop a fuller appreciation of San Francisco history. All the cemeteries are located side by side, so you can chose your own route. We give one way to make the circuit:

WOODLAWN

Start with Woodlawn Cemetery, which has an unusual Baby Section. In the midst of it are gilded plaster statues of Snow White and the Seven Dwarfs. The sign behind them reads, "Children's Sanctuary," and quotes the Bible verse: "And he said, Suffer the little children to come unto me, for such is the kingdom of heaven." On the sign is a bronze bas relief of a boy and a girl, seen from the back, reaching their hands toward the clouds.

Children's Sanctuary

Continue on the road, moving deeper into the cemetery. On your right you can see the stone of one of San Francisco's most colorful characters. His persona is reflected in his plain granite marker, which reads: "Norton I, Emperor of the United States and Protector of Mexico, Joshua Abraham Norton (1819–1880)."

Emperor Norton, a rice merchant, was once worth a quarter of a million dollars. Trying to corner the market, he bought high, but months of cargo ships all came in at once, and Norton was ruined. At that point he found it expedient to proclaim himself Emperor. To support his royal kingdom, he collected 50 cents a month from sympathetic merchants — though the owners of the Palace Hotel did not allow him to set up his headquarters there as he had commanded them to do. Instead, he lived in a boarding house and patrolled the streets in a plumed hat and military uniform on his bicycle, a small, dark-bearded regent with a preoccupied scowl.

Over the years Emperor Norton issued various manifestos, including one declaring the need for a bridge across San Francisco Bay and another demanding a pay raise for local sailors. As befitting his royal position, he tried to get Queen Victoria to marry Abe Lincoln and commanded that Maximilian of Mexico, whom he saw as a rival, be put to death. Emperor Norton himself dropped dead at the corner of California and Dupont Streets. The *San Francisco Chronicle* announced, "Le Roi Est Mort," and flags flew at half-mast in the city. When Lone Mountain Cemetery was broken up in 1934, the Emperor's remains were brought to Woodlawn with appropriate ceremony.

Because of Emperor Norton's interest in bikes, once a year a motorcycle gang from up in the mountains and mining country comes down to pay their respects to him. Like everybody else, they end up at that historic watering hole of mourners, Molloy's.

Nearby is a nice bronze cameo of **John Michael Eckfeldt** (1831–1874), for many years an officer of the United States Mint. An unusual feature is the marble drapery, complete with tassel, half hiding Eckfeldt's portrait, as if it has just been pulled back to give a quick glimpse of him.

Across the way from Emperor Norton is the flat gray granite bed of **John D. Daly** (1842–1923), founder of Daly City, the town adjoining Colma. It has a population of 37,000, all living.

Also buried in this cemetery is **A. P. Hotaling**, a whiskey wholesaler whose building made it through the Earthquake of 1906. It was the only thing left standing in five square miles. In answer to critics who felt that the Earthquake occurred because San Francisco had become a Sodom and Gomorrah, one wag came out with poem: "If God spanked San Francisco because it was so frisky, Why did he level the churches and save Hotaling Whiskey?" The original warehouse is still there.

Also in Woodlawn, close to the road, is a rose garden where next of kin and others sprinkle the ashes of people who prefer to be outdoors rather than locked away in crypts. The concept is interesting, and the roses are thriving, but it is nevertheless startling to look at the ground and see bits of bone. Four tall marble columns mark the way into the garden.

OLIVET

The most striking monument in Olivet Cemetery is John Stoll's tall black-granite monolith erected by the Sailors' Union of the Pacific for its members. Here a stern, determined steersman grasps the wheel as water submerges his body and a wave cloaks his shoulders. Only his head, chest, and hands which steer the ship are free. He is heroically fighting the gale or perhaps rising from the sea to be honored here. The inscription around it reads: "And the sea shall give up its dead. From every latitude here rest our brothers of the Sailors Union of the Pacific."

In the same cemetery, closer to the front entrance, is an unusual monument, "In Memory of Showfolks of America,

Sailors' Union of the Pacific monument

1945." It shows a montage of a clown, Ferris wheel, and buildings in the background and is painted in primary colors. Buried in the ground around the monument are the circus people in whose memory it was erected, with the epitaph, "That they may rest in peace among their own." The site was originally purchased in 1918 to bury 56 show-folk who died in a train wreck in Indiana.

HILLS OF ETERNITY AND HOME OF PEACE

These two Jewish cemeteries are divided only by an interior road. On the Hills of Eternity side there is only one personality of note, but it is someone who comes as a surprise to many people. The marker of **Wyatt Earp** (1848–1929) now lies flat on the ground, an upright version having been stolen three times. Earp was buried in a Jewish cemetery by his sister **Josephine** (1861–1944), who was married to **Max Weiss** (1870–1947).

The gunfighter gained his reputation first by working as a police officer in Wichita and Dodge City, Kansas, then as an armed guard for Wells Fargo in Tombstone, Arizona. In 1881 Earp, his three brothers, and a friend, Doc Holliday, were involved with the Clanton gang in the shoot-out at the O. K. Corral in Tombstone. Although there was some controversy as to which faction were actually the criminals, Holliday and the Earps were eventually exonerated on the grounds that they had been acting as peace officers. After the O. K. Corral, Earp took to the road, establishing saloons in Nevada and Alaska before settling in California. He received public notice once again when he refereed a boxing match between Tom Sharkey and Bob Fitzsimmons wearing a six-shooter in the ring. No one questioned his decisions.

To locate Wyatt Earp, drive down the road between the two cemeteries to the rough-hewn mausoleum of **C. Meyer**. Walking along the path, look for a boulder which has two carved marble doves peering into a book in which the name **Sophia Isaacs** (1837–1907) is engraved. Earp is slightly forward and to the right of her monument.

Across the road in Home of Peace, along the same row as Earp's marker but at the end by Middle Road, is the large mausoleum of **Levi Strauss** (1830–1902). The outside is plain granite with two very fat columns. Inside is a wonderful marble statue of two angels surrounding a cameo of his mother. Strauss himself remained a bachelor. The structural work below the surface is deep, several hundred cubic yards of cement to keep the mausoleum from shifting or uprooting during an earthquake.

Levi Strauss, a dry-goods merchant, initially sold Genoese cloth in San Francisco to make sails but soon teamed up with tailor Jacob Davis to manufacture work pants. The metal studs, which helped keep the jeans from splitting under pressure, were a stroke of genius, though at first, when the cowboys stood around the campfires at night, the stud in the crotch area would heat up and create a painful reaction. When word reached Strauss and Davis, the offending rivet was quickly removed.

This cemetery has a number of charming turn-of-the-century monuments, including a beautiful marble portrait "In memory of **Natalie**, oldest daughter of Isadore and Marie Shirpser. Born in Germany 1846, Lost on steamer 1865." There is also a bas relief of a soldier on horseback on the marker of **C. C. Keene**.

In this vicinity are members of the **Sutro** family. **Adolph Sutro** (1830–1898) was a benevolent patriarch dear to the hearts of San Franciscans. A massive man with huge white mutton-chop whiskers and a heavy German accent, he invented a drilling process to drain the water out of silver mines and stop drownings. He used his earnings from the Comstock Mine to acquire nearly 10 percent of San Francisco real estate.

Happy to share the wealth, Sutro gave the Mt. Parnassus Hill area to the University of California and established Sutro Heights west of the city. On Sundays visitors could pay 10 cents and stroll around his formal gardens or rent bathing suits and swim in Sutro Baths. Each of his six pools, under glass, was kept at a different temperature. Sutro also helped establish an electric trolley line to bring visitors from the city for 5 cents instead of the 20 cents charged by the Southern Pacific.

When the SP took over the line, and Collis Huntington raised fares, Sutro protested — then ran for mayor on the Populist ticket and won. Huntington got more than he bargained for. Fueled by encroaching senility, Sutro made the downfall of the Southern Pacific his primary issue and succeeded in getting Congress to defeat a major refunding bill.

Inside the large mausoleum near the front entrance to Home of Peace is one more notable San Franciscan. Go into the second entrance and straight toward the stained-glass window at the end. On the bottom right, three sections from the end is **Herbert Fleishhacker** (1872–1957).

Financier Fleishhacker was forced to retire from his Anglo–London–Paris Bank under a cloud. Though legally exonerated of dipping into the till, he still had to liquidate his assets to repay creditors. He returned to favor when he established the San Francisco Zoo, inspired, it was alleged, by the smells of the animals he encountered on a trip to India. Near the zoo was built the largest saltwater swimming pool in the world, also Fleishacker's donation. Unfortunately, at one thousand feet long the pool was impossible to heat. It is now a parking lot.

Isaias W. Hellman's (1842–1920) huge structure is in a circular area of mausoleums. Hellman was one of the founders of Wells Fargo Nevada Bank.

HOLY CROSS

As you drive into Holy Cross Cemetery and enter the circle, you will see on your right, across from Assumption Chapel, the impressive mausoleum of **James Graham Fair** (1831–1894). It has a semicircular design with his name beneath a scabbard; on top there is a shallow bas relief of an angel looking into a book.

What the angel finds written in the book about James Fair may not please her. "Slippery Jim," one of the four big winners in the Comstock Lode, had the unendearing habit of planting misleading market tips to help drive up the value of his holdings. During his purchased term as United States senator from Nevada, his wife caused a sensation by divorcing him for chronic adultery. When Fair died in 1894, his will was contested by many, including a "widow" with her own version and a copy of a marriage contract. Fair's

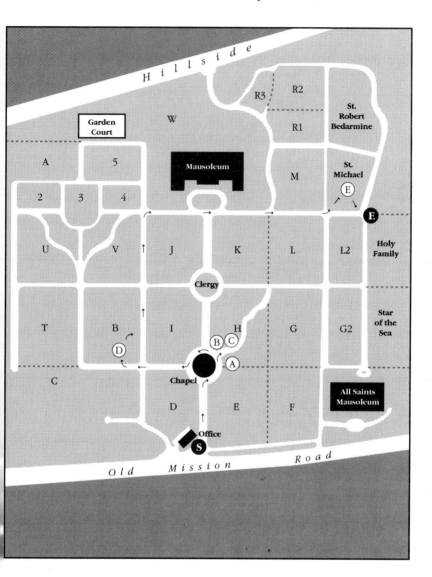

A John Gately Downey
B James Graham Fair
C A. P. Giannini
D Eugene Schmitz
E George Moscone

three remaining children (his oldest son had committed suicide at 27) had the foresight, however, to bribe a California Supreme Court justice with $400,000 to settle the $50 million estate their way.

William S. O'Brien (d. 1878), one of Fair's partners, is also buried in Holy Cross. A former gold miner turned bartender in the financial district, O'Brien got his tips from conversations overheard in the Auction Lunch Saloon. Unlike his partners, Fair, James Flood, and John Mackay, however, O'Brien was thankful to retire and quietly enjoy his wealth. He died a bachelor, the first of the Big Four to check out.

Directly to the right of the Fair mausoleum is **John Gately Downey** (1827–1894), the seventh governor of California. He has a large cross, and his long-bearded cameo in bronze on the front. Downey, an Irish-born druggist, spent most of his life in Los Angeles, where he helped establish a public-library system, horse-drawn streetcars, a railway connection to San Francisco, and the University of Southern California. As governor (1859–1861) he kept the Port of San Francisco from falling into private hands and handled the position well — but his sympathy for the South during the Civil War ended his career.

In January 1881 a Southern Pacific passenger train plunged down a ravine in the Tehachapis. The governor's wife, **Maria Jesus Guirado Downey**, was one of the 20 passengers killed. He never recovered physically or psychologically from the accident and her loss.

If you walk down the path between the two mausoleums, three markers down on your left is the white bas relief of a grieving woman with a cross and Christ's head in a circle above it. It is the last resting place of **Amadeo Peter Giannini** (1870–1949), who died at 79 when what started as hoarseness from a cold ended as a fatal heart attack.

If any banker can be considered a hero of the frontier, A. P. Giannini qualifies. As a boy on a 40-acre ranch near San José, he saw his immigrant father brutally murdered over one dollar. Perhaps from that point, he determined to champion the cause of small landowners and hardworking immigrants. His Bank of Italy (later the Bank of America) began in a converted saloon and emphasized small loans to farmers and laborers. After the 1906 San Francisco Earthquake struck, he rescued his $2 million in gold and securities by burying them in a farm cart under heaps of vegetables and driving calmly through crowds of drunken looters. Giannini invested heavily in the movie industry when it was still considered a fluke and in the Golden Gate Bridge

A Victorian cluster

when Stanford professors were saying it wasn't going to last.

In Section B, count three rows of markers over and about 18 markers up to reach the white marble monument, about three feet high, with a cross and circle. It belongs to **Eugene Edward Schmitz** (1864–1928) and his wife, **Julia Driscoll**. The landmark at the edge of road designating his row is a huge rough-hewn cross belonging to **Eugene P. Murphy**.

"Handsome Gene" Schmitz did not intend to be a crooked politician. He was first a violinist and orchestra leader. But political boss Abe Ruef decided that Schmitz's German–Irish good looks and charisma were what San Francisco wanted and got him elected mayor for three terms (1901–1907). Schmitz charmed the socialites, and Ruef paid off the bribes. Although Schmitz behaved heroically during the Earthquake, the ruins brought certain things to light. The new city hall, built at enormous cost, was allegedly found to have the bathroom drains emptying into the basement. It was destroyed by the Earthquake in 30 seconds, causing someone to comment, "That's what happens when you mix bad politics with bad cement."

Schmitz, sensing the climate, left for a European vacation. When he returned, he was indicted for bribery, convicted, and sentenced but got off on a technicality because he was indicted as Eugene Schmitz, not Eugene Schmitz, Mayor of San Francisco. Like his eastern counterpart, Gentleman Jim Walker of New York, he was admired by his constituents anyway and was subsequently elected supervisor in 1917 and 1921.

Across the way is a section for nuns. The old stones are identical, giving the sisters' names, their orders, and "R. I. P." Most of them died around the turn of the century. A larger marker commemorates the **Sisters of Notre Dame of San Francisco**, and **Sister Aloyse of the Cross**, their Mother Superior, who died in 1894.

George Moscone (1929–1978) has a simple in-ground red marker that reads, "We love you Dad," placed by his four children. To locate it go to the statue of St. Michael slaying the dragon in the center of the section and count down five rows of markers toward the entrance.

A week after the mass suicides in Guyana originating from Jim Jones' People's Temple in San Francisco, the city was rocked again by the double slayings of George Moscone and Harvey Milk. (See Chapter 13 for San Bruno/Golden Gate, where their killer, Dan White, is buried.) A native San Franciscan, Moscone first practiced law, then became involved in Democratic politics. He came down on the liberal side, opposing cuts in welfare and mental-health programs. From the board of supervisors he moved to the state senate, then back again to San Francisco as mayor. During his tenure he kept the baseball Giants from moving to Toronto and survived a recall election by conservatives.

Moscone's greatest stumbling block was crime. Opposed to the death penalty—his father, a San Quentin guard, had showed him the gas chamber, which horrified him—Moscone was criticized as being "soft on crime." The number of violent robberies in the city was considered unacceptable, and the conservative element was angry at Moscone's appointment of homosexuals to political positions. The city polarized. Finally even metal detectors and police supervision of City Hall were not enough to save George Moscone from the crazed wrath of a Dan White.

On the way out, you may notice the monument of **L. Lerceri**. It has a white marble statue of what appears to be a saint, an older man with a dog by his side, pulling up his robe on one side to reveal his leg and boot. He has a surprised and stunned look on his face as he gazes into the distance. The bas relief below him shows an anchor, a cross, a ribbon bow with fringe, and flowers.

DIRECTIONS TO COLMA: Take Route 280 south from San Francisco and exit onto Route 82 to the exit for Colma. The cemeteries are located along El Camino Real.

WYATT EARP
1848-1929.
JOSEPHINE EARP
1861-1944.

PEACE BE WITH YOU ALL

Mountain View

*There are more things in San
Francisco's Chinatown than are
dreamed of in heaven and earth.*
— FRANK NORRIS

MOUNTAIN VIEW CONTAINS few famous people but is a
pleasant example of a Victorian cemetery and provides
many attractions for an afternoon's stroll. Every familiar
funerary symbol is represented here, from marble scrolls
with engraved names to lambs, urns, and melancholy angels. These more interesting monuments are located primarily in the back section to the right of the cemetery and
up on the ridge to the left.

To locate Mountain View's most famous person, Frank
Norris, drive down the main road to Section 12. Catty-
corner to the **Edson-Adams** mausoleum is the family plot
of the author. His marker reads "Beloved by his brothers in
Phi Gamma Delta who cherish his memory and testify their
gratitude for his devotion to the fraternity."

FRANK NORRIS *b. March 5, 1870, Chicago; d. October
25, 1902, San Francisco.* It is no accident that Frank Norris
was memorialized by his fraternity brothers. Up to the
moment of his death, he was the golden-haired college boy
who played the banjo, adored practical jokes, and went on
occasional binges. He made up nicknames for his "brothers," acted in their plays, and wrote the ritual for the first
annual "pig" dinner, celebrated by the Phi Gamma Deltas
ever after as The Norris. When he died at 32 life was still a
marvelous adventure.

Norris was born in Chicago, where his father was a jewel-
er, and moved to California when he was 14. As a teenager
he was found to have some gift for drawing, and his father
arranged for him to study art in London and Paris. But
Frank quickly became sidetracked by the romances of King

Arthur and his knights. Instead of studio painting he spent his days in the museum studying various kinds of armor and wrote long illustrated fantasies which he mailed home to his brother Charles. When one of these was intercepted by his father, the elder Norris ordered Frank home.

His education was continued in a more conventional way when he entered the University of California in 1890. Although he detested the academic program, he entertained himself with the fraternity and discovered Zola. Frank quickly made plans to become an American Romantic Realist, although he did not describe himself this way until much later. As one critic explained it, "He is not concerned with the drama of the broken teacup because such dramas do not exist for him. . . . His attention is held only when there is a great deal of china broken at once and he prefers heavy restaurant ware and thick clay pitchers to Royal Copenhagen demi-tasses."

Unable to pass math, Frank left the university to spend a year at Harvard. He was already at work on two of his novels, though it would be several years before the first was published. Instead, in 1895 he made the first of two adventure trips, both of which would have disastrous consequences for his health. In South Africa, as correspondent for the *San Francisco Chronicle*, Norris was captured by the Boers, suffered a severe attack of African fever, and was finally expelled from the country. His second foray was to Cuba in 1898 for *McClure's Magazine*. It brought him the horrible sights of war and another bout of fever.

Meanwhile his books had begun to be published. *McTeague*, considered his masterpiece, was brought out in 1899 by Doubleday, McClure & Company. The story of a money-hungry dentist who eventually murders his wife was made into the movie *Greed* in 1923 by Erich Von Stroheim and is considered a classic. Reviews of the book were mixed, with William Dean Howells leading the cheering section and Miss Nancy Huston Banks of *The Bookman* lamenting the fact that her hopes that "the celebration of the painful and unclean had passed from fiction forever" had once again been dashed.

The other Norris novel which, in retrospect, won critical notice was *The Octopus*, whose title referred to the railroad as it devoured California farmland and created bloody conflicts. Its sequel, *The Pit*, the second in a planned trilogy on the theme of wheat, was about the grain speculators in Chicago and was less vivid. The third book, *The Wolf*, which shows the relief of famine by the distribution of wheat, was never written. Norris' other books, tossed off between masterpieces, ranged from melodramatic to dreadful. *A Man's Woman* (1900) is universally considered the worst.

In the months before he died, Norris and his wife, Jeanette, were planning a trip around the world by tramp steamer to research *The Wolf*. Because she suffered from frequent stomach ailments, she had an appendectomy before they embarked. A month later, when Frank complained of an attack of indigestion, she suggested appendicitis, and he laughed it off. The doctor agreed with Jeanette, but Norris refused to take them seriously until he was doubled up with pain. The operation revealed advanced peritonitis and gangrene. The adventurer fought bravely, but the fever attacks that had weakened his constitution took the fight away from him.

Also in Section 12, but closer to the road and to the entrance gates, about the third full row of markers up, is a monument with a square, a cylinder, and a ball on top, all in brown. It commemorates **Emma Marwedel** (1818–1893) and has the epitaph, "She loved little children." Marwedel, a San Francisco educator, was active in the early kindergarten movement, founding many schools based on the theories of Friedrich Froebel. These stressed pleasant surroundings, physical activity, and close observation of nature.

Up on Mausoleum Row (Section 35), the first large memorial with the filigreed work is to **Samuel Merritt**, MD, (1822–1890) who, besides being a physician, was a "shipmaster, philanthropist, regent of the University of California, mayor of Oakland, and founder of the Samuel Merritt Hospital."

The statuary on the memorials nearby is interesting, but the most striking mausoleum, especially when seen at a distance, is that belonging to the **Bradbury** family, which has a nearly life-size young marble angel standing outside the dark doors. The flat roof is surmounted by a pyramid whose shape is echoed by smaller decorations at the base of the stairs.

Charles Crocker (1822–1888) lies in a Greek temple designed by the architect Arthur Page Brown. Crocker, a beefy dry goods store owner, ended up as one of the Big Four owners of the Southern Pacific Railroad. To get there, however, he had to race with his Chinese crews against the Union Pacific. He lost workers in avalanches and accidents, sacrificing safety to speed, but won the financial support of the US government. The mausoleum was commissioned by his wife, **Mary Crocker** (d. 1889), who, while personally supervising the construction, lay down for an afternoon nap and never awoke.

Bradbury family mausoleum

Going down the road to the next row of markers, in Section 27, look for a bronze cameo profile of "Our Sister Rosalia LaBastida de Coney (1844–1897), beloved wife of Brother Alexander K. Coney, 32nd Consul General of Mexico." Next to her is a marker with the inscription, "Under the foundation stone is deposited the heart of Dr. Ignacia Herrera y Cairo, ex-governor state of Jalisco, Mexico, murdered May 21, 1858, A martyr to the cause of Freemasonry." On top of this marker is an inscription to **Edwin A. Sharman** (1829–1914), who was a father of Oakland Freemasonry.

Going along the lower row of mausoleums, you will find the requisite Egyptian pyramid — most older cemeteries have at least one — this one a memorial to the **Miller** family and dated 1896. On the door, however, is a bronze cameo of a young and beautiful woman with the name Evie above it. The memorial appears to have been built for her. Her real name was **Einnim H.**, the wife of **C. O. G. Miller**, who died in Oakland on March 28, 1896, at 30 years.

Also along this row is the mausoleum of the **Ghirardelli** family, a name familiar in the San Francisco area as owners of the early chocolate factory, now Ghirardelli Square. Nearby is a mausoleum with upright torches and an hourglass symbol with wings denoting passage of time, a wreath, and a young woman mourning against a lectern, clutching flowers and a shawl.

Returning to leveler ground, drive through some of the older sections to your left for more individualized markers. A number of them are evocative, including that of Captain **William Lund**, "A Native of Norway. Lost at sea Oct. 1884, Aged 32 years." The stone bears a tilted anchor at the top.

Behind the main mausoleum is the sandstone pyramid of **William McKendree Gwin** (1805–1885). The structure is distinguished by two male Egyptian heads with wigs and necklaces rather than by the usual sphinxes. Dr. Gwin was trained as a lawyer and a doctor, though he never practiced medicine. He came to California in 1850 for the express purpose of ushering her into statehood and becoming her first US senator in the process. In Congress Gwin was able to provide California with all the accouterments necessary for a new state. Although he was criticized severely by contemporary historians as "avaricious" and "unprincipled," the twentieth century has recognized his achievements and judged him more kindly.

As you return to the entrance gate, you will notice that the slightly untended look of the older sections — some neglected memorial fountains are only empty blue saucers in the ground — gives way to a spiffiness of mowed grass and working fountains. Up in the front is a mausoleum which is still in use, and whose most famous resident is **Henry John Kaiser** (1882–1967).

Henry J. Kaiser was a living inspiration, a man with an aphorism for every occasion. His early success in highway contracts and paving in the Northwest was based on his slogan, "Find a need and fill it." He found a need for a $20-million road project in Cuba and spent his time there dreaming of building the Hoover Dam — a project he finished two years ahead of schedule. ("There's only one time to do anything and that's today.") After turning out freighters during World War II by using innovative prefabrication techniques, Kaiser turned his attention to cars. But although he avowed, "In the Frazer there is the heart of Joe Frazer, and in the Kaiser you will find the soul of Henry Kaiser," the Kaiser–Frazer Automobile Company ran off the road soon afterward.

Kaiser was rumored to sleep only three hours a night. When he went to Hawaii for a vacation in 1954, he immediately saw its potential and created a $350-million resort and housing development. Henry ("Pink is a happy color.") Kaiser decorated his Hawaiian Village Hotel in that shade, a color which matched his Lincoln, jeeps, bulldozers, and view of the world. He died in his sleep at 85.

Also in Mountain View is missionary **William Taylor** (1821–1902). He is chiefly remembered now for introducing eucalyptus seeds from Australia to California — a blessing or the opposite, depending on whether or not one likes the pungent odor smelled everywhere in San Francisco in the spring.

DIRECTIONS TO MOUNTAIN VIEW: Take the San Francisco–Oakland Bay Bridge and exit onto Route 880 into Oakland. The cemetery is located northeast of the city at 5000 Piedmont.

House Tours

> *How assiduously nature seeks to remedy these labored art blunders. She corrodes the iron and marble, and gradually levels the hill which is always heaped up, as if a sufficiently heavy quantity of clods could not be laid upon the dead.*
>
> —JOHN MUIR

LIKE THE EARLY pharaohs of Egypt, the settlers of northern California preferred to be buried close to the things they loved. In Luther Burbank's and John Muir's case, the significant objects were not jewelry and golden goblets, but the gardens they had cultivated and the wildlife they had nurtured. Jack London's Wolf House was destroyed the night before he was to move in. The remains stand near his gravesite as a monument to his dreams. Viewing the homesteads where these innovators lived and worked, and where their remains now lie, provides a fuller understanding of their lives than a trip to a cemetery alone would.

All of the homes on this house tour are north of San Francisco. Each is a pleasant day's outing from the city. Visiting Luther Burbank in Santa Rosa, you may want to stop at the Pioneer Cemetery and the Ripley Museum as well. Jack London, in Glen Ellen, is located near Sonoma in the heart of wine-tasting country. A visit to John Muir in Martinez could be combined with a stop in Berkeley.

LUTHER BURBANK HOME

When you reach the home of Luther Burbank, enter the gardens first. You will be able to see, depending on the season, some of the Burbank creations: the white Shasta Daisy, Red-Hot Poker flowers, plumcot, kiwi fruit, and the

"Paradox" Walnut — so named because it is a fast-growing hardwood. The brick alcove on Santa Rosa Avenue contains a number of memorial plaques, such as:

> Luther Burbank, March 1849–April 2, 1926.
>
> In memory of our citizen of the world whose love for youth and growing things is expressed in the work done in these gardens. The perpetual ownership of these grounds is now vested through the generosity of Mrs. Burbank and the City of Santa Rosa.

The small country cottage of Luther Burbank gives a feeling for the horticulturist, placing him in the center of his belongings. His tastes were simple, running to rustic furniture and the Victorian accessories of his time. Many of the striking painted tiles on display were collected by his wife. Scattered through the house and Burbank's study are prints of his creations and photographs showing him with many people, including Henry Ford, and Helen Keller, to whom he is presenting a Shasta Daisy.

Burbank is buried under a large Cedar of Lebanon tree in the side yard, a tree which he particularly loved and which he grew from seed. The fact that it was not expected to survive made it even more precious to him. By special permission his wife, who died in 1977, is also buried under the tree, along with their pet dog.

LUTHER BURBANK *b. March 7, 1849, Lancaster, MA; d. April 10, 1926, Santa Rosa.*

> BURBANK, *v.t.* to modify and improve (plants or animals), esp. by selective breeding . . . figuratively, to improve (anything, as a process or institution) by selecting good features and rejecting bad, or by adding good features.

Luther Burbank was his father's thirteenth child. His mother was his widowed father's third wife. Of 14 siblings half died by their teenage years. It was not an auspicious start for a man whose name was to become world famous and also enter Webster's Dictionary as a transitive verb.

Yet the life surrounding Burbank in the early years proved stimulating. Horticulture was in his blood and his environment. Burbank's mother was a Burpee by birth (cousin W. Atlee was to become a supporter of Burbank's), and her father was a successful gardener who died while resting from his green labors at the age of 87. On his father's side he learned of the natural sciences from his uncle Levi, who was an associate of Louis Agassiz. From his brother George he learned the grafting of apple branches and excitedly watched the Baldwins ripen.

A slight, slim, and sensitive youngster, Burbank was hypochondriacal throughout life, perhaps as an outgrowth of

Burbank house and burial tree

so many sibling deaths. His religious upbringing mellowed over the years, moving from fundamentalist Baptist to the Unitarianism of his grandfather. But when he was 19 his Baptist upbringing came into conflict with Darwin's *Variations of Animals and Plants under Domestication*, a book which Burbank felt to be the most influential he ever read.

With Darwin as his guide, he started experimenting with the artificial selection of certain plants. Within a short time he experienced his greatest success. Finding an extremely rare seed pod on an Early Rose potato, he carefully cultivated the seeds and then began the process of selection. By the time he was 24 he had developed the Burbank potato. Today, whether you pronounce it *potato* or *potahto*, it is still most likely to be a Burbank you buy and cook, the most widely grown potato in the country.

This success garnered recognition for Burbank. He moved to California, where his thriving nursery business mirrored the agricultural growth of that state. Introducing exotic varieties, especially from Japan and Australia, and then developing hybrids from them through selection, Burbank flourished. His New Creations catalogue was a huge success, and the large nursery companies bought his offerings at high prices. They in turn propagated the varieties and sold them to the public. Burbank's catalogue is notable for its prose as well—the copy bears the same personal, intimate imprint attempted by many of today's mail-order catalogues.

With Burbank's fame came a host of reverential admirers. Hagiographers appeared, and Burbank was canonized. He was a genius, his work the equivalent of vegetative alchemy. Burbank came to believe his press. He developed a grandiose view of himself as a messiah, a Napoleon of the garden, and did little to temper his extravagant notices.

Scientists and fellow nurserymen were both jealous and less impressed. Some of Burbank's creations were less than he claimed, and others appeared to be existing varieties merely renamed. His techniques were not altogether unknown, and his record keeping, crucial to genetic work, was exceedingly sloppy. Furthermore, his scientific knowledge was not of a high order. What Burbank accomplished was done through an exceptionally keen and practiced eye and an intuitive sense for choosing the right plants for further propagation. His genius lay in his hard work and his ability to short cut the standard scientific method of hybridization. With uncanny ability he could select the very best prospects for hybridizing, thus accelerating development of the desired hybrid by several years. He also developed far more varieties than anyone else. Even today, with 60 intervening years of further improvements, there are many Burbank varieties to be found: plums, peaches, nectarines, quinces, and the Shasta Daisy.

Burbank first married at age 41. Henpecked and then threatened, he fled to the workshop above the stable for two years. After six years of less-than-connubial bliss, Burbank was happily divorced. His second marriage was to his secretary, Elizabeth Waters. He was 67, she was in her mid-twenties. A hybrid marriage and perhaps, therefore, a contented one.

Burbank's last years were controversial. He was under siege for his exaggerated claims (most notably his "spineless" cactus), and yet still idolized by many. His opinions were sought on every subject from parenting (he loved children but had none) to jazz (he hated it). He created further controversy and alienated many of his followers with his public expression of Unitarian humanism. Decrying the harsh God of fundamentalism, he proclaimed a love for all things living.

In 1926, aged 77 and optimistic for another good year, Burbank suffered a heart attack and gradually succumbed, falling into a coma from which he never awoke.

SANTA ROSA RURAL CEMETERY

If you have time while visiting Santa Rosa, you may want to take a look at the Santa Rosa Rural Cemetery, an important repository of pioneer history. It is located along Franklin Avenue; directions are available at the Burbank House. First surveyed in 1879 and used as a burying ground since the 1880s, the cemetery also contains 21 varieties of roses, and plant species native to California.

As you enter, you will see a simple gray granite marker inscribed, "In memory of those who died in the Disaster of April 18, 1906." It commemorates 75 known Santa Rosa victims of the San Francisco Earthquake, and four unknown. Off to the side an older monument says, "May their souls rest in peace. Amen." In remembering the San Francisco Earthquake, many people do not realize that Santa Rosa, 60 miles north, was also hit hard. Though there were no tall city buildings there, many homes and lives were lost.

Unfortunately the cemetery looks as though the Earthquake happened yesterday. But the cataclysm in this case appears to have been vandalism. Many upright marble markers have been broken off at the base and lie on the ground. As you wander around, look at those as well. You will see epitaphs such as that on **Warner**'s (1891) stone: "Safe, safe at Home," and "At rest." There are representations of downturned torches, symbolizing the extinction of life, and the sheaves of wheat which show that the deceased reached a ripe old age.

After the fall

A rare carved wooden marker with a rough floral design has survived, commemorating **A. C. Freeland**, who died May A.D. 1851, age 41 years. It has a swirling design resembling a lasso beneath the name. Nearby is the marker of **Susan Dickey** (1810–1873) showing clasped hands and the verse:

> She's gone, she's left this world of woe
> For regions of eternal love.
> T'was God who called her from below
> To join in praising him above.

The history of hard times can be read between the stones. The monument of **Melley Ann**, wife of **J. J. Lane**, who died in 1864 at 28, laments:

> Dear children, too, your mother kind
> Must go and leave you here behind:
> May Jesus deign your souls to raise,
> To join and sing his lasting praise.

Also in the plot is **Louisa** who died at four, born when Melley Ann was only 16.

The plot of **John David Cooper** (1835–1917) and his wife is even more poignant. At the front of the bed are the stones of the eight children they lost: two in 1878, at 2 and 5 years old; two in 1882, a newborn and a baby of 20 months; two sons, 10 and 17, in 1887; and in 1888, twin girls, Alpha and Ada, who died the same day they were born. Four markers have lambs, two have fingers pointing upward, the last is round and plain. Even in an age when disease snuffed out small lives like a puff of wind over a candle, the Cooper family's misfortune seems extreme.

The very tall stele of **John Richards** (1824–1879) is interesting because of its history. A former slave who became a barbershop owner in Santa Rosa, Richards was so highly esteemed that a large funeral procession accompanied his casket to the cemetery.

Some of the other names scattered through the burial ground represent early Santa Rosa's most prominent citizens. **Anabel McGaughey** was the city's first woman doctor. **Thomas Geary** was elected to Congress during the Grover Cleveland administration. **Frank Doyle**, president of the Exchange Bank, was known as the "Father of the Golden Gate Bridge." **Emma Marie Fick Kopf**, the first female deputy sheriff of Sonoma County, is also here.

JOHN MUIR HISTORIC SITE

The home of John Muir is located in Martinez, just off the freeway near Alhambra Road. To understand Muir's life here one hundred years ago, however, you will need to block out such encroachments of civilization. That becomes easier as you wander around the grounds, visiting the vineyards and orchards which contain apricot, pear, quince, cherry, peach, lemon, orange, almond, and walnut trees.

Muir's house itself is an attractive gray-green Victorian with forest-green trim. Its furnishings are typical turn-of-the-century oak, but there is a wonderful hall piece which has carvings of herons on either side. In the dining room is an impressive oak breakfront. The second-floor bedrooms show the governess' room, a nursery alive with antique puzzles and games, and Muir's own bedroom. The study has his desk, several bookcases, a typewriter on a stand, and etchings strewn across the rug. The wastebasket is full, with several balled-up sheets nearby on the floor, indicating his work style.

The most wonderful thing about the attic is its musty smell. Old furniture is still stored here. From the attic you can climb a narrow flight of stairs into a lookout tower and ring the bell that hangs there. The tower was used by Muir for early-morning meditation.

At the time of his death, John Muir was buried on his property about a half-mile away. (Take Alhambra Road to the right turn on Alhambra Valley Road to Strenzel Lane, at the back of the orchard.) But in the intervening years, progress has separated him from the land which he loved. In the same way that the freeway has grown up around his original home, a residential area now surrounds Muir's burial plot. Muir's plain stone has his dates and a thistle design, as does the marker of his wife, **Louie Strenzel Muir** (1847–1905). The larger monument is to her parents, the **Strenzels**. A chainlink fence surrounds the area.

JOHN MUIR *b. April 21, 1838, Dunbar, Scotland; d. December 25, 1914, Martinez, CA.* John Muir began his love affair with nature early. By the age of 3 he was accompanying his grandfather in explorations of the Scottish countryside and ocean shore. Stored at the sharp edge of his memory, these experiences were readily evoked by the sights, sounds, and smells of nature in California. Muir's early life was far from being an idyll, however. Frequently into mischief with other boys of the town, he earned regular, methodical beatings at the hands of his father, a stern, fanatical Christian. At both home and school, Muir discovered an "educational system based on leather." In Muir's case, the application of leather only fostered further rebellion and resentment, a cycle which continued into Muir's adult life.

Ever searching for the right sect, the elder Muir decided on the Campbellite Disciples of Christ and moved his family to Wisconsin in 1849. For young John, the farm entailed long days of work, frequent righteous beatings, and, occasionally, a chance to explore his new environment. Muir's trials included the job of chipping through 80 feet of sandstone to find water for the farm. The work took months and almost cost him his life. In return for the stone removed, Muir built a will of rocklike calm and endurance.

Muir's mind first drew attention by the devices that he invented on the farm. Upon leaving for the University of Wisconsin, he took some of his contraptions with him, including his early-rising machine, a kind of hands-on alarm clock which cleverly tipped the sleeper out of bed at the prescribed hour. This, combined with his farmer's beard and naiveté, made him a most recognizable figure at the university. More important, he became exposed to scientific ideas of the day.

Unable to remain in school and unwilling to return home, Muir headed for Canada in 1864 in order to avoid the Civil War draft. The trip made way for Muir's epiphany. Journeying alone through a large swamp near the end of day, tired, hungry, and with no prospects for the night, Muir encountered a rare orchid (*Calypso borealis*). Framed against yellow moss and glowing white against the oncoming night, the beauty of this remote flower gave Muir not only emotional release but also the awareness that nature existed for its own sake, not merely to satisfy man.

Three years later, Muir had returned to the United States and suffered through a period of blindness, the result of a workplace accident in Indianapolis. Upon recovering his sight, he left industrial work for good. His senses once again finely attuned to nature, Muir embarked on a journey, a "grand Sabbath day three years long." On the way he sharpened his philosophy, deciding that man lent no more completeness to the universe than "the smallest transmicroscopic creature that dwells beyond our conceitful eyes and knowledge." Muir believed that each creature and plant existed for its own happiness. Such was the basis for his philosophy of conservation.

California was not intended to be the final destination of Muir's extended sabbath, but it proved to be a most fortuitous one when he discovered the Yosemite Valley for himself. It was a transcendental relationship which lasted for several years; Muir conquering "unclimbable" peaks by himself, allowing his will to surmount his fear as he bounded through the rocks and along the cliffs — literally hopping and leaping to some inner musical rhythm, his arms spread as if he were ready to step aloft. He supported himself in the valley first by tending sheep ("hoofed locusts" to Muir) and then by operating a saw mill. He became known locally as a lone, eccentric expert on the region and guided an inspired Emerson through the valley. Studying the glaciers of the valley, Muir controverted conventional scientific thought when he theorized that the valleys of Yosemite were glacial in origin. The amateur was substantially correct.

Muir's transcendental romps through Yosemite inspired similar flights of speech and writing. Although sometimes grandiosely verbose, Muir's writing more often gives full expression to his inspired surroundings. According to his listeners, his speech was even more moving in its ability to convey Muir's impassioned universe. Indeed Muir's writings on nature became gospel for readers across the country, exciting many to a first appreciation for the wild outdoors and helping to ignite a whole back-to-nature movement.

With age Muir gradually became domesticated and settled down to married life with his wife and two daughters in Martinez. He was never a true scientist, but more an acute observer. President of the Sierra Club from its inception in 1892 until his death, he became a leading defender of the wilderness. His work inspired presidents and Congress to set aside vast tracts as parkland. He even led Teddy Roosevelt through Yosemite; two of the century's greatest talkers camping under the pines, awaking excitedly to find four inches of snow on their blankets.

And so Muir continued, through the death of his wife in 1905, fighting for the preservation of nature. He lost his last battle, that of trying to preserve the Hetch Hetchy Valley from damming, but he could find solace in the size of the battle. He had spread the word, and his legacy has stayed with us — Nature — "Life at work everywhere, obliterating all memory of the confusion of man."

JACK LONDON PARK

In the Jack London Museum is the author's battle cry:

I would rather be ashes than dust. I'd rather that these sparks should burn out in a brilliant blaze than that I should be stifled by dry rot. I would rather be a superb meteor, every atom of me in magnificent glow, than sleepy in permanent planet. The proper function of man is to live, not to exist. I shall not waste my days in trying to prolong them, I shall use my time.

The building which houses the museum was originally the House of Happy Walls, finished in 1922 by Charmian London. Although her husband had died in 1916, much of the furniture in the house was designed by both Londons and custom built for the ill-fated Wolf House. The Dictaphone and the roll-top desk are from London's original study; the other furnishings give a glimpse of style in the 1920s. The photographs give a sense of the man himself.

Because the project was so close to London's heart, the ruins of Wolf House are worth a visit. The trails are well marked, although there are signs warning of rattlesnakes and poison oak. If these don't deter you, take the half-hour walk deep into the woods. Even in ruins, the framework and the immense stone chimneys are impressive. The house contained 15,000 square feet and included 26 rooms and nine fireplaces. A reflecting pool was built into the interior, and within the four floors were such areas as a Stag Party Room, servants' quarters, fireproof manuscript vault, music alcove, gun and trophy room, Charmian's apartments and sundeck, and Jack's sleeping tower at the top.

At the ruins there is a picture of what Wolf House looked like and a quote from Jack London: "My house will be standing, act of God permitting, for a thousand years." God or man did not permit it. The night it was completed in 1913 it burned to the ground at 2:00 A.M. It was a stunning loss, financially and emotionally. Jack London claimed he would rebuild. He never did.

To reach the Londons' grave, you will need to go in the opposite direction from Wolf House, again following the markers. At the site there is the following sign:

> Jack London once remarked to his wife Charmian and his sister Eliza that, "I wouldn't mind if you laid my ashes on the knoll where the Greenlaw children are buried. And roll over me a red boulder from the ruins of the big house." On November 26, 1916, in a silent ceremony Charmian London placed her husband's ashes on the chosen knoll under this stone. After she passed away in 1955, Charmian's ashes were also laid to rest here.

The stone itself is overgrown with moss and ferns and other foliage at the base. Located behind a natural-wood picket-fence enclosure, it is identified by a sign as "Jack London's grave."

Boulder marking Jack and Charmian London

JOHN "JACK" GRIFFITH LONDON (JOHN CHANEY) *b. January 12, 1876, San Francisco; d. November 22, 1916, Glen Ellen, CA.* Jack London's adventurous life was tumultuous before he saw the light of day. His father, William Henry Chaney, was a vagabond astrologer. A man of many liaisons, few commitments, and no children, he urged his mistress, Flora Wellman, to abort her pregnancy. Refusing, she instead made two sensational suicide attempts. The attendant publicity and the impending responsibility caused William to flee to Oregon. Flora remained in San Francisco, an object of sympathetic curiosity, and gave birth to Jack.

Eight months later Flora married John London. Limited as a breadwinner due to Civil War injuries, he was nevertheless kind to Jack. Flora, however, was too busy for her son. Rarely showing affection, she ruled the house by hysteria. Her spiritualist seances garnered the family a reputation for being odd, and her get-rich-quick schemes drove them into poverty. At first Jack withdrew, but by the time he was 15 he was in open rebellion against the regimen of familial support and duty. He turned to oyster pirating, drinking, and brawling. Though short, he was broad shouldered, quick, and tough, and he learned to survive. At 17 he escaped slum life by signing on as a sailor on a sealing schooner. On board he read during every free moment and witnessed the slaughter of the seals. This barbarism, enacted solely for the luxury of fashionable coats, sharpened Jack's feelings and views as to man's nature and the spoils of the rich.

Upon his return he earned his first money through writing: a $25 prize for a sketch about his sailing adventures. He then pursued work as a laborer, briefly marched with Kelly's Army (a group of two thousand unemployed men marching toward Washington, DC), bummed on the rails, and spent time in jail for vagrancy. He saw and experienced firsthand the worst of life for the poor man: police brutality, hunger, theft, violence, homosexual rape. His later novel, *The Road*, a forerunner of Steinbeck's and Kerouac's road novels, laid out these experiences. Jack's socialist leanings took firm root, and using his talents as a brilliant speaker, he soon became a leading socialist in the Oakland area. It was through local meetings that Jack met Anna Strunsky, a Russian Jew, whose like sentiments and sharp mind drew them together. Despite the attraction, Jack impulsively married another woman, Bess Madern, in 1900.

Oddly, for Jack's strong good looks and sexual magnetism allowed him a wide choice of women, the marriage was one of practicality. Jack wanted an earth-mother type to raise his children and tend the home, and Bess was glad to act in this role. Such practical moments were rare in Jack's life of unbounded enthusiasms and passions, and no more than four months after the wedding he was writing more passionately than ever to Anna. In the next two years Jack fathered two daughters and pursued his romance with Anna. The two played at Abelard and Heloise, writing "fictionally" of their passion in *The Kempton–Wace Letters*. Escaping both love and marriage, Jack traveled to London, where he lived as and wrote of *The People of the Abyss*, a shocking exposé of working-class life in London. Upon his return he wrote his most famous book, *The Call of the Wild*, and then, in need of money, sold his rights to the publisher for $2,000. The book went on, of course, to sell millions.

Soon Jack was in love again, this time with Charmian Kittredge. Plain, five years his senior, a woman with liberated views and an adventurous spirit, she would attempt anything that Jack would. With her spirit and femininity, she won Jack over, though it was not that easy. Jack first left to cover the Russo–Japanese War and then started another affair upon his return, while Bess started a divorce action. Jack married Charmian in 1905 the day after his divorce became final.

Jack continued to pursue his own brand of socialism. While decrying the conditions of the common man, he also supported white supremacy and adapted the teachings of

Spencer and Darwin to support his views. Jack periodically outraged his fellow socialists with his contributions of yellow journalism to the Hearst papers. His racist views were an overcompensation for the uncertainty of his roots: his early poverty, his missing father, and his eccentric mother.

Jack also overcompensated through an obsessive concern with his body. He took inordinate pride in his masculine appearance, but he abused his body during his many adventures. Over the years he suffered from alcoholism, scurvy, yaws, psoriasis, pyorrhea, and gonorrhea. He took arsenic treatments for yaws, but these eventually compounded his problems by damaging his kidneys. Continued drink and overeating (raw duck) only exacerbated the condition. Jack also suffered from intestinal problems and increasingly took heroin, morphine, and opium as analgesics.

As his health declined over his last 10 years, he stayed remarkably active. Under the influence of Charmian he broke away from The Crowd, a group of Bohemians and pretenders headed by his good friend George Sterling. He matured emotionally and spent more time with Charmian both in their travels throughout the Pacific and on their ever-growing ranch. The ranch became his last great passion and his final resting place. On November 22, 1916, Jack died of an overdose of morphine. Whether his death was by suicide is not clear, but the point is moot, for even Jack's magnificent energy could not have carried him on much longer.

DIRECTIONS TO LUTHER BURBANK HOME: From San Francisco drive north on Route 101. On reaching Santa Rosa, exit on 3rd Street to the right. Turn right again on Santa Rosa Avenue, and continue until you come to the house, at Sonoma Avenue.

DIRECTIONS TO THE JOHN MUIR HISTORIC SITE: From San Francisco, take Route 80 north to Route 4 (John Muir Parkway). Turn left on Alhambra Avenue. The house is located at 4202 Alhambra, Martinez

DIRECTIONS TO JACK LONDON PARK: From San Francisco take Route 101 north to Route 116 going east. Turn left into Route 12 north to Glen Ellen and follow signs to Jack London Park.

Carmel Mission and Garden of Memories

Great eucalypti, black amid the flame,
Rise from below the slope, above his name.
The light is vibrant at their edges, clings,
Running in all ways through quick whisperings,
Falling in secrecy athwart each stone.
Under a little plaque he waits alone.

—YVOR WINTERS

CARMEL MISSION

Of the twenty-one missions scattered along the coast of California, San Carlos Borromeo was said to be the favorite of Junípero Serra, father of California missions. Besides being the second mission he founded, this is the one he selected for his last resting place. His cell-like quarters, containing a primitive wooden table and chair, a pallet for sleeping, and a crucifix hanging on a leather thong, are open to visitors.

Carmel Mission is more beautiful now than in Father Serra's lifetime. The Moorish-style church, built from sandstone from the nearby Santa Lucia Mountains, was completed in 1797, after his death. It is doubtful that in the early struggling days there was such a profusion of roses, lantana, canna lilies, and salvia on the grounds or around the fountain. And, of course, Father Serra never saw the magnificent sarcophagus created in his honor.

On reaching Mission San Carlos Borromeo, go first into the basilica to the main altar, which shows a polychromed wooden crucifixion scene and other carved figures in surrounding niches. At the foot of the altar are the remains of Junípero Serra, his successor Father **Fermín Lasuén** (d. 1803), and two other Franciscan missionaries, **Juan Crespi** (d. 1782) and **Julian Lopez** (d. 1797). Juan Crespi was first a student of Junípero Serra in Majorca. Following his mentor to the New World, he achieved recognition as diarist of the Gaspar de Portolá expedition. In 1772 he suffered a mental and physical collapse from which he never fully recovered.

Fermin Lasuén, an old friend of Serra's, was a Franciscan with determined views. When they were brought together in 1775 at Carmel, Lasuen wrote back to Mexico that the padre was irascible and difficult to work with. When Serra offered him administration of the mission at Capistrano, Lasuen was insulted, feeling a location farther north was preferable. Yet he went on to make the mission one of the most notable in the chain.

Outside the sanctuary to the right is a floor marker for **José Antonio Romeu**, an early California governor who died in 1792. Next to him is a commandant of the Presidio, **Hermengildo Sal** (d. 1800).

It is in lives such as these that California's earliest history is found:

MIGUEL JOSÉ JUNÍPERO SERRA *b. November 24, 1713, Petra, Majorca; d. August 28, 1784, Carmel.* In contrast to the hardships of the second half of his life, Junípero Serra spent his early days in comfort in beautiful Majorca. His boyhood was idyllic and sun filled. As the first child of his parents to survive beyond babyhood, Miguel José was gently nudged in the direction of the church. He excelled in Latin and theology and became a Franciscan priest in 1731. To mark his profession, he chose the name Junípero after Brother Junípero, the close companion of St. Francis, whose warm, impulsive, childlike nature irritated everyone but St. Francis. There also the connotation of the rugged hardiness of the juniper tree. The family name Serra (saw) was retained with the image of "cutting down all the works of the Devil."

For the next 18 years, Father Serra taught and ministered at the Church of San Francisco, waiting to become a missionary to the New World. He went at the first opportunity. After a sea voyage of 99 days, he embarked at Vera Cruz and began the walk to Mexico City. On this journey he received the poisonous bite—probably from a brown recluse spider—that was to plague him the rest of his life. The immediate effects were swelling, fever, and nausea, but the wound on his leg remained swollen and permanently ulcerous.

Although the invasion by one culture of another can be traumatic, Father Serra brought sensitivity to his missionary work. He was gentle with the Mexican Indians. Rather than attack their idol Cachum, Mother of the Sun, he competed with Cachum by setting up the 14 Stations of the Cross in visual form, creating colorful processions during Holy Week, and staging Nativity plays by the children at Christmas. Several years later, Serra was presented with the statue of Cachum, no longer an object of awe. He took it back to the archives in Mexico City.

After almost nine years in the Sierra Gorda, Serra was recalled to the College of San Fernando in Mexico City. He was less tolerant of the comfortable lifestyle he found there. A slight, swarthy man, he scourged his own body from the pulpit, beating his breast with a rock and burning his skin with lighted tapers. In an effort to bring the complacent to repentance, he stripped to his waist and lashed himself with a chain. On one occasion, as the congregation wept, another man grabbed the chain from him and beat himself, crying, "I am the ungrateful sinner before God who should do penance, and not the Father." The man died of his wounds.

Because of his dramatic sermons, Serra was in great demand as a speaker. He limped on his painful leg all over Mexico and jumped at the chance to join an expedition into Alta California coordinated by Governor Gaspar de Portolá. While the Franciscans were spreading salvation, Spanish soldiers had been giving away smallpox and syphilis. Yet the soldiers and the priests were interdependent. Because of the small number of military troops, missionaries were expected to Christianize the Indians into submission. The soldiers were pledged to provide protection for the Franciscans against Indian attack.

Father Serra was depressed by the San Diego Indians. Coarse and unattractive, they pilfered the sails of the supply ships and snatched the blankets from the priests' beds. None of them wanted to be baptized. When Serra moved on to Monterey and Carmel, he left behind no converts. But the missionaries soon found that if winning the Indians was difficult, working with the Spanish governors was worse. Serra was constantly battling Fages, then Rivera, and De Neves, for foodstuffs and soldiers for protection. There was also conflict over choosing mission sites. In 1776 De Neves disputed Junípero Serra's authority to bestow the rite of Confirmation. The priest, having been given papal permission, did so anyway.

Serra began his last round of mission visits in 1783. His ulcerated leg made walking impossible, and he suffered

Memorial to Father Junípero Serra

from the respiratory weakness which would eventually kill him. But at San Diego, which had blossomed in the intervening years, he was able to perform the 984th baptism and record the 606th confirmation. After visiting the other missions, he returned to Carmel. The following summer he died. According to custom, his body was washed and dressed in his homespun Franciscan habit, and he was placed barefoot in a plain wooden box. He was given a last tour of the mission that he loved, then lowered into a grave next to his old friend, Juan Crespi.

Move into the adjoining room to see the memorial to Junípero Serra. Created in bronze, the sarcophagus was unveiled in 1924. It is the work of sculptor Jo Mora. Created in the gisant, or recumbent, form so popular in Westminster Abbey and St. Denis in Paris, it depicts Father Serra laid out on his back, hands folded in prayer. His feet rest on a bear representing the young state of California. Father Crespi, cowl off to show his tonsure, stands at Serra's head. Fathers Lopez and Lasuen kneel at the other end. The sides of the sarcophagus show the early work of the missions in delicate bas relief. Below are Indian and Spanish workers about two feet high. There is also a cameo of the priest.

The cemetery outside the basilica is small, sheltered by olive and pepper trees and entered through a sandstone archway. Over 2,300 Indians are buried here, including Old Gabriel, who helped build the church. His marker depicts an angel carrying a wreath in one hand, her finger pointing upward as she ascends into heaven.

Standing prominently in the center of the cemetery is a plain wooden cross on tiles. It has two lances moving upward from the base to form a V and a sponge — symbolism for the lance that pierced the side of Christ when He was hanging on the cross and the sponge which, after He cried out that He was thirsty, was cruelly filled with vinegar and raised to Him. It is dedicated "in memory of the 2,364 Christian Indians and 14 Spaniards who were interred in this cemetery between the years 1771 and 1833. Within the church are interred 168, both Indian and Spanish."

The mounds in the cemetery, approximately 18 inches high and covered with green growth, represent mass plots rather than individual burials. In those turbulent early days, there was no leisure for such refinements as separate coffins, flowers, or carved markers, which in any case were not part of the Indian culture. Many of the mounds are outlined in abalone shells, most of their iridescence long worn away.

GARDEN OF MEMORIES

In contrast to the beauty of Carmel Mission, the Garden of Memories seems, at first, an unprepossessing cemetery. It is in the business area of Salinas and appears dully modern—a place you would go to visit John Steinbeck, then leave quickly. But to do so would be to miss a whole era of early pioneer tombstones, some with fascinating Victorian carvings. These are in the oldest part of the cemetery which was founded in 1860, the part that is closest to the road.

On the large **Weaver** monument right near the road is a bas relief of **Freddy E. Weaver** (1881–1917) on his horse. Just behind him is an empty marble crib which says only "**Bertie**." On the back are his dates: May to July 1883.

Thomas Etchels's marker (1805–1873) has a hand reaching down holding a chain, with the broken part falling back to earth. On either side are tassels.

One of the next markers you will see is an ornate Woodman of the World monument to **Charles Keith Shepard** (1878–1906). It has a tree trunk, a dove, a sign hanging from a peg with Shepard's information, and below it an ax and mallet over ferns—all carved in marble.

On the huge **Smith** stele is a bird with a note in its mouth that says, "Over there." Underneath it reads:

Go take our messages of love
To wife and mother, pretty dove.

The next side has an infant on the half shell, with:

Life's pilgrimage commencing here
Prepares for us that brighter sphere.

The third side shows a carving of a very ornate bouquet with roses, sweet peas, and a calla lily right in the middle, and the words:

These precious flowers in their bloom
Shed fragrance o'er the silent tomb.

The final side has a stylized wicker fruit basket with cherries and grapes hanging out the sides and the inscription:

Pilgrim on the road to heaven
Enjoys the fruit which God has given.

In the front bottom of the marker are the verses:

A few short years of evil past,
We reach the happy shore.
Where death-divided friends at last
Shall meet to part no more.

The monument is to **Virginia V. Smith** (1836–1880).

Notice the bronze statue about two feet tall of **James E. Graves** (1832–1909), native of Kentucky. The statue shows him wearing a peaked western hat. Nearby is a carved marble monument showing a tiny child resembling a doll sitting in a niche, her feet peeking out from under her dress. It is "Sacred to the memory of **Leila**, Daughter of Thomas and Sarah Graves, died December 31, 1871, at two months and 24 days."

An attractive marker in this area is that of **Richard Lund** (1848–1879). It has a ribbon at the top bearing the word "Farewell" and two clasped hands emerging from ornate cuffs. Another marker, to **Donna M.**, wife of **Charles Chamberlin**, who died in 1875 at 21 years, has the epitaph:

Our darling dwells on the other shore.
He has claimed her as his own.
And in perfect peace and love she dwells
Before the great white throne.

Also in this area is the Civil War monument of **G. W. Bryant**. who died April 3, 1872, from wounds received September 19, 1863, at the Battle of Chicamauga while fighting in the Confederate Army. It pictures several rifles loosely joined together and a Confederate Army bag. Bryant was 33 years old when he died.

Right by the side of the road is an in-ground bronze marker that shows two very beautiful angels floating toward each other with their arms outstretched to what was at one time probably a standing vase. It is the monument of **Jessie A. Adams** (1882–1935). Also by the road is the stone for **Bartholomew Burke**, "a native of Galway, Ireland," who died in 1873 at the age of 40. Elegant tracery adorns the niche which holds a representation of Jesus.

Close to the back road is the tall monument of the **Patton** family. On the front is a remarkable three-dimensional carving of a little boy riding a pony, toy sword at his side, dog on the ground beside him. It is the memorial of **Judson M. Patton** who died August 16, 1881, at age 12.

Looking around this section you will see a number of other poignant stones and carvings, here and just across the road. To reach the monument of John Steinbeck move to the back of the section on the right side and look for a short, rounded holly tree about one-third of the way down until you come to a large marker with the name **Hamilton** (Row 60, Grave 27). The marker designated as John Steinbeck's is smaller. Near the Steinbeck monument is a charming marble remembrance which says simply, **LULU**, with the words, "Gone but not forgotten."

JOHN STEINBECK *b. February 27, 1902, Salinas; d. December 20, 1968, New York City.*

> Whan of IX wyntre age
> I toke siege wyth Kinge Arthurs felyship emonge knyghtes
> most orgulus and worshyppful as ony on lyve.

So wrote John Steinbeck in the dedication of his last book, *The Acts of King Arthur and His Noble Knights*. Not only did he take up the sword and shield at age 9, but he kept the siege throughout his life. Malory's tale of the knights of the round table had a hypnotic effect on Steinbeck. It was a world that entered his fiction through symbolism time and again. He felt himself a part of this knight or that; he recognized their good and their evil; their indecision was his. He felt some of Galahad but "perhaps not enough. The Grail feeling was there, however, deep planted. . . ."

That Galahad was not enough present at times seemed like an understatement, for too often Steinbeck could be impatiently disdainful and arrogant, a supercilious observer of a grail-less world. These attitudes were perhaps a defense against his diffidence and his homeliness. Indeed all through his life he would be plagued by periods of self-deprecation.

John grew up in Salinas, the third child of John and Olive Steinbeck. From birth he heard his uncles recite Shakespeare and Bunyan. His father, a man of several talents, was well known for his story telling. Olive, a teacher of Irish descent, pushed young John too early into reading "books [which] were printed demons." His mind caught on, however, and his abilities flowered with the discovery of King Arthur.

John did well in high school and entered Stanford University in 1919 but was not emotionally prepared and encountered academic problems. He dropped out several times, working in between at the Spreckels factories in the San Francisco area and at ranching jobs and factory work, all of which gave him exposure to the working poor of the area. His experiences were to play an important role in his future works. To his credit he stubbornly pursued his writing throughout his desultory college career. He left Stanford without a degree and for good in 1925 and headed east. Meeting with little success in either love or journalism in New York, he did receive encouragement regarding some short stories he had written. He returned west and holed up in the Sierra Nevadas through two isolated winters before finishing his first novel, *Cup of Gold*, in 1928.

The book fared poorly, but by 1930 Steinbeck had the support of Carol Henning, his first wife, and, even more important, he had come under the influence of Ed Ricketts, a young biological scientist whose sharp intellect was to shape and define, for years to come, Steinbeck's philosophy and aesthetic. Relentlessly prodding John, Ricketts began to bring him around to a Darwinian view of nature and to see that man's primary struggle was between himself and natural surroundings.

The year 1933 saw John's first success, with the highly praised long story, *The Red Pony*. Two years later he was guaranteed financial success with *Tortilla Flats*, which reached the best-seller lists and was sold for movie rights. The book also marked the beginning of Steinbeck's reputation as a social critic, a writer with a humanitarian interest in the plight of the poor. *In Dubious Battle*, published shortly thereafter, brought Steinbeck even more into the political limelight, this time with a scolding from both the left and the right for his condemnation of both ideologies as being self-serving rather than serving the interests of the poor.

In the meantime Steinbeck visited the migrant farm workers' camps in California, viewed conditions, and learned the realities and psychology of vigilante behavior from a sympathetic camp administrator, Thomas Collins. The information was to form the basis for John's most famous novel, *The Grapes of Wrath*. Published in 1939, it was dedicated to Carol and to Tom Collins, and was an instant success and cause célèbre. The Joad family became famous. Their story was taken to Hollywood, and the movie became a classic. Other Steinbeck stories made the silver screen, most notably *The Red Pony*, with its stunning Copland score. Steinbeck also made it to Broadway, with the adaptation of "Of Mice and Men" his biggest hit.

Steinbeck remarried twice, having two sons, Thom and John IV, by his second wife, Gwendolyn Conger; but he stayed married longest to Elaine Anderson Scott, whom he wed in 1950. In his later years the critics, often ambivalent, became increasingly hostile. Their hostility was fueled when Steinbeck won the Nobel Prize in 1962. Nevertheless the public remained loyal, and Steinbeck's books remained best sellers. Buoyed by the prize and the success of *Travels with Charley*, Steinbeck also took pleasure in becoming a confidant of LBJ during his presidency. In poor health, Steinbeck died of a massive heart attack in New York City. His ashes were scattered over the land and ocean by Pacific Grove. A champion of the fight, albeit without the grail, the knight Jehan Stynebec de Montray had returned home.

DIRECTIONS TO CARMEL MISSION: Take Route 1 south from San Francisco and exit onto Junipero Avenue below the exit for the 17-Mile Drive. The mission is on your right.

DIRECTIONS TO GARDEN OF MEMORIES: Take Route 101 and exit at John Street for several blocks until you come to Abbott Street. The cemetery is located at 760 Abbott Street, Salinas.

Sources

Agee on Film. James Agee. New York: McDowell and Obolensky, 1958.

American Epitaphs Grave and Humorous. Charles L. Wallis. New York: Dover, 1973.

The Art of W.C. Fields. William K. Everson. New York: Bonanza Books, 1967.

The Barrymores. Hollis Alpert. New York: Dial Press, 1964.

Bing Crosby, The Hollow Man. Donald Shepherd and Robert F. Slatzer. New York: St. Martin, 1981.

Black Popular Music in America. Arnold Shaw. New York: Schirmer Books, 1986.

California: Land of New Beginnings. David Lavender. New York: Harper & Row, 1972.

California People. Carol Dunlap. Salt Lake City: Peregrine Smith Books, 1982.

A Cast of Killers. Sidney D. Kirkpatrick. New York: E.P. Dutton, 1986.

Cecil B. DeMille. Charles Higham. New York: Scribners, 1973.

Citizen Hearst. W.A. Swanberg. New York: Scribners, 1961.

City of Nets. Otto Friedrich. New York: Harper and Row, 1986.

The Disney Version. Richard Schickel. New York: Simon & Schuster, 1985.

Disney's World. Leonard Mosley. New York: Stein & Day, 1985.

Doug and Mary. Gary Carey. New York: E.P. Dutton, 1977.

Dreiser. W.A. Swanberg. New York: Scribners, 1965.

Fatal Charms. Dominick Dunne. New York: Crown, 1987.

The Film Encyclopedia. Ephraim Katz. New York: Perigee Books, 1979.

Frank Norris. Franklin Dickerson Walker. New York: Russell & Russell, 1963.

A Gardener Touched with Genius. Peter Dreyer. New York: Coward, McCann & Geoghegan, 1975.

The Great Jazz Pianists. Len Lyons. New York: Morrow, 1983.

The Great Pianists. Harold C. Schonberg. New York: Simon & Schuster, 1963.

Groucho and Me. Groucho Marx. New York: Bernard Geis, 1959.

Groucho, Harpo, Chico and Sometimes Gummo. Joe Adamson. New York: Simon & Schuster, 1973.

Harlow. Irving Shulman. New York: Bernard Geis, 1964.

The Hearsts. Lindsay Chaney and Michael Cieply. New York: Simon & Schuster, 1981.

His Picture in the Papers. Richard Schickel. New York: Charterhouse, 1973.

Hollywood Heartbreak. Laurie Jacobson. New York: Simon & Schuster, 1984.

The Hollywood Murder Casebook. Michael Munn. New York: St. Martin, 1987.

Humphrey Bogart. Nathaniel Benchley. Boston: Little, Brown, 1975.

In the Shade of the Juniper Tree. Katherine and Edward M. Ainsworth. Garden City: Doubleday, 1970.

The Intricate Music. Thomas Kiernan. Boston: Little, Brown, 1979.

Inventing the Dream. Kevin Starr. New York: Oxford University Press, 1985.

The Jack Benny Show. Milt Josefsberg. New Rochelle: Arlington House, 1977.

Jack, A Biography of Jack London. Andrew Sinclair. New York: Harper & Row, 1987.

Jayne Mansfield and the American Fifties. Martha Saxton. Boston: Houghton Mifflin, 1975.

The Jazz Tradition. Martin Williams. Oxford: Oxford University Press, 1983.

John Steinbeck, The Voice of the Land. Keith Ferrell. New York: M. Evans and Company, 1986.

Jolson, The Legend Comes to Life. Herbert G. Goldman. New York: Oxford University Press, 1988.

Keaton, The Man Who Wouldn't Lie Down. Tom Dardis. New York: Scribners, 1979.

The Killing of the Unicorn: Dorothy Stratten 1960–1980. Peter Bogdanovich. New York: Morrow, 1984.

Ladies and Gentlemen—Lenny Bruce!! Albert Goldman and Lawrence Schiller. New York: Random House, 1974.

Lanza, His Tragic Life. Raymond Strait and Terry Robinson. Englewood Cliffs, NJ: Prentice Hall, 1980.

Laurel and Hardy. Randy Skretvedt. Beverly Hills: Moonstone Press, 1987.

Least of All Saints: The Story of Aimee Semple McPherson. Robert Bahr. Englewood Cliffs, NJ: Prentice Hall, 1979.

Liberace. Bob Thomas. New York: St. Martin, 1987.

The Life of Raymond Chandler Frank MacShane. New York: E.P. Dutton, 1976.

Long Live the King. Lyn Tornabene. New York: Putnam, 1976.

Marilyn. Gloria Steinem and George Barris. New York: Henry Holt, 1986.

The Marx Brothers. Kyle Crichton. New York: Doubleday, 1950.

The Memoirs of an Amnesiac. Oscar Levant. New York: Putnam, 1965.

Movie Star, A Look at the Women Who Made Hollywood. Ethan Mordden. New York: St. Martin, 1987.

Nat King Cole. James Haskins with Kathleen Benson. Briarcliff Manor, NY: Stein & Day, 1984.

Natalie. Lana Wood. New York: Putnam, 1984.

Natalie & R.J. Warren G. Harris. New York: Doubleday, 1988.

The New York Times.

Nimitz. E.B. Potter. Annapolis, MD.: Naval Institute Press, 1976.

Nothing in Moderation, A Biography of Ernie Kovacs. David Walley. New York: Drake Publishers, 1975.

Our Father Who Art in Hell. James Reston, Jr. New York: Times Books, 1981.

San Francisco at Your Feet. Margot Patterson Doss. New York: Grove, 1964.

Spencer Tracy. Larry Swindel. New York: World, 1969.

Sweetheart, The Story of Mary Pickford. Robert Windeler. New York: Praeger, 1974.

The Talking Clowns. Frank Manchel. New York: Franklin Watts, 1976.

This Is Hollywood. Ken Schessler. La Verne, CA: Ken Schessler Publishing, 1987.

Valentino. Irving Shulman. New York: Trident, 1967.

W.C. Fields by Himself. Commentary by Ronald J. Fields. Englewood Cliffs, NJ: Prentice Hall, 1973.

Zanuck. Leonard Mosley. Boston: Little, Brown, 1984.

Index

Permanent Californians was designed by Julia Rowe and Summer Hill Books. It was typeset by Dartmouth Printing Company in ITC Garamond Light. It was printed on Finch Opaque, an acid-free paper, by Bookcrafters.